BULLETIN OF THE UNIVERSITY OF WISCONSIN

NO. 638

HISTORY SERIES, VOL. 3, No 2, PP. 137-392

THE MINING ADVANCE INTO THE INLAND EMPIRE

A COMPARATIVE STUDY OF THE BEGINNINGS OF THE MINING INDUSTRY IN IDAHO AND MONTANA, EASTERN WASHINGTON AND OREGON, AND THE SOUTHERN INTERIOR OF BRITISH COLUMBIA;
AND OF

INSTITUTIONS AND LAWS BASED UPON THAT INDUSTRY

BY

WILLIAM J. TRIMBLE,

Professor of History and Social Science,
North Dakota Agricultural College
Sometime Fellow in American History,
The University of Wisconsin

A THESIS SUBMITTED FOR THE DEGREE OF DOCTOR OF PHILOSOPHY
THE UNIVERSITY OF WISCONSIN

MADISON, WISCONSIN
1914
PRICE 40 CENTS

CONTENTS

			PAGE
CHAPTER	I.	Introduction: The Region and the Movement..	7

PART I

A SURVEY OF THE HISTORY OF THE MINING ADVANCE INTO THE INLAND EMPIRE, 1855-1870

CHAPTER	I.	The Incipient Rush to Colville and the Indian Uprising of 1855-6	15
CHAPTER	II.	The Rush to Fraser River	24
CHAPTER	III.	Preparations for a Decisive Advance of the Frontier	32
CHAPTER	IV.	Cariboo, Kootenai, and the Upper Columbia	46
CHAPTER	V.	The Mining Advance into Idaho, Eastern Oregon, and Montana	62

PART II

ECONOMIC ASPECTS OF THE MINING ADVANCE

CHAPTER	VI.	Methods of Production and Organization of Industry	87
CHAPTER	VII.	The Product and its Utilization	101
CHAPTER	VIII.	Transportation	119

PART III

SOCIAL ASPECTS OF THE MINING ADVANCE

CHAPTER	IX.	Components and Characteristics of Society	139
CHAPTER	X.	Education and Religion	168

PART IV

LAW AND GOVERNMENT

CHAPTER	XI.	The Establishment of Government and Law in British Columbia	187
CHAPTER	XII.	The Evolution of Order and Law in the American Territories	215
		Bibliography	248
		Index	

PREFACE

This study has been made possible by the use of the stores of a number of libraries, both public and private, and by the generous co-operation of friends who are interested in history.

No more earnest and efficient public service is rendered in our time than that by librarians. The author desires to make cordial acknowledgment of the unfailing helpfulness of the staffs in charge of the libraries of the University of Wisconsin, the University of Idaho, the University of California, and of the North Dakota Agricultural College; of the city libraries of Spokane, Seattle, and Portland, and of the collections of the Montana Historical Society, the Oregon Historical Society, the Provincial Library and Archives of British Columbia, and the Academy of Pacific Coast History. In particular I wish to extend my thanks to Mrs. Ethel McVeety, Librarian of the North Dakota Agricultural College, Mr. Frederick J. Teggert and Mr. Porter Garnett of the Academy of Pacific Coast History, and to Mr. E. O. L. Scholefield, Provincial Librarian of British Columbia.

Generous access has been given to the valuable private collections of Hon. C. B. Bagley, of Seattle, Mr. Justice Martin of Victoria, and his Honour, Judge Frederick W. Howay of New Westminster.

No one who has felt the kindly spirit and received the suggestive criticism of Professor Frederick J. Turner (now of Harvard University) can fail to be grateful. Acknowledgments are particularly due to Professor Turner, and also to Mr. T. C. Elliott, of Walla Walla, Washington, Hon. W. J. McConnell, of Moscow, Idaho, Judge W. Y. Pemberton, of Helena, Montana, Judge F. W. Howay, of New Westminster, British Columbia, and to Professor Frederick L. Paxson, of the University of Wisconsin. These gentlemen read my manuscript patiently and critically and furnished many helpful suggestions.

I am indebted also to Messrs. McConnell, Pemberton, and Bagley for pioneer reminiscences and illuminating suggestions. This sort of assistance was courteously extended, likewise, by Mr. Holter, of Helena, Major J. G. Trimble (lately deceased) of Berkeley, Cal., and Dr. James S. Helmncken and Mr. Gilbert Malcolm Sproat of Victoria.

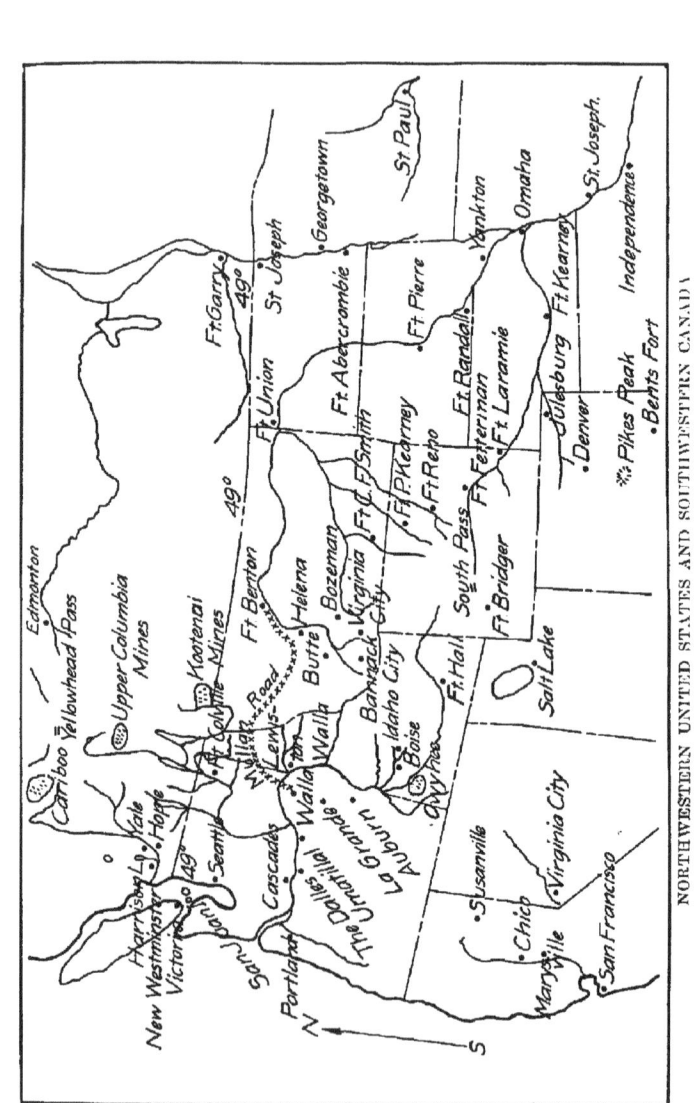

NORTHWESTERN UNITED STATES AND SOUTHWESTERN CANADA

THE MINING ADVANCE INTO THE INLAND EMPIRE

INTRODUCTION

THE REGION AND THE MOVEMENT

For almost a decade after the discovery of gold in California, the precious metal industry in the United States was carried on extensively only within that state. The decade following 1858, however, was characterized by the expansion of the industry on a large scale into many parts of the Rocky Mountain area. In this process of expansion certain movements or fields may be differentiated for convenience of study. One movement took place to the Southwest, another into the Pikes Peak region, a third into Nevada, and a fourth into the far Northwest. The last is plainly differentiated from the other movements either because of location or character of development, while the various districts which it reached were well connected by homogeneity of population and relationship of development. It is difficult, however, to find for this movement a name at once sufficiently succinct and comprehensive.

It should be made plain at the outset of this study that the term Inland Empire, as applied in the title, is used more as a convenient name for a movement than as a precise geographical designation. The region with which we are concerned includes (in terms of present political boundaries) the southern interior of British Columbia, eastern Oregon and Washington, western Montana, and Idaho. When this region began to attract wide attention about the time of the Civil War in the United States, because of a series of great mining "rushes", it was known vaguely in the East as the "Northwest", while along the western coast it was spoken of frequently as the "Northern Interior".

Today it is generally included in the term Pacific Northwest, and it might, perhaps, well be designated as the interior of the Pacific Northwest. But differentiation is often made in the United States between the Pacific Northwest and British Columbia; and so, in the absence of any definite term applicable to the whole region under consideration, I have ventured to make use of one commonly applied only to the central area within this region. Yet a growing use of the term "Inland" in southern Idaho and of the "Inland Empire of British Columbia" may give some sanction to wider application for the sake of convenience. Its extension to the Missouri slope of Western Montana, however, is defensible only from the point of view that the development of the early mining industry in that quarter formed a part of the general movement into the Inland Empire.

Considered as a whole, this vast region possesses very considerable physiographic unity. Diversities, to be sure, are to be found, as, for example, between southern and northern Idaho; but the country is clearly differentiated from the eastern plains and from the western coast. The latter distinction is most clearly marked,—travelers emerging from the dense fir forests of the coast to the plateau of the interior, either by way of the Columbia or the Fraser, observed that the trees (here of pine) became far less dense or disappeared altogether in great bunch grass plains, that the rainfall was much less, that peculiar terraces were found along the rivers, and that instead of the "canoe Indians" of the coast, there now appeared a better type, the "horse Indians". The inland plateau itself is distinctive. Covering the country from far into British Columbia to the confines of Nevada and California, and from the Cascades to the Rockies, is an immense lava formation of many layers. Its average depth is estimated at 2,000 feet, and its extent 200,000 square miles.[1] Rising above the lava

---

[1] *Bulletin U. S. Geol. Sur.* No. 108, p. 11. This monograph is by I. C. Russel, one of the best authorities for the physiography of the Inland Empire. Professor Russel characterizes the lava formation as follows: "This vast inundation of lava is one of the most remarkable and, I may say, one of the most dramatic incidents in the geological history of North America. It is safe to assume that all of the lava poured out by volcanoes within historic times, if run together, would make but a small fraction of the mass under which the region drained by the Columbia is buried."

plateau are the partially submerged peaks and mountain ranges of the primeval country, and on the eastern border the lava thins out into gulfs and bays among the Rocky Mountains.[2] In the Rocky Mountains or in the off-shoots westward from these mountains—the Owyhee, the Boise, the Salmon River, the Bitter-root, and the Cariboo ranges, and the Okanogan highland—were located the various mining camps about which we are to study.[3] From the Rockies flowed the three great river systems which became important factors in transportation to these camps—the Missouri, the Fraser, and the Columbia. The two latter are much alike. Both are noted for the swiftness of their current and the ruggedness of their canons; both swing far northward, and both receive from the East a great tributary (in the one case, the Thompson, in the other, the Snake); both have fine navigable stretches in their upper courses which, as the rivers plunge from the plateau, are interrupted by formidable obstacles; and both form magnificent waterways from the last of these obstacles to the ocean. The districts drained by these systems, likewise, have much of physiographic similarity. The Line of 49', the boundary between British Columbia and the American territories, was drawn at right angles, so to speak, to the physiographic inclination of the country. *From the point of view of physiography it would seem that there was not sufficient differentiation north and south of the political boundary materially to modify the development of society.* In other words, so far as the country was concerned, the development of institutional life was likely to be identical.

Civilized society took possession of this region both north and south of the Line through a great movement of miners, which occurred in the decade following 1855. Previous to that year, it is true, there had been within the region such forerunners of civilization as fur traders, explorers, and missionaries, and

---

[2] An important phase of the geology of Montana is discussed in *Some Volcano Ashbeds of Montana*, by J. P Rowe, *Mont. Univ. Bull.* No. 17, Geol. Series, No. I, 1903

[3] A succinct and satisfactory treatment of the physiography of British Columbia is that by Geo. M. Dawson, in *Geol. Sur. of Canada*, Vol. III, pt. II, pp. 5R-15R. A bibliography is appended.

through its southern part had proceeded the immigration on the Oregon Trail; but the institutions of civilized society had not been established upon the soil of the Inland Empire. These the Mining Advance produced.

The advance of the miners into the British and American portions of the region was practically contemporaneous, and the various rushes were interrelated. "A flood of picks and pans" (as writers in the midst of events styled it) spread over the country in successive waves, beginning with the Colville country in 1855. Between 1858 and 1866 rushes occurred (using present political designations) in British Columbia to Fraser River, Rock Creek and the Similkameen, Cariboo, Kootenai, and the Upper Columbia; in eastern Oregon, to John Day River and to Powder River; in Idaho, to the Nez Percés mines, Salmon River, Warren's Diggings, Boise, and Owyhee; and in Montana, to Grasshopper Creek, Alder Gulch, and Last Chance. There was constant migration between these various camps, which political boundaries did not seriously interrupt.

The general unity of the movement was greatly increased by the presence everywhere of Californians. It is true that in different fields different outcroppings (if the phrase be permissible) of population appeared. Thus in Cariboo, for example, the British element was more apparent than in most camps south of the Line; men from Missouri and Colorado were conspicuous in Boise Basin, while still another admixture was formed by the people from Minnesota who came to Montana. But a stratum of Californians was to be seen everywhere, and these produced throughout the region a similarity in methods of mining, in manners of society, in interests, and in the sort of institutions that tended spontaneously to spring up.[4]

There are three points of view, the statement of which may be of value in considering the mining advance into the Inland Empire.

---

[4] Californians, of course, went to most American camps, and there were also relationships between many of the camps of the region we are studying and Nevada and Colorado. But the main point which is here sought to be made is that *in the constituent elements of the population of the mining camps north and south of the Line, there were not sufficient divergencies wholly to account for variations in types of institutions.*

[146]

In the first place, this movement was part of the formation and advance of an *eastward moving frontier*. American population, which had advanced westward up to 1840 in comparatively gradual and connected movements, in the decade 1840-50 leaped to the Willamette and the Sacramento; now it was recoiling eastward and in this recoil was meeting the old frontier, which was still advancing westward. In this beginning of the fusion of frontiers there was an interesting commingling of men reared in the East and of the men habituated to Californian ideas and usages. New problems were created (among which the condition of the Indians was the most grave), new industrial and social forces were generated, and older ones reshaped or accentuated.

A somewhat elated poem of the time, published in Montana, indicates the swiftness of change wrought by this meeting of frontiers:

"The star of Empire Westward takes its way;
When Bishop Berkeley wrote *was* very true,
But were the Bishop living now, he'd say
That brilliant star seems *fixed* to human view.

"From Eastern hives is filled Pacific's shore—
No more inviting sun-set lands are near;
The restless throng now *backward* pour—
From East to West they meet, and stop right here.

"Away our published maps we'll have to throw—
The books of yesterday, today are lame

. . . .

"And towns and roads are made on every side,
In shorter time than books and maps are bound."[5]

A second point of view in the consideration of the mining advance is that it was a movement based, primarily, on a single industry. Whether north or south of the Line, in British Columbia, Idaho, or Montana, men talked of mines, struggled for

---
[5] H. N. Maguire in the Montana *Post*, republished in the Owyhee *Avalanche* Feb. 10, 1866.

mines, and founded their laws and institutions on mines. Other forms of industry were subsidiary to mining. (By mining, of course, is here meant mining for the precious metals.) The growth of this industry in this region, moreover, was related to the evolution of the industry in other sections, and, therefore, adequate treatment should include reference to the more important phases of the general development then going on in precious metal production.

The third and principal point of view of this study is that of comparison between British Columbia and the territories to the south during the period of the mining advance. While there would seem to be sufficient unity in the history of the whole region, during this period, to justify an attempt to treat it as a whole and to segregate it from other movements of the time, yet the main thesis here offered is that, in spite of unifying natural tendencies, the accidental political Line did cause deep cleavage in the formation of institutions. *In two similar parts of the same region, with a population having many of the same elements and occupied in the same industry, distinct differentiation did occur; and the phases, sources, and tendencies of this differentiation will be a recurring theme in this history.*

The plan of presentation contemplates: (1) a survey of the history of the mining advance; (2) special treatment of its economic and social aspects; (3) consideration of problems of government.

PART I

A SURVEY OF THE HISTORY OF THE MINING ADVANCE INTO THE INLAND EMPIRE, 1855-1870

CHAPTER I

THE INCIPIENT RUSH TO COLVILLE, AND THE INDIAN UPRISING OF 1855-1856

Ft. Colville, which for thirty years had been the chief inland post of the Hudson's Bay Company, became the first important center for mining development in the Inland Empire. It stood on the east bank of the Columbia on the second terrace back from the river, and in 1855 comprised a stockade which partially enclosed a dwelling house, several rude huts, a blacksmith shop and a few storehouses,—all made of squared logs and all somewhat decayed. The chief clerk of this establishment was Angus MacDonald, an intelligent Scotchman, and the habitues of the place were some twenty Canadians and Iroquois Indians. Three miles from the Fort was a good flour mill, in which was ground wheat raised by the French settlers, whose scattered farms dotted for nearly thirty miles, the beautiful Colville valley.[1] The mining district of which this fort became the center had no definite limits, but was held to comprise in general the territory lying east of the Columbia and between the Spokane and Pend d'Oreille Rivers.[2]

Who first discovered gold in this region, we do not know nor is the question important. Various roamers through the wilderness,—explorers, French-Canadians, mountain men,—with interest sharpened by the discoveries in California, had happened on gold in divers localities, but their discoveries had brought no results.[3] In the late summer and fall of 1855, how-

---
[1] Stevens's *Report on the Hudson's Bay Co.*, 33rd Cong. 2nd Sess., Gen. Doc. Vol 7, No. 37, p 8. *Life of Stevens*, Vol. 1, p. 348.
[2] Olympia *Pioneer and Democrat*, Sept. 28, 1855.
[3] Thus McClellan had discovered gold on the Wenatchee in 1853 and Findlay or Benetsee in Montana in 1852, *Pacific Railway Reports*, Vol. 12, p. 120; *Contributions to the Historical Society of Montana*, Vol. 2, p. 121. The first discovery on the Pend d'Oreille was made by Walker, a half-breed. Letter of Judge B. F. Yantis, Olympia *Pioneer and Democrat*, Nov. 23, 1855.

ever, a movement occurred to the vicinity of Ft. Colville, which had some of the characteristics of a genuine miners' "rush," and which ushered in the gold era in the Inland Empire

Considerable numbers of the citizens of Oregon and Washington participated in this movement and prospected in the Colville mines in the fall of 1855. The interest was increased by business stagnation in the Willamette and on the Sound[4] Some idea of the extensiveness of the movement may be inferred from scattered notices: "Suddenly all eyes turned to Colville," said the *Olympia Pioneer and Democrat*. "Many of our best men have gone prospecting." Governor Curry wrote to General Nesmith that many Oregon citizens had gone to the Pend d'Oreille mines; Steven's messenger, Pearson, met a company of ten or fifteen men near the Umatilla River on their way to the mines; Stevens, himself, a little later enrolled eighteen miners in his "Spokane Invincibles;" Yantis reports twenty men at work on one bar; organized parties explored the country under the leadership of well known citizens.[5] It is apparent, therefore, that at that time a movement took place of some magnitude.

The reports brought back, a number of which were made by reliable and conservative men, were of such a nature as to inspire further efforts. It seemed that gold could be found almost anywhere between the Spokane and the Pend d'Oreille, but that the deposits were small and superficial.[6] Still, men made with pan and rocker three to six dollars per day, and a few twelve. Explorations many miles up the Pend d' Orielle failed to show any large deposits, but MacDonald at Fort Colville told the miners that chances were better farther up the Columbia—a suggestion not without fruit in the later discovery of mines on Fraser River.[7]

The difficulties in the way of the miners, however, were great. The gold was light "float" gold, for the economical col-

---

[4] Deady, *History of the Progress of Oregon after 1845*, Ms., p. 37; *Olympia Pioneer and Democrat*, Sept 14, 1855.
[5] *Id.;* 34th Cong., 3rd Sess., Ex. Doc, Vol. 9, No. 76, p. 158, Oct. 16, 1855; *Pioneer and Democrat*, Sept. 28, 1855, and Nov. 23, 1855.
[6] Report of Col. Anderson, Olympia *Pioneer and Democrat*, Sept. 28, 1855.
[7] *Report* of Judge Yantis, *id.*, Nov. 23, 1855.

lection of which quicksilver and the sluice system were needed. Supplies were scanty and men were living on flour and coffee.[8] There were no suitable roads from the Sound over the precipitous mountains, and steamboat traffic on the Columbia was just starting. Hence, transportation was not yet organized, and organized transportation is vital to the success on a large scale of distant mining operations. But the most baffling obstacle to the adventurers was difficulties with the Indians.

The Indians of eastern Washington, in number about twelve thousand, were not to be despised as enemies. Living in an exhilerating climate, on an elevated plateau, thoroughly accustomed to the use of the horse, and having a variety of food, they constituted in physique and mind a fine race.[9] The Nez Percés, inhabiting, for the most part, the country lying eastward from the present city of Lewiston, Idaho, were the largest and best ordered tribe, and, though not wanting in warlike qualities (as Joseph's warfare subsequently proved), they were nevertheless distinguished for their friendship to the whites. *This peace policy of the Nez Percés should be emphasized as the most important fact in the history of the Indian wars of the Inland Empire.* North of the Nez Percés lived the Coeur d' Alenes, Spokanes, Pend d' Oreilles, and Flatheads. A third group was to be found south from the Nez Percés, and consisted of the Walla Wallas, Cayuses, and Umatillas. Over the Blue Mountains was the desert country in which roamed the Shoshones—banditti they above all other tribes. Another group, important particularly because of the position it occupied, was the Yakima. The Yakima country lay west of the Columbia—between that river and the Cascade Mountains. The position was central, therefore, both to the Sound Indians and to the tribes of the farther interior and the principal chiefs of the tribe were related to the chiefs in both regions. Moreover, this

---

[8] *Report* of A. B Stuart, *id.*, Sept. 9th, 1855.
[9] Many writers of the time comment on the marked differences between the Indians of the interior and the "fish" Indians of the coast, who lived almost exclusively on salmon and who traveled in canoes. Travelers in British Columbia made the same observation. For example, Kipp, *The Indian Council at Walla Walla*, p. 6; Anderson, Alex C., *Handbook and Map to the Gold Regions of Frazer's and Thompson's River*, p. 6.

territory lay directly in the path of the mining advance.

The head chief of the Yakimas, Kamiakin, who was charged by the whites with being the chief instigator and organizer of the Indians in their efforts to stay the white advance, was an Indian worthy of note. All accounts agree that in physique and countenance he was impressive. He was tall and athletic, though somewhat slovenly in dress. His face, generally gloomy and thoughtful, lighted up wonderfully in speech, "one moment in frowns, the next in smiles, flashing with light and black as Cerebus the same instant." Speech with him, however, was rare, for he had the demeanor of a grave, proud man. He refused to be baptized as a Catholic, because he would not put away his surplus wives. Jealous of his rights and especially watchful against attempts to acquire the Indian lands, he traveled widely, striving to arouse the Indians to their peril. He may be regarded as an Indian statesman, who with devotion to the customs of his race and love for the superb land in which he lived, tried as best he might in feeble Indian fashion to unite the unorganized tribes against the dreaded white advance which he saw now impending.[10]

The Indians of the Inland Empire were, indeed, in bad plight. The tribes of the east had been pushed ever farther westward, but with both frontiers closing in upon these Indians, whither should they go? Everywhere throughout the tribes was the fear of being dispossessed of their lands and everywhere uneasiness. This dread and uneasiness extended to the Indians on the Sound. The whites, after the outbreak of hostilities, claimed that a general conspiracy had long been brewing and that Kamiakin was the arch conspirator; but it is evident now that conditions in different localities had made matters ripe for desperate measures on the part of the Indians without any deliberate plan of action.[11] They shrank from the coming of white settlers and especially of miners, for they knew something of the troubles that had befallen the Indians

---

[10] References on Kamiakin: Winthrop, Theodore, *The Canoe and the Saddle*, p. 237; *Life of Stevens*, Vol. 2, p. 38; *Indian affairs Report*, 1854, p. 234; Wright to Wool, *Message and Documents*, 1856-7, pt. 2, p. 160.

[11] *Remarks of J. Ross Browne*, 35 Cong., 1 Sess., App., p. 494.

in California.[12] Chiefs of the Yakimas, Cayuses, and Walla Wallas had said to Gen. Alvord at The Dalles in 1853 that "they always liked to have gentlemen, Hudson Bay Company men or officers of the army or engineers pass through their country, to whom they would extend every token of hospitality. They did not object to persons merely hunting, or those wearing swords, but they dreaded the approach of the whites with ploughs, axes and shovels in their hands."[13] It can readily be seen, therefore, that, with the Indians feeling thus, the coming of the miners to Colville was likely to precipitate hostilities.[14]

Another cause of the Indian outbreak, however,—so army officers in particular claimed,—was the treaties made by Governor Stevens in the summer of 1855. A great council was summoned by him to meet at Walla Walla, which was attended by large numbers of the Nez Percés, Cayuses, Walla Wallas, Umatillas, and Yakimas. All of the tribes were suspicious and semi-hostile at this council, except the Nez Percés; and even of them a faction plotted with the malcontents. Kamiakin vehemently opposed any cession of land and rejected all presents from the whites. But at length the friendliness towards the whites on the part of the majority of the Nez Percés under the leadership of their head chief, Lawyer, prevailed, and treaties were signed which provided for the forming of three reservations and the paying of large annuities. The Nez Percés were to receive the beautiful country lying mainly between the Snake River and the Bitter Root Mountains; the Yakimas were to have their homes in the valley of the river that bore their name; and the remaining tribes were assigned tracts in eastern Oregon.[15]

These treaties were subjected to bitter denunciation by army officials, who claimed, as mentioned above, that they were a main

---

[12] Also Wool in *Message and Documents*, 1856-7, pt. 2, Rpt. Sec'y of War, p. 88.
[13] *Life of Stevens*, Vol. 2, p. 025.
[14] See on this Roder, Capt. Henry, *History of Bellingham Bay*, MS, pp. 19 and 20.
[15] A pleasant narrative of this council is that by Lawrence Kipp, *The Walla Walla Council, Indian Pamphlets*, Vol. 14, No. 10, and republished in *"Sources of the History of Oregon"*, F. G. Young, editor. A good account is found also in *Life of Stevens*, Vol. 2, pp. 34-65. Text of treaties is given in 57 Cong., 1st Sess., No 542, p 521-531.

cause of the war which broke out in the fall of 1855.[16] Their ratification was delayed for four years by the Senate, in part because of the large annuities provided. John Sherman said that the government might more cheaply bring all the Indians to New York and board them at the Hotel St. Nicholas. But Stevens's course was in reality statesmanlike. Although the Donation Act was to expire by limitation, December 1, 1855, there was still time for settlers to take up claims. Under this act Congress had authorized settlers to take claims before any attempt had been made to extinguish the Indian title. Moreover, Stevens, foreseeing the impending advance of the whites and, as chief advocate of the northern route for the Pacific railway, favoring settlement, believed that the reservation system was the only refuge for the Indians.[17] At any rate these treaties were the first definite step under government sanction in preparation for white occupation of the Inland Empire.

The suspicions, regrets, and resentments aroused in the minds of the Indians by these treaties perhaps contributed to the outbreak of war. The chances of trouble of course were increased from the fact that the main passes from the Sound to the eastern country, as we have before mentioned, lay through the Yakima country. The Indians later, in extenuation of their course, claimed that the miners en route had violated their women; Stevens tried to verify this statement, but was unable to do so.[18] All accounts claim that the miners were from a good class of citizens on the Sound. The first to be killed were Mattice and Fantjoy or Fanjoy, "both respectable men from the state of Maine." The attacks on separate individuals continued incessantly during September. It is to be noted that the exasperation on the part of the whites caused by such attacks lay not alone in lives actually lost, but also in making lines of travel so insecure as to hinder development of the country. The total number of men lost, however, was not inconsiderable to a small community; one newspaper on the Sound

---

[16] For example, Wright to Wool, *Message and Documents*, 1856-7, p. 160.
[17] For a statement of Steven's policy see *Rpt Com. Ind. Af.*, 1854, pp. 247-249.
[18] *Message and Documents*, 1856-7 Wright to Wool, p 152, May 30, 1856; 35 Cong. 1st Sess., App. 491.

counted up thirteen of the residents of the immediate vicinity who were known to have been slain and reported several others missing.[19] Matters came to a climax when A. J. Bolon, agent for the Yakimas, was murdered by Qualchien, nephew of Kamiakin. Thereupon, Major J. G. Haller led a company of regulars into the Yakima country only to be driven out with considerable loss. At about the same time some of the Sound Indians took to the war path, and the war became general.

The details of the war of 1855—56, though stirring and interesting, may be found elsewhere.[20] A chronological resumé of the events directly concerning the interior country 1855—56 would include: the calling out of large numbers of volunteers both in Oregon and Washington in the fall of 1855; the expedition of Major Raines into the Yakima country; the daring return of Stevens from the Blackfoot council; a decisive engagement between Indians and Oregon volunteers in the Touchét valley in December; a surprise by the Indians at the Cascades in March of 1856; an expedition by Col. Wright into the Yakima country; a fight between Washington Volunteers and Indians in Grande Ronde valley; a second council by Governor Stevens at Walla Walla, and an attack by the Indians on himself and escort; and, finally, the establisment in the fall of 1856 of Ft. Walla Walla.

The policy of General Wool, who, as commander of the Department of the Pacific, was supreme military head in this war, is worthy of note, especially from the point of view of the mining history. Volunteers, called forth by the governors both of Washington and Oregon, took very active part in the campaigns, much to the disgust of General Wool. He claimed that the war had been precipitated by the treaties of Stevens, that the volunteers had entered it largely in order to plunder the Indians, and that citizen speculators had fostered it for the purpose of getting more money into the country from the Federal Government. In pursuance of his position towards the volunteers and the work of Stevens, he issued the following

---

[19] Olympia *Pioneer and Democrat*, Oct. 19, 1855.
[20] Meaney, Edmund S., *History of the State of Washington*, pp. 176-202; Bancroft, H. H., *Works*, Vol. xxxi, pp. 108-200.

order: "No emigrants or other whites, except the Hudson Bay Company, or persons having ceded rights from the Indians, will be permitted to settle or remain in the Indian country, or on land not ceded by treaty, confirmed by the Senate and approved by the President of the United States.

"These orders are not, however, to apply to the miners engaged in collecting gold at the Colville mines. The miners will, however, be notified that should they interfere with the Indians, or their squaws, they will be punished or sent out of the country."[21]

This order is interesting from at least two points of view. In the first place, Wool regarded the interior country as a natural reserve for the Indians, who might there be separated from the whites on the Sound by the Cascade Range, "a most valuable wall of separation."[22] In the second place, he excepted from his order the miners—the most immediate cause of trouble. Why did he make this exception? Certainly he had no special favoritism to show these men, for they were most likely to defeat the policy at which he aimed From a legal point of view, the miners were at that time simply trespassers upon the public domain.[23] It may be surmised that the custom of the miners of unconscious trespassing and their claim of implied recognition to such right on the part of the United States, may have influenced this martinet to make the relaxation in their favor.

The attitude of the military, however, did stay further mining development south of the Line for a period. Since the Indians were unchastised and murderers such as Qualchien were not surrendered for trial, the hostility of the Indians was such as to make the interior country unsafe. In traveling through it, all parties had to exercise "Constant watchfulness and care;" so much so that it was unsafe for the passage of pack trains or for prospecting.[24]

In several respects, however, this war helped to prepare for

---
[21] 34th Cong. 3d Sess., Vol. I, pt. 2, p 169.
[22] See further on this point, *Life of Stevens*, Vol. II, p. 226.
[23] Blanchard and Weeks, *The Law of Miners, Minerals and Mining Water Rights*, p. 92; Davis, *Historical Sketch of Mining Law in California*, p. 213.
[24] R. H. Lansdale in *Report Com. Ind. Affairs 1857*, No. 154, p. 377.

later advance. The military operations in the upper country and the establishment of Ft. Walla Walla stimulated the development of transportation on the Columbia, and particularly so in efforts to overcome the difficulties at the Cascades and the Dalles. Moreover, the warrants of the war debt for the services of the volunteers, which, it was assumed, would be paid by the general government, circulated as an inflated medium of exchange and formed capital wherewith to promote enterprises of all sorts. A thoughtful observer writes: "Portland I think was quite slow and dull until this Indian war concentrated a good deal of business here. There were a good many operations and of course a large portion of this scrip was concentrated here. Traffic and the impetus to business given by it, was felt here."[25] The war claims amounted to no less than $6,000,000, of which sum not quite half was finally paid. This formed a large addition of capital for the scanty populations of the Willamette and the Sound.[26]

---

[25] Deady, *Hist. of the Progress of Oregon after 1845*, Ms., p. 37.
[26] A good statement concerning this war debt is found in the *Financial History of Oregon*, by F. G. Young, *Some Features of Oregon's Experience with the Financial Side of Her Indian Wars of the Territorial Period*, Quar. of Oregon Hist. Soc., June 1907, Vol VIII, No. 2, pp. 182-190.

CHAPTER II

THE RUSH TO FRASER RIVER

The magnificent domain now known as British Columbia in 1855 was all but untouched by civilization. Over it the Hudson's Bay Company was still paramount. The mainland they held by virtue of an exclusive license to trade, and Vancouver Island they owned as a colony by Parliamentary grant. The chief factor of the company, James Douglas, was also Governor of Vancouver Island. The principle post was Victoria, where a few houses clustered around the fort of the company. On the mainland the posts of chief interest to this history were: Ft. Langley on the south bank of the Fraser, twenty eight miles above the mouth; Ft. Hope sixty miles farther up, its sight a "lovely plateau ......, environed with lofty and shaggy mountains;" Ft. Yale, the extreme head of steamboat navigation on the lower River, twelve or fifteen miles above Ft. Hope; and Ft. Thompson, far in the interior on Thompson River.[1] Roads there were none, save the Hudson's Bay Company's brigade trail up the Fraser. The interior of the country, cut off by the cañons above Ft. Yale, was inconceivably remote, unknown, and inaccessible.

The more remote and inaccessible a country might be, however, the more alluring it often seemed to miners. Stimulated in part no doubt by the suggestions of Angus MacDonald, of Colville, gold seekers ranged northward from the Colville mines in the fall of 1855.[2] As example of one of these adventurers we may mention James Taylor, of Olympia, who with

---

[1] A clear map showing these posts is found in Bancroft, *Hist. Pac. States*, Vol. XXVII, p. 177.

[2] Indians, indeed, had been bringing into Kamloops small quantities of gold since 1852. De Groot, *British Columbia; its condition and prospects*, p. 4.

a small party made his way by Nachess pass to the Colville district and thence, in August, 1855, struck across the Okanogan country and penetrated as far as Thompson River.[3] MacDonald wrote to Governor Douglas, on the first of March 1856, that gold had been found in considerable quantities on the Columbia within British territory, and that he believed that valuable deposits would be discovered; and this information Douglas transmitted to the Colonial Secretary.[4] But the disposition of the Indians towards Americans in the summer of 1856 hindered further development for a time.[5] The Indians themselves, however, did some work.[6] The developments of 1857 are summarized by De Groot as follows: "During the summer and fall of 1857, a number of persons, being mostly adventurers from Oregon and Washington territories, of the Colville mines, together with a sprinkling of half breeds and Canadian French, formerly in the company's service, made their way into the country on the upper Fraser, where, prospecting in the neighborhood of the forks, they found several rich bars, on which they went to work, continuing operations with much success, until forced to leave from want of provisions on the approach of cold weather. Coming to Victoria, or returning whence they came, these men spread abroad the news of their good luck and laid the foundation for the excitement that soon after followed."[7] Douglas, also, noted the excitement abroad, particularly in the American territory.[8]

By the latter part of March, 1858, the news from Fraser River was of such character as to produce a real furore on the Sound. On the twenty-second, the *Herald* at Steilacoom issued an extra in which it announced that miners on Fraser and Thompson Rivers were making from eight to fifty dollars per day, and that the Indians were friendly. Within a week mills were compelled to shut down from lack of laborers, and vessels were deserted. All the hands at the Bellingham coal mines

[3] Victoria *Gazette*, July 10, 1858.
[4] Hazlitt, *Br Col & Van. Id.*, p. 128.
[5] Letter of Douglas, Oct. 24, 1856. *Id*, p. 129.
[6] Dec. 29, 1857 *Id.* p. 130.
[7] De Groot, *British Columbia; Its Condition and Prospects*, p. 13.
[8] Letter of Douglas, Dec. 29, 1857; Hazlitt, *Br. Col. and Van. Id.*, p. 130.

quit work.[9] Soldiers deserted. Around Victoria nearly all the floating populace left.[10] The villages of the lower Sound stirred with new life: Port Townsend was "like a bee hive;" Whatcom took measures for cutting a trail from that place to intersect the Hudson Bay Company's Brigade Trail, and weeks of labor were consumed on this trail before it was found not feasible. As shiploads of miners from California came pouring into the various ports, many towns aspired to be the "San Francisco" of this northern movement. Whatcom and Sehome at first took the lead, and later Semiamoo, out near Point Roberts, attracted attention. In all these places throngs gathered, faro banks sprang up, and speculation in lots throve; but finally the advantages of Victoria and the policy of Governor Douglas smothered these ambitious booms.

Meantime, there was in progress from California one of the most remarkable "rushes" in the history of mining movements.

Conditions in California at this time were favorable for a swift and great exodus of population to a promising field. The exportation of gold, which by 1853 had mounted to $57,330,000, had fallen in 1857 to $48,976,000.[11] Moveover, the conditions and methods of production were changing. At first it had been comparatively easy for men to find good claims which could be cheaply worked; or, if they were compelled to work temporarily for another, there was no sense of inferiority to the employer on the part of the laborers. But now, with the exhaustion of the surface placers, there was increasing necessity for the employment of capital on a large scale and of resort to corporate methods in order to work the deep diggings. In the attempt to engage in operations on a large scale many individuals had hazarded and lost previous gains and were now burdened by debt. Many small claims were yielding only very moderate returns in comparison to those of flush times, and new claims were to be found only after long, expensive, and uncertain prospecting. Men who had been accustomed to large returns and to independence became restive and dis-

---

[9] *Puget Sound Herald*, Mar. 26, 1858
[10] *Letter of Douglas*, March 22, 1858; Cornwallis, *New Eldorado*, p. 255.
[11] *Mineral Resources*, 1867, p. 50.

couraged in working for less than "wages," but greatly resented being forced to work as employes. Consequently, many were eager for opportunities in a new country which might bring back the freedom, enthusiasm, and easy gains of the earlier time.[12]

A vehement belief spread through the mining counties that Fraser's River would repeat these earlier experiences. Miners, to be sure, were somewhat skeptical of new fields, because they had been badly mistaken in several disastrous excitements. But trusty delegates in this case reported back to some of the camps the richness of the new fields, and secret notes from former comrades often authenticated the reports of the newspapers. Moveover, there was a theory that farther north gold fields became richer (as had been the case in California), and that fine gold discovered in the lower parts of a river betokened great deposits farther up. The reports of the "flour gold" of the bars of the Fraser, therefore, brought conviction and enthusiasm.

Accordingly miners from the interior thronged all roads to Stockton and Sacramento, and at these places crowded into steamers for San Francisco. Some of the mining counties lost a third of their population; business was badly deranged and general bankruptcy was anticipated; claims that in March would have brought one thousand dollars would not bring one hundred dollars in June.[13] Not only the miners who poured into San Francisco were intent on Fraser River, but many of the inhabitants of that city accompanied them northward. Common laborers, bricklayers, carpenters, printers, cabinet makers, merchants, gamblers, and speculators in real estate, as well as miners, crowded to three times their capacity vessels whose seaworthiness was often doubtful.[14] Fares to Victoria were for the "nobs" $60, for the "roughs," $30. Steamboat owners of course made money rapidly. A careful estimate placed the number who went from California to Victoria dur-

---

[12] This paragraph is based upon an article by J. S. Hittell in *Overland Monthly*, May, 1869, Vol. II, pp. 413–417, Downie, Maj Wm., *Hunting for Gold;* De Groot, *Br. Col; Its Condition and Prospects*.

[13] Hittell, *Cariboo, Overland Monthly*, May, 1869.

[14] "Times" correspondence, *Hazlitt, Br. Col. and Van. Id*, p. 147.

ing the spring and early summer at twenty-three thousand, while probably eight thousand more proceeded overland.[15]

As ship after ship discharged its crowds at Victoria or at Esquimault (a fine harbor three miles from Victoria), a lively town sprang into existence around the staid Hudson's Bay quarters. Hundreds of tents occupied the picturesque slope, while more permanent dwellings and stores were swiftly put up. Speculation in lots was rife. A newspaper, the Gazette, was soon established. Crowds of miners continually coming and going, auctioneers shouting their wares, the calls of dray men,— all the bustle and stir of business,—recalled to many minds early days in San Francisco.

These miners at Victoria, however, were still far from the mining region. To get to it the Gulf of Georgia first had to be crossed, and then the Fraser ascended for a hundred miles and more. In the absence at first of adequate transportation, hundreds of the adventurous enthusiasts entrusted themselves to hastily made boats and canoes, in which they ventured to encounter the dangerous tides and currents of gulf and river. Later, steamboats ascended to Hope and Yale.

The first miners on the Fraser found rich and easy diggings. The gold occurred in the "bars" of the river.[16] The lowest bar worked was Fargo bar, which was about fifteen miles above Ft. Langley.[17] From there clear up above the cañons above Yale a succession of rich bars was uncovered, the richest district being in the vicinity of Ft. Yale. In this district on Hill's Bar the discoverer made six hundred dollars in sixteen days, and two other men took out two hundred and fifty dollars in a day and a half. From many points came reports of rich returns, and old Californians declared they had never seen such diggings.[18] All along the Fraser were evidences of activity and industry, and the future seemed full of hope.

Meantime, steps had been taken to ensure law and order. In December, 1857, Douglas had issued a proclamation which assert-

---
[15] Nugent's *Report*, Ex. Doc. 35th Cong. 2nd Sess., Vol. XII, No. 3, p 26.
[16] "Every mine over which a river extends when in its most flooded state." Gold Mine Regulations, Macfie, *Van. Id. and Br. Col.*, p. 532
[17] Mayne, *Br. Col. and Van.* Id., p. 93.
[18] "Times" correspondence. *Hazlitt, Br. Col. and Van. Id.*, pp. 134–140.

ed that "all mines of gold...... whether on the lands of the Queen or of any of her Majesty's subjects, belong to the Crown", and required that a miner should take out a license before digging for gold.[19] Douglas at first questioned whether it was a wise policy to admit without requiring an oath of allegiance, large numbers of "foreign population, whose sympathies may be decidedly anti British," and he issued a proclamation in May, 1858 which, to say the least, attempted sufficiently to safe-guard the interests of the Hudson's Bay Company.[20] This proclamation warned all persons from engaging in trade for Fraser River and from navigating boats thereon, except by license and sufferance of the Hudson's Bay Company. The sufferance, which cost six to twelve dollars per trip, was issued on condition that the vessel owner using it should transport only the goods of the Hudson's Bay Company; that he should import no powder nor utensils of war, except from the United Kingdom; that he would receive no passengers except such as had licenses to mine, and that he would not trade with the Indians.[21]

Douglas acknowledged that his authority to make this proclamation was questionable; but strongly claimed that the Hudson's Bay Company's right of exclusive trade with the Indians implied exclusive trade of all sorts.[22]

But Her Majesty's Secretary of State for the Colonies instructed him that he should "oppose no obstacle whatever" to the entrance of foreigners and repudiated the claim of exclusive trade rights for the Hudson's Bay Company.[23] The rush of population to British Columbia, however, had decided the Imperial Government to terminate the license of exclusive trade with the Indians by which the mainland was held by the Company; and, on August 2, 1858, the act was passed by which the colony of British Columbia was established. The governor of the new

---

[19] Cornwallis, *The New Eldorado*, p 349.
[20] Despatch of Douglas, May 8, 1858 *Id* p 356.
[21] *Letter of Stevens to Sec'y of State*, July 21, 1858, *Id* 324–5.
[22] Despatch of May 8, 1858. *Id* 258–9; Rights of Hudson's Bay Company, *Id.* pp. 296–400.
[23] Despatch of Sir E Bulwer Lytton, July 1, 1858. *Id.* 367. These restrictive measures of Douglas were called to the attention of the U. S. Federal authorities, who sent to Victoria as special agent, John Nugent. Nugent's report censures Douglas. 35th Cong., 2nd Sess., Vol. XII, No. 3.

colony was to have temporarily absolute power, subject to the Queen in Council.[24] Douglas was invited to become Governor on strict condition that he sever all connection with the Hudson's Bay Company, and he accepted.

With powers now plainly defined and old relations with the Company severed, Douglas turned resolutely to the formidable task before him. A gold commissioner and assistant gold commissioners were appointed; proclamations were issued having force of law for the regulation of the mines and the survey of lands; order was decisively kept; the great undertaking of providing routes of transportation into the interior was entered upon. Vigilance and energy were shown in all directions.

The establishment of government may have been made somewhat easier by a swift recession of the tide of population which had burst into the country. The miners, indeed, were confronted by a most disconcerting phenomenon. The first operations had been carried on in the spring and early summer, when the water was low; but high water in the Fraser comes with the melting of the snows in the mountains by the summer sun. The river has an enormous rise in the summer months; at Ft. Langley it is fourteen feet, and higher up much greater—at Pavillon, for example, it rose in 1859 eighteen feet in a single night.[25] Such a rise of course submerged most of the bars and stopped work. Some of the miners resolutely determined to wait for lower water; others, facing every danger and privation, prospected far into the interior; but the great majority, finding expenses heavy and prospects poor, returned to California—there to classify Fraser River as the most colossal of humbugs.[26]

In spite of all these disappointments, however, the rush to Fraser River accomplished very important results. The rule of the Hudson's Bay Company west of the Rockies was ended; British Columbia with its outlook on the Pacific, had come into being; prospectors were pushing farther and farther into the interior toward Cariboo and Kootenay; an inter-oceanic railway

---

[24] For a copy of the Act, see Appendix to Cornwallis, pp. 317–322. Bill in final form, *British State Papers*, 1858–59, pp. 789–42.
[25] Mayne, *Br. Col. and Van. Id.*, p. 86.
[26] One gets some idea of the bitterness of feeling in regard to Fraser River from Angelo's *Idaho*.

on English soil was begining to be talked of and with it the federation of British North America.[27] England's participation in the life of the Pacific Coast was assured. "However we may regard the advent of England upon our shores" wrote a thoughtful Californian, "or whatever estimate we may set on the value of her possessions in this quarter, one thing is certain, we have now got to meet her on this side of the globe, as we have met her on the other, and encountering her enterprise and capital; her practical, patient industry and persistence of purpose, dispute with her for the trade of the East and the empire of the seas."[28]

---

[27] Cornwallis, *New Eldorado*, Chapter VIII; Speech from the throne, 1858, Bancroft, *Hist. of Pac. States*, Vol. XXVII, p. 642.
[28] De Groot, *Br. Col.; Its Condition and Prospects*, p. 4.

CHAPTER III

PREPARATIONS FOR A DECISIVE ADVANCE OF THE FRONTIER

While the foundations of British Columbia were being laid in this rush of 1858, events were taking place south of the line which ended General Wool's peace policy, pacified the interior, and opened it to settlement.

It will be recalled that Wool had excepted miners when he had declared the upper country closed to settlement, and in spite of the hostility of the Indians and the apathy of the soldiery, some miners continued their work, especially in the vicinity of Colville. These felt the need of protection from the Indians and of some form of government for themselves. Accordingly, a meeting was held at Colville, Nov. 23rd., 1857, in the log store of F. Wolff. A petition was drawn up praying for the location of a company of soldiers in the valley, and a rude governmental organization was effected.[1]

Influenced by this petition, by reports that two miners had been killed by the Indians, and by a desire to punish some Indian depredations on the stock at Ft. Walla Walla, Colonel Steptoe, in command at that fort, determined on a reconnaissance to Colville. The expedition, which started May 5, 1858, consisted of about 175 men—dragoons, mounted artillery men, packers, and Indian guides. Although they took along two howitzers, the equipment was poor, the troopers being armed with the old Yager rifles or with musketoons, and the supply of ammunition being insufficient. The route was by the old Nez Percés trail to Red Wolf Crossing, just below the present city of Lewiston, Idaho, and thence northward towards the

---
[1] A full account of this meeting appeared in the Portland *Oregonian*, Jan. 30th, 1858.

Spokane. The northern Indians, particularly the Coeur d' Alenes and the Spokanes, already hostile in feeling because of friction with the miners and because of rumors of the construction of a new military road (the Mullan Road) through their country, desired to have the Snake river the boundary of the Indian country and wished no troops to come north of it; they were incensed, therefore, to a degree of which Steptoe had no conception, and the more because he, instead of marching directly to Colville by the accustomed trail, chose one far to the east which ran near much-valued camass grounds.[2]

The expedition had proceeded to the vicinity of Filleo Lake, some eighteen miles south of the present city of Spokane, when the way was blocked by Indians (mainly Coeur d' Alenes), and the whites turned aside and encamped by the lake. So hostile was the attitude of the Indians that Steptoe determined to retreat next morning. Soon after the retrograde movement began next morning (May 17), firing commenced and a running fight ensued for several miles. Steptoe finally made a stand on a hill overlooking the Tohotonimine (or Pine) Creek.[3] Two commissioned officers and six men had been killed and eleven wounded, by the time the hill was reached. By nightfall only two rounds of ammunition were left to each man. The situation was indeed desperate, for Walla Walla, the nearest point of succor, was ninety miles away, and the Snake river intervened. A flight by night was determined upon. The dead were buried, the howitzers were dismantled, and the stores abandoned. The command rode all night and reached Snake River next day. There they were helped by the Nez Percés, and finally reached Walla Walla in safety.[4]

---

[2] *Letter of Father Joset to Father Congiato, Report of Sec'y of War*, 1858, p. 355

[3] This hill adjoins the village of Rosalia, Wash.

[4] Sources for the Steptoe expedition: *Report of Secretary of War* for 1858; *MS of Father Joset* (In Nichols' *Indian Affairs*).

Accounts from survivors: Michael Kenney in Spokane *Spokesman-Review*, May 12, 1901; John O'Neill, *Id.*, April 2, 1906; Thomas J. Beall in Lewiston *Teller*, March 14, 1884. (See also, *A Pioneer Soldier of the Oregon Frontier*, in Oregon *Hist. Quarterly*, Sept., 1907.)

A secondary account is found in *History of the State of Washington*, by Edmund S. Meaney, pp 212-214.

I am indebted for personal recollections of this affair and also of the Wright

This attack on regular soldiers made it evident to Gen. Clarke, who had succeeded Gen. Wool in command of the Department of the Pacific, that the Indians must no longer be dealt with in temporizing fashion. He at once began concentrating troops from all parts of the Pacific coast and planned an effective campaign. The command of the expedition against the Spokanes, Coeur d' Alenes, and allied tribes was given to Colonel George Wright, and a cooperating force was ordered to proceed into the Yakima country under command of Major R. S. Garnett.

Colonel Wright (afterwards General) both in this campaign of 1858 and later as commander of the Department of the Pacific in the troublous times of the Civil War, proved himself an officer of more than ordinary wisdom and usefulness. His appearance was not particularly martial, though dignified; for he was rather short in stature and corpulent in figure. His military operations were very carefully conducted, and he exacted from his soldiers strict discipline. In his dealings both with the soldiers and the natives he was stern, but very just. Unostentatious and not given to worry, he pursued his duty quietly and patiently, but at the same time with energy and promptitude.[5]

While Wright was collecting and drilling his forces at Walla Walla, several expeditions bound for Fraser River ventured into the hostile territory. The first of these companies to start was that headed by David McLaughlin, which set forth from Walla Walla early in July. A German who strayed from camp was promptly murdered by the Indians, and near the boundary line along the Okanogan River a fierce fight took place, in which three Californians were killed. As the company numbered one hundred and fifty men, however, it was able to push

---

expedition to Major Trimble, Mr. Beall, and to Mr. William Kohlauf. Mr Beall went over the ground of the fight with me

[Since the above was written there has appeared a careful work by B F. Manring, entitled *The Conquest of the Couer d' Alenes, Spokanes, and Palouses.* It contains much valuable source material both for the Steptoe and the Wright expeditions.]

[5] This characterization of Wright is based on conversations with Major J G Trimble and on an editorial in The San Francisco *Daily Bulletin* of June 30th, 1864.

through. Other companies proceeded under Pearson, Steven's old express rider, and Joel Palmer, formerly superintendent of Indian affairs. Misfortunes beset the former, but the latter went through very successfully.[6] The largest company probably was that headed by "Major" Mortimer Robertson, which left the Dalles the latter part of July.[7] Most of the members were from California, but there were a number from Oregon and the "States". Among them were carpenters, blacksmiths, etc., ready, it was said, to build a city. They numbered 242 and were given a regular organization into six companies. This array reached the Fraser mines without trouble.[8] These expeditions broke the way for an important overland commerce betweeen Oregon and Washington, and British Columbia.[9]

Wright was ready to take the field the latter part of August. His force consisted of five hundred and seventy regulars, thirty friendly Nez Percés, and one hundred employes. A fort was constructed at the mouth of the Tucanon, and here Snake River was crossed. Thence the expedition struck northward, every precaution being taken to guard against surprise. The Indians were found concentrated at Four Lakes, sixteen miles southwest of the present city of Spokane.[10] Here had come Yakimas, Spokanes, Coeur d' Alenes, Pend, d' Oreilles, and representatives of many other tribes. Kamiakin, himself, was present. As the troops moved to the attack on September first, they admired the dashing horsemanship and picturesque appearance of the "wild array" of the Indians.[11] The infantry opened the battle. The men were now armed with the new minie rifle, which carried farther than the Hudson Bay carbines of the Indians and the conditions of the Rosalia fight, therefore, were reversed; the Indians were dismayed to find their firing apparently of no effect on the soldiers, while that of

---

[6] Bancroft, *Hist. of Pac. States*, Vol. XXVII, pp. 367-369.
[7] Robertson had failed to get through in an earlier attempt. *Puget Sound Herald*, July 16, 1858
[8] *Weekly Oregonian*, Aug 7th, 1858..
[9] The most important element in this traffic was cattle and it is at this time that the cattle business of Oregon and of interior Washington begins to assume large proportions. (Conversation with Hon. C. B. Bagley.)
[10] The battle took place near the present village of Medical Lake.
[11] See Kip's *Army Life on the Pacific*, pp. 55-56 Kip's account of the expedition is readable and reliable.

the latter was deadly. As the red men wavered, the day was decided by the dragoons, who, eager to avenge their former defeat, dashed upon the enemy. The Indians scattered in flight. Eighteen or twenty of them were killed and many wounded, while the whites lost none.

Five days later Wright marched for the Spokane River, fighting nearly all the way. The Indians burned the grass and fought from the cover of the smoke, but they were skillfully pressed back. Kamiakin, in the course of this skirmishing, was almost killed by being hit on the head by a large limb of a tree, which was torn off by a howitzer shell.

The spirit of the Indians was beginning to break under these defeats, and they were further cowed by an incident which occurred on Wright's march eastward along the Spokane River on his way to the Coeur d' Alene mission. He captured eight hundred horses, which the Indians hoped to regain by stampeding, but Wright encamped two days and killed the whole band. So, by the time the mission was reached and a council summoned, the Indians gathered in subdued mood. They agreed not to molest the whites any more and to give hostages for good behavior. On his way back, while encamped on Lahtoo Creek, Wright sent a detachment to the Steptoe battle field to bring the remains of those who had fallen there. Other proceedings at this camp changed the name of the creek from the beautiful softness of "Lahtoo" to the rough symbolism of "Hangman". To the camp one evening came Owhi, chief of the Yakimas, brother-in-law of Kamiakin. He acknowledged that his son Qualchien was near by. Now, Qualchien Wright particularly wanted to get hold of, for it was he that had slain Bolon, and he had been conspicuous the last summer in attacking miners. Owhi was put in irons and word sent to Qualchien that if he did not come to camp at once, his father would be hanged. Into camp, therefore, he came boldly, dressed so gorgeously as to make the soldiers stare. Wright's account makes no mention of the fierce struggles of Qualchien, when seized, nor of how he died cursing Kamiakin; the stern soldier wrote: "Qualchien came to me at 9 o'clock this morning and at 9.1/4 a. m. he was hung." The evening of the same day six Palouses met the same fate. In the course of the expedition the total number of the hanged reached sixteen. Owhi, however did not meet that death, but was shot while attempting to escape on the way back to Walla Walla.

The stern measures of Wright, with the successful cooperation of Garnett in the Yakima country, brought permanent peace to the Indian country, except for the forays of the bandit tribes of Southern Idaho. These events of the summer of 1858, indeed, were very important in the history of the settlement of the Inland Empire, for they cleared the way for the advance of the frontier.[12] General Clarke at first had been in favor of Wool's policy of keeping settlers out; but the conduct of the Indians, in attacking the troops, the emigration through the country to British Columbia, and the knowledge that it would be impossible to stay the advance of the miners and of accompanying agricultural settlers, determined him to reverse Wool's policy and to recommend the confirmation of Steven's treaties.[13] General Harney, who succeeded Clarke in October of 1858, issued an order reopening the Walla Walla valley to settlement, and in March of the next year the treaties of Stevens were ratified. The carrying out of the terms of these treaties in the founding of agencies, the payment of annuities, etc., of course helped to reconcile the Indians; while at the same time the establishment of new Ft. Colville in 1859 and the operations of the Boundary Commission, with its large escorts, completed a military cordon around them.[14]

---

[12] This Indian uprising seems intrinsically more important than the better-known outbreak of Chief Joseph. The former was an effort to stay the white advance of like nature with the efforts of Pontiac, Tecumseh and Black Hawk; while the episode of Joseph was a desperate and unreasonable, though brilliant, outbreak against going on to the prescribed reservation, and is akin to such episodes as that of Geronimo.

[13] 35th Cong., 2nd Sess. App., p. 206.

[14] Kamiakin escaped over the Bitter Root Mountains and lingered among the Pend d'Oreilles. In the winter of 1858-9 Father De Smet was sent to try to induce him and some other chiefs to come in. He found the once wealthy chieftain and his family in pitiful poverty and misery. Kamiakin "made an open avowal of all he had done in his wars against the government, particularly in the attack on Colonel Steptoe and in the war with General Wright" * * * "But he repeatedly declared to me and with the greatest apparent earnestness, that he was no murderer." The worn Indian came with the priest nearly to Walla Walla and then vanished. He finally settled down on a farm on the shore of Rock Lake in Whitman county, Washington. There he spent his old

The Boundary Commission, consisting of both British and American representatives, began its work in 1857 and completed it in 1861. Their labors resulted in a clear definition of the Line of 49' through timber and over mountains from tidewater to the summit of the Rockies. The line was marked by frequent clearings, twenty feet or more in width and half a mile or more in length, the aggregate length of these clearings amounting to almost half the total distance.[15] The plain marking of the boundary was useful to the government of British Columbia in the enforcement of its new tariff laws. Just at the time, therefore, when settlement was beginning in a region of essential physiographic wholeness, government drew sharp its artificial line.

The fixing of the boundary line on land was made difficult only by obstacles of nature, but the choice of the proper channel among the islands which lay off the mainland, produced the San Juan crisis of 1859.[16] This grave incident gets its significance largely from the mining advance, in connection of course with the geographical situation. The island had a very strategic position, since it commanded the route from Victoria to the mouth of the Fraser. The settlers who precipitated the difficulty were mainly American miners, who, on their way back from the Fraser diggings, had "squatted" on the island.[17] To the British Governor the possession of this strategic island by the Americans, especially since they already formed so large a proportion of the populace over which he ruled, seemed intolerable; on the other hand, to the United States British Columbia loomed on the Pacific as a rival, and possibly dangerous, power.

---

age H died in the later seventies and was buried on a knoll above the lake. Kamiac Creek flows near his home, while a few miles eastward a long sinuous butte is still called Kamiac Butte. The foregoing account is based on De-Smet's report (*Sen. Doc.* 36th Cong. 1st Sess. Vol. II, No. 2 pp. 98-107.) and on conversations with pioneers who knew Kamiakin.

[15] A realistic picture of the sort of opening cut may be seen in the frontispiece of Mayne's *Br. Col. and Van. Id.*; the basic account of the work of the commission is that by Baker, *Bull. U. S. Geol. Sur.*, No. 174.

[16] Official documents for the San Juan affair are found in 36th Cong., 1st Sess., Vol. V, No. 10, pp. 1-75; also Douglas, *Correspondence Book*, MS. p 22, Aug. 1859. The best secondary accounts are Meaney, *Washington*, pp. 240-254 and Bancroft's, *History of the Pacific States*, Vol. XXVII, pp. 605-639.

[17] Gosnell, *Sir James Douglas*, p. 280; Meaney, *History of Washington*, p. 244.

In the light of this occurrence the building of the Mullan road assumes an important aspect. The years 1859 and 1860 assuredly were marked by attacks on the problems of transportation both north and south of the Line. The establishment of new posts in the latter region, the necessities of the new reservations, and the need of supplies for the Boundary Commission, as well as the incoming of miners and immigrants, called for better means of communication.[18] But the possibility of war with Great Britain and the necessity in that event for a more expeditious and safer route for transportation of men and supplies to the northwest than by sea, constituted a strong motive in the War Department for furthering the new road.[19]

The plan of a road to connect the headwaters of the Columbia had been conceived by that empire builder, Stevens, who wished to open a northern route for emigration and to nourish sentiment in favor of a northern Pacific railway. He secured an appropriation from Congress of $30,000 in 1855. Meanwhile, Lieutenant John Mullan, who had been left by Stevens in the Bitter Root Valley to continue explorations in that region, discovered the easy pass over the Rockies which bears his name. Mullan, an indefatigable and enthusiastic path breaker, had done more than any other man to explore thoroughly the tangled country between the Missouri and the Spokane, and, at the instance of Stevens, he was placed in charge of the construction of the road. Delayed by the Indian war of 1858, the road was pushed through in 1859 and 1860 and completed in 1862. Its total length was 624 miles and the cost of construction $230,000. It was well constructed, substantial log bridges being built, rocky stretches blasted, and many miles of forest leveled. Before it was completed, a body of three hundred soldiers was brought west over it, and soon it began to be used by the miners.[20]

The road itself, however, was only a part of a comprehensive plan which included testing and developing the navigation of

---

[18] In the Department of Oregon there were 2158 U. S. troops in 1859, Sen. Doc. 36th Cong 2nd Sess., Vol. II, No. 2, 610–11.

[19] See report of Sec'y. Floyd, 36th Cong. 2nd Sess. Vol. II, No. 1, p. 687.

[20] Mullan, *Report on Military Road*, pp. 34–35. Wash. Gov't. Printing office, 1863.

the Missouri and of the Columbia. The house of Chouteau & Company of St. Louis, with some aid from the government, sent the first steamboat to Ft. Benton in 1859.[21] The same year the *Colonel Wright* was launched on the Columbia, the first steamboat above The Dalles. In the previous fall Ruckel and Olmsted constructed a wooden tramway around the Cascades at a cost of $114,000—one of the first steps toward the development of the Oregon Steam Navigation Company's system.[22] Both the Missouri and Columbia river lines in a few years had an immense traffic in the transportation of miners and miners' supplies.

The great movement of the miners south of the line, however, was not to come until 1861. In the period 1858 to 1860 all that was here worthy of note in mining was a revival of interest in the Colville mines and recurring efforts on the Wenatchee. The towns of Puget Sound were particularly interested in the latter region, and they were so keenly hopeful that mines would be found in American territory so situated as to boom them, that they became excited at any news favorable to their hopes. In 1858 "highly important" news from the Wenatchee brought forth an extra of the *Steilacoom Herald*, and at Seattle rumors of the same sort in 1860 led to displaying of flags, firing of guns, and general rejoicing. Town lots for sale in the latter the day before at $100 rose to "an almost unwarrantable price."[23] But the Wenatchee mines proved evanescent and the Sound country, except for settlers who eddied in from the Fraser River currents, made comparatively slow growth during the mining period.

There was, however, during 1859 and 1860 very considerable activity in the extension of the mining area in British Columbia. Nevertheless, these years, in comparison to the fevered efforts and ambitions of 1858, were on the whole dull, and are to be looked upon rather as a time of preparation for the future advance of the frontier than as a period of decisive

---

[21] Account of this trip in *Contributions to Historical Society of Montana*, Vol. VII, pp. 253–6.
[22] Portland *Advertiser*, Sept. 18, 1858.
[23] San Francisco *Daily Bulletin*, Sept. 26, 1860.

achievement. As preparatory to further advance, however, the extension of the mining area in British Columbia was not without significance and took place in two directions.

The first of these movements was up the Fraser to the region of the Quesnelle River. Some of the miners who stayed after the recession of the tide in 1858, continued work on the old bars of the Fraser, while others pushed far northward, a number striking eastward up the Thompson, but the main portion sticking to the Fraser. There were good diggings near Cayoosh or Lilloet and on Bridge Run, but the most promising territory was that of the remote Quesnelle, into which miners pressed in considerable numbers in 1859-60.[24] A detailed estimate by the *British Colonist* in the winter of 1859-60 of the population along the Fraser, on the Douglas-Lilloet route, and above Lilloet placed it at 1175, and this was largely increased the next summer, especially on the Quesnelle.[25] The distances to be travelled, however, were great, and the difficulties of transportation immense. No miners in America had yet faced such formidable obstacles as these who were now toiling toward the heart of British Columbia. Yields, while variable, were on the whole encouraging, but it was almost impossible to get supplies. In the spring of 1860 flour on the Quesnelle cost $125 per barrel and bacon $1.50 per pound. Tools were not to be had.[26] The arrival of packers from Oregon, however, in June (among them the indefatigable General Joel Palmer) relieved the situation and brought a reduction of 25-50 per cent.[27]

The other important scene of mining activity in British Columbia at this period lay east of the Cascade mountains near the boundary, along the Similkameen River and Rock Creek. These diggings were first discovered by soldiers of the Boundary Commission in the fall of 1859, and high hopes were entertained of them.[28] Early in the following spring large numbers of men came from The Dalles, Walla Walla, the Sound, the

---

[24] A good account of this movement is to found in Bancroft, pp. 447-461. *History of Pacific States*, Vol. XXVII.
[25] Quoted in San Francisco *Daily Bulletin*, Feb. 1st, 1860.
[26] *Id.* May 30th, 1860.
[27] San Francisco *Daily Bulletin*, June 19, 1860.
[28] Bancroft, *Works*, Vol. XXXI, *Wash. Id. and Mont.*, p. 232.

Willamette Valley, and from northern California. Heavy shipments of goods were made, 120 pack animals and horses leaving The Dalles in one day.[29] Two embryo towns sprang up, with the usual sprinkling of saloons, "hotels," and stores. A few men did very well, but the rich diggings did not prove extensive; the larger portion of the miners scattered to other fields, and this district proved not very valuable.

The great problem of the Government of British Columbia at this time, it can readily be seen, was to facilitate transportation to the remote regions to which the miners were penetrating, and this both for the sake of development of the regions themselves (with consequent revenue), and in order that Victoria might compete in trade with the Dalles and Portland. Remarkably effective aid to the government in the solution of this problem, and in other tasks as well, was furnished by a detachment of the Royal Engineers.[30]

This corps was sent from England in 1858 by order of Sir. E. Bullwer Lytton, then Her Majesty's principal Secretary of State for the Colonies. It was under Lytton's guidance and care that the new colony came into being, and it may be interesting to note that the library which the Engineers took with them was selected by the author of *"The Last Days of Pompeii."* The detachment "was a picked body, selected out of a large number of volunteers for this service, and chosen with the view of having included in their ranks every trade, profession, and calling which might be useful in the circumstances of a colony springing so suddenly into existence. And although it is called a detachment of the Royal Engineers, there were four men in it who did not belong to the Royal Engineers at all—namely, two of the Royal Artillery and two of the 15th Hussars—included for the purpose of forming the nucleus of an artillery corps should the exigencies of the case so re-

---

[29] San Francisco *Daily Bulletin*, Feb. 18, 1860.
[30] Mention may be made here of the explorations made by Capt Palliser under the auspices of the Royal Geographical Society. Palliser in 1859 went from Edmonton by way of Kootenai Pass to Ft. Colville The object was to find a suitable pass for a railroad, but no such pass was then found Beggs, *Hist. Br. C*, p 448; Bancroft, *His. Pac States*, Vol. XXVII, p. 643; *Paper Relative to the Exploration by the Expedition under Captain Palliser* (1858), and *Further Papers* (1860).

quire."[31] In all there were about one hundred and sixty men, and they were under the command of Colonel R. C. Moody.

The first duty with which Colonel Moody was charged was the selection of a site for the capital of British Columbia. "On sanitary, on commercial, on military, and on political grounds" he chose a thickly wooded eminence on the north bank of the Fraser River. The town which began to grow in 1859 on this site was at first called Queensborough, but later was named New Westminster.

On two occasions the Engineers took part in strictly military movements. The first occasion occurred in connection with a jealous dispute between two magistrates at Yale and Hill's Bar. Conspicuous in this dispute was Ned McGowan, who, as a resident of California, has been under the ban of the Vigilantes. At a distance the affair took the appearance of an uprising of the rougher Americans, and Douglas took instant steps for thorough suppression Twenty-five of the Engineers and a force of marines, accompanied by Chief Justice Begbie, went to Yale. The trouble proved at close range a complete fiasco, serious only for the heavy cost to the colony for sending the troops; nevertheless it suggested the sort of treatment that would be given to disturbers of the Queen's peace [32] Another occasion arose the next summer at the time of the San Juan affair when fifteen of the Engineers were ordered to the scene of trouble.

The great work of the corps, however, was in coping with the problem of transportation. The developments on the upper Fraser and the Quesnelle emphasized the necessity of some way for improving transportation to a point beyond the cañons of the lower Fraser. A route had been discovered in 1858 which proceeded by way of Harrison River and Lake and a chain of small lakes to Cayoosh on the Fraser. But there were considerable stretches of portage at various places on this route,

---

[31] *The Work of the Royal Engineers in British Columbia*, by His Honour, Frederic W. Howay, p. 3. This is an excellent and elegantly executed monograph, which gives an interesting and reliable account of the work of the engineers. I am indebted to Richard Wolfenden, I. S O, V. D., Printer to the King, for a copy Colonel Wolfenden was, himself, a member of this detachment of the Engineers.'

[32] *Id.* p. 485

which required the making of trails and roads. By the cooperation of Gov. Douglas and the miners a trail had been made in 1858. The Engineers deepened the channel of Harrison River and constructed a substantial road between Douglas and Little Lilloet Lake,—a "work of magnitude" wrote Douglas, "and of the utmost public utility."[33] A trail was laid out by them, also, to Similkameen, afterwards widened out into a wagon road. Their monumental work, however, was done on the great trunk road from Yale to Cariboo, the most difficult portions of which were constructed by them. These sections were fairly carved from the great rock walls of the Fraser.

Besides their services in road building, the Engineers laid out all the important towns and made surveys of the public lands. Their work is thus summarized by Judge Howay:—"All the important explorations in the colony were performed by them; the whole peninsula between Burrard Inlet and Fraser River was surveyed by them; all the surveys of towns and country lands were made by them; all the main roads were laid out by them; some of these, including portions of the Cariboo Road, the Hope-Similkameen Road, the Douglas-Lilloet Road, and the North Road to Burrard Inlet were built by them; practically all the maps of the colony and of sections of it were made from their surveys, prepared in their drafting office, lithographed and published by them at their camp; they formed in 1862, the first building society in the colony; they designed the first churches (Holy Trinity Church and St. Mary's Church, New Westminster) and the first school-house in the colony; they designed the first coat of arms and the first postage stamp in the colony; they established the first observatory, and to them we owe the first systematic meteorological observations in the colony, covering a period of three years; they formed the Lands and Works Department, the Government Printing Office, and printed the first British Columbia Gazette; they aided in the maintenance of law and order; and their commanding officer was the first Chief Commissioner of Lands and Works, as well as the first Lieutenant Governor."[34] No such record of multi-

---
[33] *Id.* p. 7
[34] *Id.* pp. 9 and 10.

farious activities can be assigned to any one body of men south of the line in preparation for or participation in the mining advance.[35]

---

[35] The letters of Governor Douglas, it must be said in deference to historical impartiality, contain some adverse criticisms of the Engineers, though these may be due in part to what we in the United States would call differences of sectional leaders, Colonel Moody representing New Westminster and Gov. Douglas Victoria. See *Correspondence Book of Sir James Douglas*, MS., pp. 71-72.

CHAPTER IV

CARIBOO, KOOTENAI, AND THE UPPER COLUMBIA

I. Cariboo

Notwithstanding the activity of the Engineers and the extension of the mining area to the Similkameen and the Quesnelle, the years 1859 and 1860 in the British Colony, as we have before remarked, in comparison with the excitement and activity of 1858 were years of dullness and discouragement. In Victoria business was poor, and the merchants regretted the departure of the California miners. The yield of gold, however, was considerable, amounting in 1859 to over a million and a half of dollars.[1] Yet there seemed danger of further decrease of population and even of the collapse of the Colony. Governor Douglas, on a visit to the upper country, in September of 1860, wrote from Cayoosh that "The fate of the Colony hangs at this moment upon a thread, abundance of the precious metal is the only thing that can save it from ruin."[2]

The abundance of the precious metal, which was permanently to establish British Columbia, came from one of the most remarkable gold fields in the whole history of mining—the Cariboo district. This district lay in the triangular area to the north of Quesnelle Lake and River, between them and the farthest bend northward of the Fraser. A good description of it has been left us by Lieutenant Palmer of the Royal Engineers: "Cariboo is closely packed with mountains of considerable altitude, singularly tumbled and irregular in character, and presenting steep and thickly wooded slopes. Here and there tremendous masses, whose summits are from 6000 to

---
[1] *Geological Survey of Canada*, 1887-88, Report, p. 23R.
[2] Douglas to Moody, *Correspondence Book*, MS. pp. 48-49.

7000 feet above the sea, tower above the general level, and form centres of radiation of subordinate ranges. This mountain system is drained by innumerable streams, of every size from large brooks to tiny rivulets . . . , which run in every imaginable direction of the compass.

"Of the Superior mountain passes—Mts. Snowshoe, Burdett, and Agnes, the latter is generally known as the 'Bald Mountain of William's Creek.' (On these there was but a scanty growth of trees, and the tops were covered with grass.)

"The headwaters of the streams radiate in remarkable manner from these bald clusters. From Mt. Agnes a circle of one and one-half miles radius includes the sources of Williams, Lightning, Jack of Clubs, and Antler Creeks."[3] Three of these creeks—Williams, Lightning, and Antler—were the more important in the mining history of Cariboo. Their valleys, in common with those of other creeks were "generally narrow, rocky, thickly wooded, and frequently swampy."

About the time that Gov. Douglas was writing his rather doleful letter from Cayoosh in the fall of 1860, the adventurous vanguard of the miners, having pushed up the north branch of the Quesnelle to Cariboo Lake and prospected the streams emptying into that lake from the north, crossed the divide into Antler Creek. Reports of marvellous finds made by these men came to the outer world during the winter. The next summer (1861) about 1500 men penetrated to this rich region, and these are estimated to have produced $2,000,000.[4] In this year Lightning and Williams Creeks were discovered and yielded fabulously.[5] At Victoria in the fall gaping crowds followed miners to the banks as they carried fortunes in canvass sacks—fortunes which promised restoration of prosperity to the city.

The years 1862 and 1863 saw the flood tide in the history of Cariboo, although the mines there continued to yield largely for some years later. About 2500 men were at work in Cariboo

---

[3] Palmer, Lieut. H. Spencer, *Williams Lake and Cariboo, Topographical Report*. Printed at Royal Engineers Press, New Westminster 1863, pp 10–12.
[4] Estimate of Dawson, *Geological Survey of Canada*, Rpt., 1887–88, p. 20B.
[5] An excellent general account of Cariboo is that of Dawson, mentioned above. For details of discoveries, Bancroft, *His. of Pac. States*, Vol. XXXII, pp 472–519, gives much valuable information, though not well organized.

in 1862 and 4000 in 1863. Most of these were laborers, who received at the ordinary rate $10 per day, but who paid $35 per week for board and for the privilege of sleeping on the floor of a cabin wrapped each in his own blanket. The rate of wages paid is proof of the extraordinary richness of the field. On Williams Creek there were at work in 1862 one hundred and sixty-nine "Companies" owning 727 claims. By the tenth of June, 1863, the number of claims was 3071. Two mining towns had arisen, Van Winkle on Lightning Creek and Richfield on Williams. Attention was being directed to quartz, and 50 claims were staked off on Snowshoe mountain in 1862. Capital was accumulated in large amounts at the mines and invested there.[6]

The yields were remarkable and can be verified better than in most camps. Of course the tales of individuals acquiring fortunes in a few months are many. For example we may cite the celebrated "Cariboo" Cameron, who went to the mines in the spring of 1862 fresh from Ontario and so unused to miners' life that men laughed at him for calling a claim a "lot." He had $500 when he left Victoria in the spring of 1862; during the summer he made $10,000 and acquired title to claims so valuable that he was able within a year to leave the colony with $150,000.[7] We are fortunate, however, in the case of the Cariboo mines, in having some official statements in regard to yields which are of very exceptional reliability and importance. These are found in reports from Mr. Peter O'Reilly, Gold Commissioner in Cariboo in 1862-63.[8]

---

[6] The sources of this account are summaries found in the London *Times*, Aug. 8 and 26, 1863.

[7] Cameron links up with some older British Columbia history. He was neighbor to Simon Fraser, the discoverer of Fraser River, and went to Cariboo at about the same time as John Fraser, a son of Simon. Cameron returned to his old neighborhood in Ontario and bought a large farm and a mill, but fortune had turned, and he lost his money. He returned to Cariboo, thinking again to wrest riches from the old gulches, but he failed, and lived on, haunting in a restless and impecunious old age various gold fields (as did Dietz, Stout, Comstock, and so many once fortunate miners), until at last he died and was buried at Barkerville. These details I have from Judge Frederic W. Howay and from Mr. Simon Fraser, a grandson of the explorer, now a resident of Fargo, N. D.

[8] The reports from the Assistant Gold Commissioners to Gov Douglas from the various fields constitute perhaps the most reliable and satisfactory sources

Writing from Richfield, May 11, 1863, Mr. O'Reilly mentions that he has been able through the kindness of Messrs. Grier and Diller to get a "short statistical return of their respective Companies," but that the latter gentleman did not want his information published in the local papers. The returns are as follows:

"The Hard Curry Claim.

"Williams Creek.

"This claim was originally preempted on the 27th of September, 1861, by three shareholders, viz: J. P. Diller, Pennsylvania, Jas. Loring, Boston, and Hard Curry, Georgia, and is still held by them in three full shares of 100 feet each.

"During a period of 17 months from the time above mentioned no satisfactory results were obtained, the time being chiefly employed in prospecting the claim. Two shafts were sunk at an aggregate cost of $7724. On the 18th of February 1863 the Company began to wash up, and from that time to the present the claim has steadily paid the following almost fabulous amounts to the fortunate share holders."

		Ounces.	Dollars.
Three days ending 21st Feb		295	$4,720
Week " 28th "		236	3,776
Week " 7th Mar		1,327	21,232
Week " 14th "		475	7,600
Week " 21st "		1,785	28,560
Week " 28th "		753	12,048
Week " 4th April		1,62	28,192
Week " 11th "		2,744	43,904
Four weeks " 18th-29th April,			
and and-9th May		1,276	20,416
Total		10,053	$170,448

"The total amount expended by the Company in working the claim from the 18th of February is $26,748, which with a previous cost of $7724 brings the total expenses to the 9th of May to $34,472, this being deducted from the gross amount

---

for the history of the early period of British Columbia mining. For more extended comment on them see the Bibliography.

taken out leaves a net profit of $135,976 or $45,325 to each share." . . .

"The number of men employed was 21 and the depth reached was 60 feet. The lead is from 12 to 15 feet wide and the strata of gravel in which gold is found is 9 feet in depth."

At present only 90 feet out of the claim of 300 have been worked."

P. O'Reilly, Gold Commissioner."

"The Grier Claim

"Williams Creek

"The original company consisted of five share holders, viz: Daniel Grier, a native of Wales, John Fairburn, Scotland, Michael Gillam, Ireland, Capt. O'Rorke, Ireland, and John Wilson, Canada West, who recorded in May, 1861, 100 feet each.

"From May to August they prospected at a cost of $3000 which included the purchase of sluices and all other material for working the claim. From August to the first week in October the net profits amounted to $7000 to the share, at which time the claims remained unworked till the 24th of May 1862. From the 24th of May 1862 to the 24th of October the total amount taken out of the claim was.............. $100,111. The total expense during that period amounted to   28,366. Leaving as net profit a sum of ....   71,745. Or to each full interest a dividend of'..........   14,349."

P. O'Reilly, Gold Commissioner."

On Nov. 27, 1863, Mr. O'Reilly summarized the results of the year in Cariboo as follows: "The number of men actually employed in the District of Cariboo north of Quesnelle River, may be set down as 4000.

"The gross amount of gold taken from the same district estimated from weekly returns obtained from claim owners on the spot, and also from personal knowledge may with safety be computed at $3,904,000.

"The quantity of provisions sent to the upper country, ascertained from the collection of road Tolls is over 2000 tons.

"The above statistics may be relied upon as being as nearly accurate as it is possible to obtain them."

Some idea of the amount of business carried on with the Cariboo mines may be derived from a statement of Mr. Cox, who succeeded Mr. O'Reilly. He wrote, from Richfield Feb. 6th, 1864, that the stock of goods in merchants' hands was,

Flour	300,000 lbs.
Beans	55,000 "
Bacon	16,000 "
Sugar	35,000 "
Tea and Coffee	30,000 "
Fresh beef	10,000 "

When we recall that nearly all of these staples (except the last) had been transported from Victoria a distance about as great as from New York to Chicago and most of that distance over rough roads and trails, we get a glimpse of the tremendous energy employed in opening up this remote region.

The importance of the business of this region to Victoria is shown from the fact that in June of 1863 it was estimated that the indebtedness of British Columbia to Victoria was $2,000,000 and that it was thought that 75 per cent. of the debt would be paid by September.[9] When the devout Bishop of Columbia visited the upper country and noted the capital invested, the ravines bridged, and the rocks blasted, he wrote: "Mountains and mighty torrents inspire the heart with reverence for the works of God; but not less instructive of the Presence of our God are all these strivings and movements of men."[10]

Williams' Creek in these years, particularly during the mining season, was a place of concentrated activity. An Englishman has left us a description of the place as it impressed him [11]

---
[9] London *Times*, Aug. 14, 1863.
[10] *Journal*, 1862-3, p. 25.
[11] Johnson, R. Byron, *Very Far West Indeed*, pp. 113-116. A cursory reading of this work is likely to make one regard it as unreliable because the style is vivid and some of the adventures so exaggerated as to seem untrue. But discrimination should be made between such stories and the description of places and scenes. The latter are corroborated by maps and by comparison with such authorities as Mr. O'Reilly and the *Occasional Papers* of the Columbia Mission.

[187]

"Across the breadth of the little valley," he writes, "was a strange heterogeneous gathering of small flumes, carrying water to the different diggings and supported at various heights from the ground by props, windlasses at the mouths, water-wheels, bands of tailings (the refuse washed through the sluices) and miners' log huts.

"On the sides of the hills the primeval forests had been cleared for a short distance upwards, to provide timber for mining purposes, and logs for the huts. These abodes were more numerous on the hill sides than in the bottom of the valley, as being more safe from removal.

"The town comprised the ordinary series of rough wooden shanties, stores, restaurants, grog shops and gambling saloons; and on a little eminence, the official residence, tenanted by the Gold Commissioner and his assistants and one policeman, with the British flag permanently displayed in front of it, looked over the whole.

"In and out of this nest the human ants poured all day and night, for in wet-sinking the labour must be kept up without ceasing all through the twenty-four hours, Sundays included. It was a curious sight to look down the Creek at night, and see each shaft with its little fire, and its lantern, and the dim ghostly figures gliding about from darkness into light, like the demons at a Drury Lane pantomine. while an occasional hut was illuminated by some weary laborer returning from his nightly toil."

"The word here seemed to be *work*, and nothing else; only round the bar rooms and the gambling-tables were a few loafers and gamblers to be seen. Idling was too expensive luxury in a place where wages were from two to three pounds per day and flour sold at six shillings a pound.

"The mingling of the noises was as curious as that of objects. From the hills came the perpetual cracking and thudding of axes, intermingling with the crash of falling trees, and the grating undertone of the saws, as they fashioned the logs into

---

Such is the verisimilitude that Mr Johnson either had actually visited the places described or had studied carefully about them [I am later informed on reliable authority that Mr Johnson did visit Cariboo]

planks and boards. From the bottom of the valley rose the splashing and creaking of water wheels, the grating of shovels, the din of the blacksmith's hammer sharpening pick axes, and the shouts passed from the tops of the numerous shafts to the men below, as the emptied bucket was returned by the windlass.''

The difficulties with which the miners of Cariboo had to contend were great. The climate, though not unhealthful, was disagreeable and at times caused serious loss and delay in mining operations. The winters were long and there were spells of intense cold, while the summer weather was variable, alternating between extremes of heat and cold. Perhaps the most unfortunate climatic feature was the incessant rains in the spring, which swept away dams, flumes, and water wheels and filled up shafts. Another difficulty arose from the geology of the country. The surface diggings served merely to attract the first discoverers; the real wealth of Cariboo lay in its deep diggings. The leads followed ancient river channels, and these were covered by the detritus of modern streams and displaced by glacial action. In consequence shafts forty to seventy feet deep had to be sunk and even then, after the expenditure of much money, there was no certainty of striking the lead. The Hard Curry Company, for example, sank their first shaft in the channel and on the lead, but the bed rock was found washed smooth; after drifting from the bottom of the shaft without success they abandoned it and sank another: it was later found that the first shaft was only ten feet from a spot where the Company afterwards took out 1224 ounces in a single day.[12] Moreover, water seeped into many shafts and could be removed only by rigging expensive pumps and windlasses. Laborers often had to work day after day in water and mud, sometimes without boots, because none could be had in camp to fit or the price was prohibitive. A man mourned greatly when he snagged a pair of boots that cost him seventeen dollars. O'Reilly reports the following prices on Aug. 15th, 1862:

---

[12] *Report* of Peter O'Reilly, May 11, 1863

```
Flour ............................$1.50 per lb.
Beans ............................ 1.50  "     "
Beef .............................50–55c "    "
Tea .............................. 3.00  "    "
Nails ............................ 3.00  "    "
Picks and shovels ................10.00 each
Lumber ...........................22c per foot
```

It is plain, therefore, that the Cariboo miners faced uncommonly severe obstacles arising from climate, geology, and scarcity of supplies. In order to meet these varied obstacles and to acquire the indispensable capital required, "Companies" were resorted to, and these became even more a marked feature of the industry of Cariboo than in other placer fields. The individual, once a camp was established, could do little except to labor for some one else or to prospect for new fields. *Some form of co-operative or organized effort is essential to the development of the mining industry, even in its simpler stages.*

All other difficulties were small, however, compared to those of transportation, and in large part dependent upon them. Not only was it necessary to transport supplies great distances into the interior, but to get them over the terrible country that lay between Quesnellemouth and Cariboo. "It is difficult to find language to express in adequate terms," writes Lieutenant Palmer, "the utter vileness of the trails of Cariboo, dreaded alike by all classes of travellers; slippery, precipitous ascents and descents, fallen logs, overhanging branches, roots, rocks, swamps, turbid pools and miles of deep mud."[13] The Bishop of Columbia had to wade through bog to his knees going into Cariboo, and on reaching Williams Creek it seemed to him like camping on a swamp.[14] It was a melancholy sight to see all along the trail the bodies of horses that had died from toil and poor feed. The absence of grass in the dense forests of the valleys was one of the greatest evils of the region, although there was good pasture on the summits of the hills. Horses

---

[13] *Report, Williams Lake and Cariboo*, p. 13. See also *Diary of Journey to Williams Creek*, Cariboo, May 1863, Macfie, 224–229

[14] *Journal*, 1862–63, p. 37.

already worn by being away from the bunch grass of the Fraser terraces during a two or three days' journey came weakened to this last terrible stretch. Sometimes a drover would lose half his train after leaving the Quesnelle, and sometimes it was impossible to use animals at all. Then men plodded through the mud and scrambled over the logs with packs of fifty pounds or more on their backs.

Great efforts were made to better communications with Cariboo in the years 1862-3. Trails were built connecting Williams Creek with Van Winkle and the latter with Quesnellemouth.[15] From Lytton to Quesnellemouth the routes followed were comparatively easy, since they were in part along the terraces of the Fraser. The portage roads on the route leading to Lytton from the lower Fraser via Harrison Lake were finished in 1863, and the great trunk wagon road to Lytton from Yale was constructed through the cañons of the Fraser about the same time. In places on this road the rocks were so precipitous that men worked suspended from the cliffs overhead. A suspension bridge was thrown across the Fraser, and navigation on that river of course expanded.[16] In 1863 the steamer Enterprise was placed upon the smooth stretch of the upper Fraser to run between Soda Creek and Quesnellemouth. Parties of returning miners who were willing to take chances built boats at Quesnellemouth which held seventeen passengers, hired an expert steersman, and ran the cañons to Yale.[17] On the lower Fraser there were ten steamers in 1863.

One of the accompaniments of this improvement in transportation and the development of the mining industry was the growth of agriculture along the roads. Farms were being brought into cultivation at various places between Lytton and Quesnelle. About Beaver Lake over a thousand acres were in crop in 1863, and along the Bonaparte River about 2000 acres were cultivated. It was thought that in a few years British

---

[15] The cost of these trails was defrayed from the revenues of Cariboo. O'Reilly paid out $25,300 for this purpose in 1863; Letter of O'Reilly Sept. 1st, 1863

[16] Resumé of these activities in Judge Howay's *Royal Engineers*, pp. 88.9

[17] Wm. Stout made seven of these perilous trips; *Reminiscences of Wm. Stout*, MS

Columbia would produce sufficient cereals for its own consumption.[18]

Victoria of course shared in the prosperity of the interior. Substantial buildings of stone and brick replaced tents and wooden buidings. Once more crowds of veteran miners were to be seen on the streets; but with them mingled unseasoned newcomers from England, for a larger portion of the immigration of 1862-3 was from the mother country than in that of 1858. Many of these novices were in straits financially, and young men of good family might be seen at manual labor. Business improved steadily. Imports rose from $2,020,000 in 1861 to $3,866,000 in 1863.[19] The combined revenues of Vancouver Island and British Columbia, which in 1859 were $73,000 and in 1860 $375,000, in 1863 were $706,000.[20] A conservative estimate of the yields of gold in 1859 places it at $1,615,000, and in 1863 at $3,900,000.[21]

The discovery and development of the mines of Cariboo, we conclude, therefore, were of paramount importance in the early history of British Columbia.

II. Kootenai.

Just as Cariboo reached the zenith of its yield in the fall of 1863, came rumors of a new field in the far southeastern corner of British Columbia. The principal diggings were upon Wild Horse Creek, which flows into the Kootenai River about fifty miles north of the Boundary.

In the fall of 1863 a prospector from Colville, named James Manning, was at the Hudson's Bay Company's post on the Tobacco Plains, when a half-breed named Finley brought in about five hundred dollars worth of beautiful gold, which he had obtained from the creek now known as Finley's Creek. Manning spent the winter near Vermilion Pass and early in the spring started prospecting various creeks. In March he joined a party of twenty men who came in by the Bitter Root Valley

---
[18] London *Times*, Aug. 26th, 1863.
[19] Harvey, *Statistical Account of British Columbia*, p. 19.
[20] *Id.* p. 10.
[21] *Geological Survey of Canada*, 1887-88, *Report*, p. 23 R

route from East Bannock, Stinking Water, and Warrens.[22] They immediately found good prospects on Wild Horse Creek and took up claims. By June there were upwards of five hundred men in the country, and in the middle of the summer, when the Assistant Gold Commissioner, John C. Haynes, arrived, there were one thousand men on Wild Horse Creek alone.

Haynes reported in August (1864) that ordinary claims were paying from $20 to $30 per day to the hand and mentioned ten companies whose average exceeded that. He issued twenty-two traders' licenses, twelve liquor licenses and over six hundred miners' certificates. In the month of August the revenues amounted to over eleven thousand dollars, of which more than one-half was derived from the customs duties.[23] In the fall there were fifty sluice companies at work, employing from five to twenty-five men each and taking out from $300 to $1000 per day. The gold was of the best grade, worth $18 per ounce. A town had sprung up called Fisherville. The Colonial Secretary, A. N. Birch, on his return from a visit to Kootenai in October took with him seventy-five pounds of government gold and rejoiced to be the first to carry gold from the base of the Rockies to New Westminster.[24]

It is significant of how the Kootenai mines were regarded in the spring of 1865 that Commissioner O'Reilly was sent there instead of to Cariboo, which had now begun to wane. In 1865, the banner year for these mines, there were from 1500 to 2000 men in the district. Fisherville, the principal town, contained 120 houses at the beginning of the season, but as the village was located on rich ground, two-thirds of it was washed away during the summer—a proceeding which caused many disputes between mine owners and house holders. Victoria Ditch, three miles long, carrying 2000 inches of water, and rendering workable 100 claims was completed at a cost of $125,000. One

---

[22] Lewiston *Golden Age*, June 4, 1864, in San Francisco *Daily Bulletin*, June 10, 1864.

[23] This account follows a narrative by Mr. Manning found among the reports of the Gold Commissioners. It is dated Sooyoos Lake, July 16, 1864, and apparently is from Mr. Haynes. See also *Report* of John C. Haynes, Aug 30th, 1864

[24] *Report* of the Colonial Secretary, A. N Birch, to Governor Frederick Seymour, Oct. 31, 1864, Macfie, 255–262, *Van Id. and Br. Col.*

shaft was sunk 90 feet. It was very difficult to estimate the amount produced in the district, because the miners would not tell their yields on account of the new export duty on gold, but it was the general opinion of miners and traders that about one million dollars was taken out. The gross revenue for the year was estimated at $75,000. On Elk Creek about 200 men were at work. But the population of the whole district was reduced by repeated rushes to the Upper Columbia, Coeur d' Alene and the Blackfoot mines, particularly to the latter.[25]

In 1866, consequently, Kootenai had clearly begun to decline. Only seven hundred men were at work on Wild Horse Creek, half of whom were Chinese. The latter had paid high prices for claims—from $2000 to $7000—and promptly met all engagements. There was considerable litigation, however, arising from the white men trying to take advantage of the Chinese.[26]

The real importance of the Kootenai mines in the mining history of the Inland Empire arose from their location, they being remote from the commercial and governmental centres of the British Colonies and easily accessible from the territories to the south. Hope, the nearest village on the Fraser, by the round-about trail that was followed, was over five hundred miles distant, and part of the trail, that from Ft. Shephard to Wild Horse Creek, was so bad that, in 1864, one of the Hudson's Bay Company trains was fourteen days in making the trip from that post and lost six horses in doing so. Lewiston, on the contrary, was only 342 miles distant, Walla Walla 408, and Umatilla Landing 453.[27] Consequently, in spite of high tariff, improvement of the British trail, and eagerness of the Government to draw trade to Victoria, physiographic considerations prevailed, and nearly all the trade was with points south of the boundary.

A marked feature of the life in Kootenai was the submission of the miners to the lawful authorities. Here were a thousand

---

[25] *Reports* of Peter O'Reilly from Wild Horse Creek, May-Sept. 1865; also resumé made Jan. 11, 1866.
[26] *Report* of Mr. Gaggin, Aug. 18, 1866.
[27] *Report* of A. N. Birch, Macfie, *Van Id. & Br. Col.* 255-262.

or two of rough miners, all collected from the American territories at the time when Montana was going through vigilante throes; government was represented by a lone magistrate with two or three constables unsupported by any possibility of aid from the Fraser; and the district was close to the boundary line, a condition permitting easy escape for transgressors. And yet the testimony of the British officials is unanimous as to the orderliness of the miners. Even before the arrival of Mr. Haynes, the miners, as usual, had taken steps to form district laws, but on the coming of the magistrate they gave him hearty support. When Mr. Birch arrived, he found "the mining laws of the colony in full force, all customs' duties paid, no pistols to be seen, and everything as quiet and orderly as it could possibly be in the most civilized district of the colony."[28] Mr. O'Reilly arrested three Americans for bringing in and circulating counterfeit gold dust, but he wrote in review of the year: "It is gratifying to be able to state that not an instance of serious crime occurred during the past season, and this is perhaps the more remarkable if we take into consideration the class of men usually attracted to new gold fields and the close proximity of the Southern Boundary, affording at all times great facilities for escape from justice."[29]

III. The Upper Columbia

The reports concerning the mining districts on the Upper Columbia, which circulated in the fall of 1865, characterized these districts as "poor man's diggings"—i. e., diggings where the deposits were superficial and workable by individuals with small capital; whereas Cariboo and Kootenai were "deep diggings," necessitating companies and capital for digging shafts, pumping, draining, and drifting.[30] Mr. O'Reilly was assigned to the Upper Columbia districts in 1866. The main diggings were on French and McCullough's Creeks, branches of Gold

---

[28] *Report* of A. N. Birch; *id.*
[29] *Report,* June 29, 1865; report, Jan. 11, 1866. The only tax that the miners tried to escape was that of the export duty on gold, not one-fifth of which was paid. O'Reilly thought it ought to be repealed. Total returns $6900. Report of Jan. 11, 1866
[30] *Report* of Mr Moberly, *Government Gazette,* Dec. 12, 1865.

[195]

Creek, which empties into the Columbia from the east, well up within the Big Bend. On arriving at Wilson's Landing in May, Mr. O'Reilly learned that a new steamer, the "49," had made its first trip from Ft. Shephard to Dalles Des Mort a few days before. The "49" proved an important factor in the transportation to this region.[31] Proceeding to McCullough's Creek, the gold commissioner found there six or seven companies, who were hindered by deep snow. On French Creek more men were found; some sanguine, others dejectedly starting to retrace their steps to Cariboo, Kootenai or Blackfoot. In all about twelve hundred men had crossed at Wilson's Landing, and this furnished a rough index to the numbers of the miners. Prices were extremely high. On trying to hire a constable, O'Reilly discovered that the wages allowed by the Government for such work were 23 cents less per day than one meal would cost, viz., three dollars. The diggings proved difficult to work on account of water and boulders, and it was apparent these were not such "poor men's diggings" as had been reported. The miners combined, however, in a "spirited way" and four or five companies worked on a test shaft, using night shifts, but they were driven out by the water at 42 feet. Fresh pumps were rigged, however, and some good yields were reported. On McCullough's Creek, by this time, fifteen companies were making from eight to twenty dollars per day to the hand. The whole district was "perfectly quiet and free from outrage of any sort.[32] The difficulties encountered, however, proved too great in proportion to the yield, and the district rapidly declined.

This movement to the Upper Columbia, insignificant compared to those to Kootenai, Cariboo, and the Fraser, may be regarded as closing the initial period of the mining industry in British Columbia. During this period, as we ought perhaps also to mention, small numbers of prospectors made their way to the far north into the Omineca district of the Skeena and Peace Rivers and to the Cassiar district of the Stickeen

---

[31] Bancroft, *His. of Pac. States*, Vol. XXVII, p. 534 Bancroft gives a satisfactory account of this movement, pp. 530-538.
[32] *Reports* of Mr. O'Reilly, May 11 to June 30, 1866.

River, and in 1871 there was considerable migration to these parts. However, the history of these movements does not lie within the range of the present study, since they may be regarded more properly as an introductory chapter to the history of mining on the Yukon.[33] The movements to Fraser River, Cariboo, and Kootenai, on the other hand, were clearly related to the movements south of the Line and were of typical and foundational importance.

---

[33] Account of the Omineca & Cassiar movements in Bancroft, *His. of Pac. States*, pp 543-564 See also *Report on an Exploration in the Yukon District, N. W. T. and adjacent Northern Portion of British Columbia*, 1887; *Geol Sur. of Canada*, No. 629.

CHAPTER V

THE MINING ADVANCE INTO IDAHO, EASTERN OREGON, AND MONTANA

Contemporaneously with the mining movements into British Columbia from 1860–66, similar occupation of new regions was proceeding in the territories to the south. The most important of these new localities were the Nez Percés and Salmon River districts in the northern part of what is now Idaho (then Washington Territory); John Day and Powder Rivers in eastern Oregon; Boise Basin and Owyhee in southern Idaho; and Deer Lodge, Bannack, Alder Gulch, and Last Chance Gulch in the present Montana. To get the location of these various districts clearly in mind not only will help in our historical survey of the movements by which these districts were occupied, but will also contribute to a better understanding of later chapters, in particular of the one on transportation.

The traveller who journeyed to the mines of the interior from the coast by the ordinary route—that by way of the Columbia—found the Columbia from the mouth of the Willamette for about forty-three miles upward a broad stream with ample depth for navigation. Then comes a gorge-like narrowing through which the river rushes with great velocity for four and one-half miles. This first obstruction constitutes the Cascades. For about forty-five miles above the Cascades there is another stretch of unimpeded navigation terminated by The Dalles and Celilo Falls. Here, "in the course of nine miles the river passes over falls and rapids and through contracted channels that completely block navigation. The fall in this distance is eighty-one feet"[1] From this point up the Colum-

---

[1] For this quotation and much of the data of this paragraph I am indebted to an excellent article by Professor Frederic G. Young in the *Annals of the American Acadamy of Political and Social Science*, Jan., 1908, pp. 189–202, on *Columbia River Improvement and the Pacific Northwest*. Quotation on p. 198.

bia 110 miles to its junction with the Snake and thence 146 miles to Lewiston there is no serious obstruction to navigation, though there are some formidable rapids.[2]

At Lewiston the cañon of the Snake takes an abrupt turn to the south, which general direction it keeps for about 200 miles, before proceeding again eastward. For about 125 miles of this southerly stretch, from the vicinity of Asotin, Washington, nearly to Weiser, Idaho, the river cañon is from 2000 to 6000 feet deep and in the vicinity of the Seven Devils Mountains assumes the grandest and most forbidding proportions. Above Weiser the depth of the cañon recedes to 200–700 feet, and the flow of the river is sufficiently gentle again to allow navigation. The rough stretch of the river just referred to and the Cascades-Dalles obstructions may be regarded as great steps in gaining the plateau regions.[3]

The mining districts of Idaho and eastern Oregon (with the exception of one far up on the John Day River, a tributary of the Columbia) were situated on the affluents of the Snake which enter it in the course of its northerly flow. The mines were not near the mouths of these affluents (which as they near the Snake partake of its cañon character), but at considerable distances up the streams. Taking first the rivers on the east side, we find farthest north the Clearwater, which empties into the Snake at Lewiston. Up the Clearwater a few miles beyond the mouth of the north fork enters from the north east Oro-Fino Creek. On this creek was the first mining district in Idaho, and in this district arose Oro-Fino and Pierce City, towns about 25 miles from the mouth of the river. A few miles above Pierce City was Rhodes Creek, famed for its richness. About sixty miles on a straight line southeast of Pierce City on the upper tributaries of the South Fork of the Clearwater was the Elk City district. The Oro-Fino and Elk City districts constituted the "Nez Percés Mines."[4] The next great

---

[2] The Snake is barely navigable also for about sixty miles above Lewiston.

[3] For description of the cañon of the Snake from Asotin to Weiser see Lindgren, Waldemar, *The Gold and Silver Veins of Silver City, De Lamar and other mining districts in Id*, 56th Cong. 1st Sess. H. Doc. 20th An. Rpt. U. S Geol. Sur. pt. 3, p. 78

[4] Maps and description of this region are found in *A Geological Reconnaissance across the Bitter Root Range and Clearwater Mountains*, by Waldemar Lindgren, U. S. Geol. Sur. Professional Paper No. 27.

tributary of the Snake to the South is the Salmon River, whose gorge, 4000 to 5000 feet deep, greatly interrupts communication between north and south Idaho. On the plateau a few miles north of the brink of the gorge, a little west of a straight line south from Pierce City and about 110 miles south east of Lewiston, were the Salmon River placers, in which Florence became the most important town. Twenty-seven miles southeast of Florence across the Salmon on the south side of the river were Warren's Diggings.[5] The next large tributary to the south, the Payette, was not the scene of mining operations, but was of some importance because of agriculture. Not far above the Payette comes the Boise, the most famous of the rivers flowing into the Snake. Care should be taken to distinguish Boise City and Boise Basin. The latter, which was a celebrated mining locality, is on the headwaters of Moore's Creek and its branches, and is about twenty-five miles northeast of the present city of Boise. Southwest from the latter site and across the Snake were the Owyhee mines, on the upper part of Jordan Creek, which is a tributary of Owyhee river. The Owyhee bends in a broad bow from southwestern Idaho into Oregon and empties into the Snake from the western side. North of the mouth of the Owyhee on the western side of the Snake in Oregon come the Malheur, the Burnt, the Powder, and the Grande Ronde rivers. Of these the Powder River furnished the only mines of considerable importance, but the Grande Ronde became early noted for its fine farms.

From the consideration of the mining districts of the Snake, let us turn to the most important of the early mining localities in the region now embraced by Montana.

The first discoveries were made on Gold Creek, a branch of the Hell Gate River, which is a tributary of the Clark's Fork of the Columbia.[6] But the placers here were not only of little importance, but more inaccessible from the southward than the great basin of the Jefferson Fork of the Missouri, where the most startling of the early developments occurred.

---

[5] For description and maps see Lindgren, Waldemar, *The Gold and Silver Veins of Silver City and other Mining Districts in Idaho*, 20th An. Report U. S. Geol. Sur., pt 3, p. 233 ff; Also *Hailey, His. of Idaho*, pp. 29–30.

[6] Gold Creek is a few miles west of Garrison, Mont.

The Jefferson basin, about 150 miles long and 100 miles wide, is drained by three branches of the Jefferson, viz., the Big Hole, the Beaver Head, and the Stinking Water or Passamari. On Grasshopper Creek, a branch of the Beaverhead, were situated the Bannack mines. Southward on the east side of the Stinking Water (into which it drains) is the celebrated Alder Gulch. The mountains southward from the Jefferson Basin are remarkably rounded and the country has the appearance of rolling agricultural land.[7] Hence it was easy for miners from Boise Basin to pass to Jefferson Basin, and the immigration from Pike's Peak and the East also found comparatively easy access. Below Three Forks, where the Jefferson, Madison, and Gallatin unite to form the Missouri, one of the largest creeks from the west is the Prickly Pear. A few miles from its mouth the Prickly Pear is joined by Last Chance Gulch, in which the city of Helena lies. Just above Helena the gulch branches into Oro Fino and Grizzly Gulches. From the heads of these gulches a low divide gives access to Nelson's Gulch, a branch of Ten Mile Creek. To Last Chance and the gulches in the vicinity came the last of the great formative rushes of the movement which we are studying.

Having now surveyed the geography of this movement south of 49°, we shall next consider the facts of the mining advance into these fields.

The discovery which initiated this movement came as a natural outcome of the pacification of the Indians by the campaigns of Garnett and Wright, the removal of the restrictions on settlement within the Inland Empire, the ratification of the treaties of 1855, and, most of all, the restless searchings of the miners from the Colville and Similkameen districts. The leading spirit in the discovery was Capt. E. D. Pierce, a prospector, who was somewhat acquainted with the Nez Percés country, and

---

[7] "In crossing the Rocky Mountains we had plenty of grass, wood and water, and the most beautiful mountain country I ever saw,—it is more like rolling prairie land covered with grass, with scattered patches of timber, and but little bed rock in sight" Letter concerning a trip from Boise to Deer Lodge, Owyhee Avalanche Jan. 6, 1866. For description of Jefferson basin see also, *Report on Mineral Resources of the U. S.* 1868, 505–509.

who had mined on the Similkameen and at Yreka, Cal.[8] A party of about a dozen men under the leadership of Pierce made a prospecting tour into the Clearwater country in the summer of 1860 and found rich prospects on Canal Gulch, a tributary of Oro-Fino Creek.[9] On the return of the party to Walla Walla, there was hesitancy in organizing for further development, because of the opposing attitude of the Nez Percés Indians—although the eastern limits of their reservation were so vaguely defined by the treaty of 1855 as to make it uncertain whether the rich ground was within the reservation. But at length Sergeant I. C. Smith outfitted about sixty men and proceeded to Canal Gulch in November. These men spent the winter there engaged in mining, building cabins, and making sluices. Forty-one claims averaged during the winter 27 cents to the pan, and in March Smith made his way out on snowshoes with $800 for his share. All through the winter letters had been sent out occasionally by the miners to their friends, and items from these were published in the papers of the Coast and of California.[10] A swiftly accelerating stream of travel consequently, started in the spring of 1861 for the Columbia and the new mines. Thus, just as the Civil War was commencing in the East, a new era of development began in the far Northwest. Early in March four or five hundred men started from Walla Walla to the mines. The town was full of pack animals and not a pick, shovel, or gold pan could be bought.[11] By June the Portland papers were protesting against so many farmers leaving the Willamette, and by September such large numbers of men had left the mining district of California as to increase appreciably the price of labor.[12] Traffic on the Columbia grew

---

[8] "The Colville gold excitement in 1858 [?] was one thing that led to the discovery of gold by Pierce on the Clearwater. They were prospecting the country all over for gold. The discovery on the Clearwater was really made by a party of Similkameen miners. Pierce had been up there I believe Pierce was an old fur trapper. He had been among the Indians a number of years. He went up there from Yreka, Cal."—Ritz, Philip, *Settlement of the Great Northern Interior*, (MS) p. 20. See also Bancroft, *Wash. Id., and Mont.* p. 234.

[9] Account of this trip in Goulder. *Reminiscences of a Pioneer*, pp. 201-2.

[10] San Francisco *Daily Bulletin*, Aug. 20, 1860; Jan. 22, Feb. 12 & 28, Mar 7 & 27, Apr. 19, 1861; Portland *Times* Nov. 24, 1860.

[11] San Francisco *Daily Bulletin*, Mar. 27, 1861

[12] *Id.* July 18, 1861 See later, *Id.* Jan 24, 1862:

swiftly. In May the Colonel Wright ran to the mouth of the Clearwater (and a little above), and two new steamers were being built. In June Lewiston sprang into existence at the junction of the Snake and the Clearwater, and from it long trains of pack animals departed daily.[13] G. C. Robbins, an observer of more than ordinary reliability, estimated in August that there were 2500 practical miners at work on Rhodes Creek, Oro Fino, Canal Gulch and French Creek, and that four or five thousand men were making a living some other way. Large amounts were being realized by various companies, particularly by Rhodes & Co.[14] Pierce City and Oro Fino became busy mining towns. As the country filled up, prospecting parties set forth to the southward; and during the summer rich diggings were discovered on the South Fork of the Clearwater, where Elk City was started; and in September excitement intensified at the news of extraordinary prospects on Salmon River[15]. In view of these wide developments the Portland papers began to look upon the mining movements in a different way than at first when they had disapproved of the departure of the Willamette farmers. "The facts in regard to the mineral riches there," said the Oregonian "which come to us from authentic sources, are absolutely bewildering;" and it predicted that there would follow "tremendous stampedes from California,—a flood of overland emigration,—a vastly increased business on the Columbia river,—the rapid advance of Portland in business, population and wealth,—and the profitable employment of the farmers of this valley."[16] A better summary of that which actually came to pass could scarcely have been written.

The prospect of largely increased immigration to the mines, however, brought added responsibility to the Indian Department, for all the mines discovered up to 1862 proved to be within the limits of the Nez Percés Indian reservation.[17] The treaty of 1855

---

[13] *Id.* July 3, 1861.
[14] *Oregonian*, Aug. 31, 1861.
[15] A good general account of these movements may be found in Bancroft, *Washington, Idaho and Montana*, pp. 234-245. For the Oro Fino region, in particular, one should not fail to read the very interesting and reliable pages of Goulder's *Reminiscences*.
[16] *Oregonian*, Oct. 26, 1861.
[17] Possibly some question as to the Salmon River mines.

had set apart an immense area bounded indefinitely by the upper part of the south fork of the Palouse River, Alpowa Creek, the Salmon River Mountains, and the spurs of the Bitter Roots.[18] In the second clause of this treaty there was a stipulation that no white men, except employes of the Department, should reside on the reservation without permission of the tribe and of the superintendent and agent. It was so evident, however, in the spring of 1861 that a large rush of the miners was under way, that an agreement was made under this proviso, April 10, 1861, between the Nez Percés and the authorities of the Indian Department, as follows: that portion of the reservation "lying north of the Snake and Clearwater rivers, the south fork of the Clearwater and the trail from said south fork by the Weippe root ground, across the Bitter Root mountains, is hereby opened to the whites in common with the Indians for mining purposes, provided, however, that the root-grounds and agricultural tracts in said districts shall, in no case be taken or occupied by the whites;" but no white person, except employes, was to be permitted to reside upon or occupy any part of the reservation south of this line.[19] Within a few weeks after the signing of the agreement, however, the arrival of steamboats made it clear that a town was needed south of the Clearwater, and Lewiston came into sudden and busy existence. A little earlier a party of fifty-two men left Oro Fino and penetrated into the unknown region of the South Fork.[20] Part of them were turned back by the incensed Indians, but the remainder discovered the Elk City district. The temper of the miners was illustrated at Oro Fino on the arrival of the detachment which had returned, when "A large and well armed party was at once organized at Oro Fino and will at all hazards prosecute their desired objects."[21] In a little while the whole country south of the Clearwater was being overrun by miners, although little real injury was done to the Indians, because of the presence of Capt. A. J. Smith, with a detachment

---

[18] Text of treaty in Keppler, C. J., *Indian Affairs, Laws and Treaties*, 57 Cong. 1st. sess. Sen. Doc. No. 452, Vol. 2, p. 528.
[19] Text of this agreement in *Report of Commissioner of Indian Affairs*, 1862, pp. 430–31.
[20] Bancroft, *Washington, Idaho and Montana*, p 240.
[21] San Francisco *Daily Bulletin*, Aug. 7, 1861.

of U. S. dragoons.[22] There was, however, great danger of hostilities breaking out, particularly as this last movement was into that portion of the country where a semi-hostile part of the Nez Percés had their homes. There were at this time three "parties" among the Nez Percés. The first under the shrewd and peace-loving Lawyer, lived in the vicinity of Lapwai and Lewiston. These had been most under missionary influence, knew something of the power of the whites, and were not averse to trading with them, but dreaded the effects of the sale of liquor. The second was found in the South Fork country and among the Mountains or Buffalo Indians, of whom the most important leaders were Joseph and Big Thunder. They were in general friendly to the whites, but dreaded intimacy with them as bringing degradation. The third party, hostile and suspicious, was composed of bands along the Salmon River, who were more or less in touch with the wild Snakes, and of whom Eagle of the Light, a pronounced enemy of the whites, was leader. A treaty which was made June 9, 1863, with the object of adjusting all difficulties, was not likely permanently to placate the last two factions, and its terms probably helped to bring on the outbreak under the younger Joseph; for they certainly left no room for Indian occupation of the Wallowa valley. Nine-tenths of the territory formerly guaranteed as a reservation was ceded, and the limits were so drawn as to exclude Lewiston, Oro Fino, Elk City, and Florence. The Indians were to receive as compensation $262,500 in addition to the sums promised by the treaty of 1855. Hotels and stage stands were to be conducted only under license from the Indian agent, and the tolls from all ferries and bridges were to be for the benefit of the tribe.[23] As no new mines were discovered within the territory delimited in this treaty of 1863, the Indians were not further disturbed.[24]

---

[22] The situation is set forth in detail by Chas. Hutchins, Indian agent, in his report of June 30, 1862. *Rpt. of Commissioner of Indian Affairs*, 1862, pp. 422-27.

[23] Keppler, *Indian Affairs, Laws and Treaties*, 57 Cong. 1st Sess. Sen. Doc. No. 452, Vol. 2, p. 644ff. See also Bancroft, *Wash. Id. and Mont.* pp. 481-492.

[24] No account of this period would be complete without mention of Wm. Craig and Robert Newell. Both were very important factors in the relations between the Government and the Nez Percés. A Biography of Craig is given in Bancroft, *Wash. Id. and Mont.*, p. 106.

The pacification of the Indians by this treaty was made all the more necessary because of the extraordinary rush to the Salmon River district, the discovery of which, in the fall of 1861, we have referred to above.[25] Immediately on the receipt of the news of this discovery at Oro Fino and Pierce City a stampede took place of all the floating populace. By the sixth of October 140 claims had been taken, and astounding results were reported.[26] Two men took out $300 in two days and two others $800; the dirt ran as high as $40 to the pan; men were making on an average $100 per day and were writing to friends in Oregon and California to hasten to this new Eldorado, where a man could have a better chance than at any time since 1849.[27] Not only the richness of the new mines, but the fact that they proved the wide extent of the gold producing country, gave to them an advertisement which drew multitudes from the Coast and started large migration from Pike's Peak and the East. November first, 1861, it was estimated that 1500-2000 miners were in the district, most of them from the surrounding camps or from the Willamette.[28]

Part of these, fortunately, withdrew before a late fall was followed by a winter of unexampled severity. The snow lasted from the 23rd of December until late in March. At Walla Walla for four weeks the thermometer ranged from freezing to 29° below, and at the Dalles 30° below was reported. It was thought that about five-sixths of the cattle in the Walla Walla Valley perished, and nearly all the sheep.[29] If such was the bitterness of the winter in the milder localities, one can imagine what the miners at Salmon River endured in their hastily constructed cabins and dug-outs at an altitude of 6,000 feet, the snow seven to ten feet deep, with insufficient provisions and all supplies cut off. Scurvy broke out, and there were men who never recovered from the experiences of that winter.[30] Hardships fell worst on

---

[25] *Supra*,—An interesting sketch of the career of Newell is furnished by Mr. T. C. Elliott in the Oregon *His. Quar.*, June, 1905.
[26] San Francisco *Daily Bulletin*, October 24, 1861.
[27] *Id.* October 14, 1861.
[28] *Washington Statesman*, Jan. 25, 1862.
[29] San Francisco *Daily Bulletin*, March 20, 1862.
[30] See Bancroft, Vol. XXXI, p. 253.

those who tried to travel, and from the Dalles to the Bitter Roots men fell victims to the frost.

But in spite of these dangers and the warnings of the newspapers, eager miners early in the spring thronged Portland and The Dalles, and five hundred of them started up the river at once on foot, many of these with only a few crackers, some cheese, and a blanket or two. As the spring advanced the numbers of the immigrants increased, and in May 3800 people departed from San Francisco for the northern mines. There were also large numbers from Utah, the States, and the Canadian provinces, the total being estimated by the *Bulletin* at 30,000.[31] At Florence, on June 1, 1862, there were recorded on the town books 1319 claims, worked by about 4200 men.[32]

A general view of this famous camp may be obtained from reports of two observers: "When on top of the mountain, which is distant some ten miles from Florence, you look eastward, and there, bounded by a high chain of snow-covered mountains, lies the basin known as Salmon River mines. It is a succession of rolling hills, none higher than 200 or 300 feet, hence the place is called a flat, having that appearance from the distance. This flat or basin resembles a gigantic inverted saucer. In or near the center lies the town of Florence."[33] Another, observing the camp from an elevated spot at a distance, thought when twilight came that he could see a thousand camp fires burning: "The sight was beautiful and I think was well calculated to give one an idea of an army in camp, dispersed over six or eight square miles of gravel."[34] In all the creeks of this basin, placer mining was feverishly prosecuted. The richest gulch was Baboon, and from this Weiser took out $6,600 in one day.[35] But while there were many astounding finds the ground proved spotted and was

---

[31] San Francisco *Daily Bulletin*, June 13, 1862.
[32] Letter of E. R. Giddings, chief clerk of surveyor general's office, *Banker's Magazine* XVII: 879. At an election that summer 1430 votes were polled and this was not more than 1/8 of the population; *Oregonian* July 21, 1862. The O. S. N Co. carried on the Columbia in 1861, 10,500 passengers and in 1862 24,500. Statement of the Secretary, *Mineral Resources*, 1868, p. 579.
[33] The Dalles *Mountaineer*, May 26, 1862.
[34] San Francisco *Daily Bulletin*, Aug. 6, 1862. For a scientific description of this basin, see Lindgren, Waldemar, *Silver City, De Lamer and other mining districts in Idaho*, 20th An. Rpt. U. S. Geological Survey, pt 3, H. Doc. pp. 232–235.
[35] Bancroft, *Works*, Vol. XXXI, p. 256.

soon exhausted. No mining camp flared up more suddenly or more intensely than Salmon River, nor flickered more quickly.

The reverse of this was true in Warren's Diggings, twenty-seven miles to the southeast across Salmon River, which were discovered early in the spring of 1862. Here the placers gave good yields for many years. Inasmuch as the large floating population of Florence, which contained many lazy and reckless men, did not cross the gorge of Salmon River, the settlement at Warren's, consisting mostly of old Californians, was distinguished for orderliness, industry, and thrift. Prices, of course at first were very high. An energetic woman, Mrs. Schultz, paid 75c per dozen for the first hair pins in the camp, but she more than recompensed herself for this by charging $3.00 per meal for board. Still when her husband wanted a newspaper, he had to pay $2.50 for a single copy. The camp grew steadily until there were 1500 men in the district in 1865, and then decreased to 500 in 1867.[36] Quartz discoveries brought some revival; but the quartz proved to be in chimneys, and not many men could be employed. At last, in 1872, the Chinamen were admitted, and much of the yield since then has come from them.[37]

Of the total yield of these various mining districts of northern Idaho it is impossible to secure exact figures. An approximation is made by Lindgren up to 1900 as follows: Elk City, five to ten million dollars, Florence, fifteen to thirty million, and Warrens certainly in excess of fifteen million; and in comparison with these yields the production of the Oro Fino mines, it is safe to say, has been not less than ten millions. A conservative estimate, therefore, would place the total production of all the mines from their discovery to 1900 at about fifty million dollars, and of this probably thirty-five millions was produced before 1870.[38]

---

[36] Hofen, Leo, *His. of Idaho County*, MS, p. 4.
[37] Of the authorities for Warren's Diggings, Hofen, *History of Idaho Co.* is best. Of the Bancroft MS. there are also Hutton's *Early Events in Northern Idaho*, Farnham's *Statement regarding Warren's and Florence*, and Mrs. Schultz's *Anecdotes*. See also Bancroft *Works*, Vol XXXI, p. 258 and scattered but valuable notices in Hailey's *Idaho* and Goulder's *Reminiscences*. For physiography consult Lindgren, *Silver City*, etc. 20th Annual Rpt. U. S. Geol. Survey, Pt. 3.
[38] *Reconnaisance across the Bitter Roots*, U. S. Geol. Survey, Professional Papers, No. 27, p. 84; *Silver City*, etc. pp. 233 & 238.

For the mines of Eastern Oregon we have no such careful reports as those of Lindgren for Idaho. The eastern Oregon mines, indeed, seem scarcely to have received the attention that their importance in building up that part of the state warrants. While there were discoveries on Malheur and Burnt Rivers, the most important centers were Canyon City on Canyon Creek (a branch of John Day's River), and at Auburn on Powder River, about ten miles southwest of the present Baker City.

The placers on the John Day were discovered in November, 1861, by a party of thirty-two men from The Dalles. Fourteen of these started back to The Dalles, but all except two were killed by the Indians.[39] A very considerable immigration followed the next year, particularly from Washoe, and settlers soon began to take up farms in the beautiful and fertile valley of the John Day.[40] Miners went to work vigorously making dams and rigging pumps, and Portland capitalists became interested.[41] In 1865 twenty-two thousand dollars per week was produced during the mining season, and in 1866 Carmany thought that the John Day mines had produced $1,500,000.[42]

The Powder River mines, also, were discovered in the fall of 1861. In June, 1862, Auburn was laid out and for a few months grew rapidly.[43] It soon had forty stores and saloons, five hundred houses, and by winter a population estimated at 3000.[44] In the dozen gulches of the district men were in June making from five to thirty dollars per day.[45] A valuable quartz lead, the Rocky Fellow, was soon discovered. Two executions occurred, one in legal form, another—that of a Spanish gambler—by the mob.[46] Settlers began taking up lands along Powder River and many immigrants or "Pilgrims" came in from the East, so that at one time there were 150 women in camp. But in 1863 the immigrants began to turn to the beautiful Grande

---

[39] *Overland Press*, March 17, 1862.
[40] *San Francisco Daily Bulletin*, Aug. 1, 1862.
[41] Id. Sept. 9, 1863.
[42] *Mineral Resources*, 1870, p. 224; Carmany, John H., *Review of Mining Interests of the Pacific Coast for 1866*, p. 9.
[43] An account of the beginnings in this locality is given by Mr. W. H. Packwood in *Mineral Resources*, 1871, pp. 179-80.
[44] *San Francisco Daily Bulletin*, December 2, 1862.
[45] Id. July 1, 1862.
[46] Id. December 15, 1862; also *Oregonian*, October 4, 1862.

Ronde valley and helped to build up La Grande, and the miners, finding that the water supply was inadequate, flocked away to Boise Basin and to other camps, and decline rapidly set in.

An interesting political development occurred, however, in 1862, when the people in the vicinity of Auburn, not being content with being an election precinct of Wasco County, organized a new county and named it *Baker* (after the famous senator of that name), elected a full set of county officers, and chose J. M. Kirkpatrick to represent them in the next legislature.[47] But the legislature temporarily refused its sanction.[48] It is significant of the growth of Eastern Oregon that in the presidential vote of 1864 the counties east of the Cascades polled 4455 votes out of a total for the State of 18,350. The political proclivities of the majority of the residents are indicated from the fact that while the state went for Lincoln by 1431 votes, McClellan carried the eastern counties by 287 votes.[49]

Auburn was a "mother of mining camps" whence prospecting parties explored in all directions.[50] The most important of these parties was that which, under the leadership of George Grimes and Moses Splawn, late in the summer of 1862 discovered the placers on Grimes' Creek in Boise Basin. The journey thither was most venturesome—the swift Snake had to be crossed, and the prowling Indians of the vast plains of the upper Snake knew no peace. Grimes himself was killed by the Indians just after the uncovering of rich prospects. We catch a glimpse from one of their number of the feelings of this little band of eleven men alone in the great wilderness far from their friends at Auburn and from the soldiers at Walla Walla: He writes simply, "We * * * carried Grimes to a prospect hole and buried him amid deep silence. He was our comrade, and we had endured hardships and dangers together and we knew not whose turn would come next."[51] They escaped in safety to Walla Walla, however, and in October were back in the Basin. During the winter other creeks besides Grimes' were found to pay, and

---
[47] San Francisco *Daily Bulletin*, June 24, 1862.
[48] *Id.* October 4, 1862.
[49] Presidential vote in Oregon, *Id* January 2, 1865.
[50] The phrase is Packwood's, *Mineral Resources*, 1871, p. 180.
[51] Splawn, in Hailey's *Idaho*, p. 42.

in the spring came a rush of unusual interest and importance. By 1864 there was a population in the Basin approximately of 16,000, one-half of whom were engaged in mining; the other half, were occupied as "merchants, lumbermen, hotel and restaurant keepers, butchers, blacksmiths, saloon-keepers, gamblers, theatrical people, lawyers, ministers, ranchers, stockmen, and transportation companies."[52]

Not only were the mines of Boise Basin very rich and easily worked (producing at least seventeen million dollars in the first four years) but also they were so situated as to encourage home-making and the upbuilding of a permanent community; although at first, it is true, most of the people, as in all placer mining communities, were intent only on making some money and getting away.[53] One reason why this region soon took on an air of permanency was that the climate of the Boise mines is much less severe than that of Florence or of Cariboo, and so towns with stable interests soon sprang up within the Basin, the largest of which was Idaho City. In the second place, a fine location for an important trading center was only a few miles distant in the Boise Valley, where Boise City was founded in the summer of 1863 and Ft. Boise established the same year.[54] The town was beautifully laid out, with wide streets, and its first promoters were exceptionally enterprising and far-sighted men. It grew rapidly into the leading city of the new Idaho Territory and became the permanent capital. A third reason for the permanent character of the southern Idaho community is found in the proximity to the mines of the fine and fertile valleys of the Payette and of the Boise, which were soon taken up by settlers. Again, the fact that this community was on the well-used Oregon trail helped to bring in a larger proportion of families; and this proportion was increased by a large migration of families from Missouri, which came to escape the pressure of war conditions.

---

[52] Hailey's *Idaho*, p. 170.

[53] Lindgren, Waldemar, *The Mining Districts of the Idaho Basin and the Boise Ridge*, 18th An. Rpt. U S. Geol. Sur. pt III, p. 655. He estimates the total production of the Boise Basin to 1896 at $44,631,800, of which $4,000,000 was quartz.

[54] Accounts of these beginnings are found in Bristol's *Idaho Nomenclature* (MS) and in Hailey's *Idaho*, pp. 88-90. An important expedition against Indians is narrated in the latter, pp. 49-60.

In Boise Basin alone there were in 1865, 799 persons under twenty-one years of age of whom 278 were girls, and 197 were children under four years of age.[55] In the last place, quartz discoveries were soon made in near-by localities, and their development called for capital and abiding population. The principal quartz districts were at Quartzburg, on the edge of the Basin, at Rocky Bar on the south Boise, and, most important of all, in the Owyhee region, southwest from Boise City, across the Snake.[56]

The party which initiated the Owyhee movement, leaving Boise in May of 1863, discovered promising placer diggings on a tributary of the Owyhee, which was named after the leader of the party Jordan Creek.[57] When the news of the discovery reached Boise, hundreds of men rushed off so distractedly for the new diggings that one correspondent facetiously reported a "special forty-eight-hour insanity for Owyhee" to have devel-

---

[55] Report of J. A. Chittenden, Territorial Superintendent of Schools, *Owyhee Avalanche*, Sept. 28, 1865.

[56] The principal sources for the history of Boise Basin, Boise City, and vicinity are the following:—
1. The Bancroft MSS. furnish:
   Branstetter, J. H., *First Discovery of Boise Basin*. (With this should be read Splawn's account in Hailey's *Idaho*, pp. 36–44).
   Bristol, Sherlock, *Idaho Nomenclature*. This is of special value for the history of the beginnings of Boise City.
   Coghanour, David, *Boise Basin*. Coghanour was an example of a thrifty, saving man.
   Butler J. S., *Life and Times in Idaho*. (With this compare Butler's chapter in Hailey's *Idaho*, pp. 183–187).
   Knapp, Henry H., Statement of Events in Idaho.
   McConnell, W. J., *Idaho Inferno*.
   Angelo's *Idaho* is a pamphlet, which, after a diatribe against Governor Douglas of British Columbia, narrates interestingly the observations of a newspaper correspondent's visit to Idaho in 1863.
2. Important newspaper sources, after the establishment of papers, are:
   The Boise *Weekly Statesman*.
   The *Idaho World*.
   The *Owyhee Avalanche*.
3. Books:
   Bowles, Samuel, *Our New West*, pp. 486–487.
   Richardson, Albert D., *Our New States & Territories*, 1866, pp. 78–79.
   Richardson, Albert D., *Beyond the Mississippi*, p. 501.
   Rustling, James F., *The Great West and the Pacific Coast*, pp. 223 & 225.
   Bancroft, Vol. XXXI, *Washington, Idaho and Montana*.
   Mineral Resources of the U. S., 1868, Report of J. Ross Browne, pp. 512–521.
   Hailey, John, *The History of Idaho*. Contains important source material.

[57] There is a resumé of the history of Owyhee in the *Avalanche*, Aug. 19, 1865.

oped.[58] The placers on Jordan Creek proved fairly productive and were worked vigorously for about two years. But the gold was of poor quality, being worth only ten to twelve dollars per ounce, and the development of the rich quartz lodes soon dwarfed the placer mining.

The first discoveries of quartz were made in July 1863. The richest section was on War Eagle Mountain. This mountain is at the head of a gulch tributary to Jordan Creek, and its summit, 5,000 feet above sea level, stands out 2,000 feet above the mining towns on the creek below.[59] On this mountain one hundred claims were "claimed, staked and recorded," in some of which gold predominated, in others silver.[60] The history of one of the veins of War Eagle Mountain deserves special consideration. This vein was first discovered in 1865 and was known as the Hays and Ray. Other parties discovered a vein (or a part of the Hays & Ray vein) which crossed the latter, the two being in form somewhat like the letter X. The later discoverers called their vein The Poorman, the name being chosen possibly to win sympathy for themselves.[61] They opened their vein exactly at the spot where it crossed the Hays & Ray, at which point there proved to be a chimney of ore marvelously rich. It ran 60 per cent. bullion, and the Poorman people took out of it $250,000 in two weeks.[62] The latter party "seeing that they would become involved in litigation, associated their company with some capitalists connected with The Oregon Steam Navigation Company, and about the same time or shortly before erected a fort at their mine called "Ft. Baker", built of logs, with portholes and other means of defense usual in such cases. The Hays & Ray had their work [i. e. of tracing connection with the Poorman vein] so nearly completed that they could commence suit, but could not give the necessary bonds."[63] They therefore gave a portion of

---

[58] San Francisco Daily Bulletin, July 17, 1863.
[59] A clear sketch map of the Owyhee district is in Bancroft's Works, Vol. XXXI, p. 417.
[60] Richardson, Our New States and Territories, p. 78.
[61] Conversation with Hon. W. J. McConnell.
[62] Richardson, Beyond the Mississippi, p. 509.
[63] Mineral Resources, 1868, p. 523. Geo. C. Robbins was the intermediary in bringing in the New York parties and "Put" Bradford the S N Co. capitalists. Maize, Early Events in Idaho, p. 7.

their interest to the New York and Owyhee Company, which guaranteed to carry the case to decision. But before trial a compromise was arrived at by which the New York and Owyhee party got the larger share. This mine in three months subsequent to the consolidation produced in net proceeds from quartz reduced in local mills $390,000. In addition fifteen tons of selected ore were sent to a smelter in Newark, New Jersey, and the bullion product ran $4,000 per ton.[64]

The special interest of these proceedings to us lies in the clearness of the call from this newly born and remote mining community to outside capital and to science. Previous to this controversy, mills had been erected by both groups of capital, the Ainsworth and the NewYork and Owyhee. The latter cost $120,000, had twenty stamps, and was under the management (in 1869) of Mr. John M. Adams, one of the first graduates of the Columbia University School of Mines.[65] The Owyhee district contained in 1866 ten mills with one hundred and two stamps. The transportation of these mills into the wilderness (300 miles of the route being by wagons from the Columbia at an average freight expense of 25c per pound) is a tribute both to American enterprise and the richness of the mines. But eastern capital was in some cases recklessly squandered, particularly through incompetent management.[66] Capitalists, it was becoming clear, must summon the aid of science and must secure more thoroughly organized control over investments in these remote regions.

A community based on the quartz phase of the mining industry naturally had more elements of permanency than one founded on the floating riches of placer gravels. Three towns along Jordan Creek came into existence progressively towards the quartz leads, culminating in Silver City. Here a Sunday school was started by the citizens, a union church was erected, and a newspaper established. Here also lived J. A. Chittenden, who was earnest in trying to start schools in the new territory and who became the first territorial superintendent of public instruction. The solid character of the development of Owyhee attracted the

---

[64] Report of W. D. Walbridge, *Mineral Resources*, 1868, p. 524.
[65] *Mining and Scientific Press*, Vol. XII, p. 279.
[66] Richardson. *Beyond the Mississippi*, pp. 510–11; also, *Mining & Scientific Press*, Vol XIII, p 343.

attention of the *Mining and Scientific Press* of San Francisco, which represented the growing stability of the mining industry upon the Coast. In its *Review* for the year 1864, it said, "Perhaps the most noticeable mining development of the past year, upon this coast, has been that of Idaho."[67] Again, speaking especially of Owyhee: "There is very good reason for believing that Idaho is destined to become a most important and permanent mining region. Thus far operations there have been conducted upon a sound basis, with very little of the speculative feature, so characteristic of new mining localities."[68]

We turn, now, to trace the advance of the miners to the headwaters of the Clarke's Fork of the Columbia and to the sources of the Missouri, into territory afterwards included in Montana. The discovery of gold in this region was due to two streams of development: that of the "Mountain men" and that of immigrants to the Salmon River mines.

The Deer Lodge Valley, on the upper waters of Clarke's Fork, had long been frequented by "mountain men" and trappers, some of whom traded during the summer far to the south with the immigrants on the great trails, and in winter continued their business with the Indians in the northern valleys. So early as 1852 a Red River half-breed by the name of Benetsee had found float gold on Gold Creek. More important was the arrival in Beaverhead valley of James and Granville Stuart in the fall of 1857. These were miners of high character who had left California for a visit to their old home in Iowa, but, hindered by the Mormon war of 1857, they had turned north with the mountaineers. Having found on this trip fair prospects at Gold Creek, they returned in the winter of 1860-61. They were disappointed in not getting supplies at Ft. Benton, and had to send to Walla Walla for picks and shovels. In May of 1862, they commenced operations, but with indifferent success.[69]

Soon parties began to arrive whose aim was to get to the Sal-

---

[67] Vol. X. p. 8.
[68] June 3rd, 1865. To the authorities for Owyhee should be added Lindgren, Waldemar, *The gold and silver veins of Silver City, De Lamar and other mining districts in Idaho*, 20th Ann. Rpt. U. S. Geol. Sur., Pt. 3, 1900, p 233 ff.
[69] This account is taken from the *Life of James Stuart* by Granville Stuart, Cont. His. Soc. Mont., Vol I, pp. 36-61.

mon River mines. Some of these immigrants came up the Missouri by boat to Ft. Benton and from there started by the Mullan Road for the Salmon River fields; others came with the Fiske overland expedition across the plains from Minnesota to Ft. Benton; still other parties from Pike's Peak[70] and Missouri, diverging from the great emigrant trail, tried to reach the center of excitement by cutting across to Salmon River, but were compelled to turn north towards Deer Lodge Valley and the Mullan Road. Explorations, of course, were taking place in all directions by these various parties, and a number of promising "diggings" were discovered.[71] Of these the most important was situated on Willard, or Grasshopper Creek, an affluent of the Missouri.

It was in August of 1862 that the first bar was discovered on this creek by John White, and towards this locality thereafter converged parties from various directions. Thus the first important mining camp in Montana started. A miner's district was organized, and a town of log huts came into existence with the name of East Bannack. The yields were good. One "pilgrim" panned out ten dollars one morning and got fifteen dollars more in the afternoon with a rocker—big wages for a man from the States. Two took out $131 in a week.[72] A fine quartz lode, the Dacotah, was discovered in December, and a rude mill was built that winter.[73] There are preserved the names of 410 persons who spent the winter of 1862-3 in Bannack City and vicinity, Dakotah Territory, and of these thirty-three were women.[74]

From Bannack there proceeded in February, a prospecting party which discovered placers completely eclipsing those hitherto discovered in Montana. It was through mere chance that the discovery was made, for these prospectors, starting as part of an expedition to the Yellowstone, had failed to make connec-

---

[70] In the phraseology of the miners "Colorado" was seldom used, but the region was spoken of as Pike's Peak, and people from that region were "Pike's Peakers."

[71] These explorations were sketched by Granville Stuart, *Contr. His. Society Mont.*, Vol. II, p. 123; see also Bradley Mss., Bk. 3, p. 281.

[72] *Diary* of J. H. Morley, MS., Sept. 15 and Oct 4, 1862.

[73] W. A. Clark in *Contr. His. Soc Mont.*, Vol. II, p. 51; also *Mineral Resources*, 1868, p 468.

[74] *Contr. Hist. Soc. Mont.*, Vol I. pp 334-354

tions with the other part of the expedition, and, after a toilsome journey ending in being plundered by Indians, had been forced to turn back. On the way back they prospected in a gulch which one of the party named Alder, and the returns were most promising. We get a glimpse of the diverse nativity of the miners from the records of these discoverers. The party consisted of the following:

Bill Fairweather, native of New Brunswick, St. John's River,
Mike Sweeney, native of Frederickstown, St. John's River.
Barney Hughes, native of Ireland.
Harry Rodgers, native of St. John's, Newfoundland.
Tom Cover, native of Ohio.
Henry Edgar, native of Scotland.[75]

Some of these men had been mining at Salmon River, and at least one in British Columbia.[76]

They found here a gold field richer than any they had worked in, for Alder Gulch produced in three years thirty millions of dollars.[77] It was populated swiftly. The principal town was Virginia City, which soon became a thriving municipality with substantial buildings, a newspaper, churches and schools, as well as hurdy-gurdys, saloons, and theatres. The columns of its first paper, The Post, give us a vivid picture of the town, as it chronicles the hosts of incoming "pilgrims," a fireman's procession of two companies with gay uniforms, a poster warning against the use of deadly weapons, and the building of water works. In one issue a prize fight is announced whereat no weapons are to be allowed in the enclosure; in another a notice is inserted that Professor Dimsdale's school will open on Idaho St., behind Mr. Lomax's Corral, "where all branches included in the curriculum of the best seminaries will be taught for $1.75 per week, and strictest attention will be given to the morals and deportment of the pupils."[78] The population of Madison County, in which Alder Gulch was situated was in 1864, 11,493.[79]

The comments of an intelligent miner give us a view of the

---
[75] *Journal of Henry Edgar, Con. His. Soc. Mont.*, Vol. III, p. 141.
[76] *Contr. His. Soc. Mont.*, Vol. VII, 197.
[77] *Mineral Resources*, 1868, p. 507.
[78] *Post*, Sept 17 & 23, 1864.
[79] *Post*, Oct. 8, 1864.

Gulch as it appeared to him while out for a walk in November of 1863. "It surprises me to see how rapidly this country improves First, two miles below here is Virginia City, a thriving village with many business houses; then one mile farther down is Central City, not quite so large; then in another mile you enter Nevada, as large as Virginia; then about a mile and one-half further Junction City. The road connecting all these 'cities' is bordered with dwellings, on both sides all along. * * * Recalling that only eighteen months ago this was a 'howling wilderness,' etc.,—truly truth is more wonderful than fiction and excels in marvelousness even the Arabian Nights, but truth and the marvelous go hand in hand when Young America finds a good gold gulch."[80]

It was in September of 1864 that a party of Georgian miners, prominent among whom was John Cowan, began regular mining operations at Last Chance Gulch. Other parties followed, particularly from Minnesota. A village sprang up in the Gulch at first called "Crab Town" and soon after Helena.[81] This village was a natural center for many rich gulches which were opened up back of it—such as Oro Fino, Grizzly, and Nelson's—and besides was well situated for trade between Ft. Benton and the mining localities farther west. Quartz was soon discovered, and in December of 1864 the celebrated Whitlatch Union vein was struck, the total yield of which up to 1876 was estimated at $3,000,000.[82] Placer mining also yielded largely in all the gulches, but was hindered by scarcity of water. One nugget of solid gold was accidentally thrown out by a sluice fork, which was valued at over $2.000.[83] A newspaper, *The Radiator*, was transferred from Lewiston, Idaho, to Helena in 1865.[84] Virginia City was gradually displaced as first in population and importance.

In three years the economic and social foundations of Montana were laid. A review of some of the salient facts and tendencies of the founding of the new community are brought out in a

---
[80] *Diary* of J H. Morley, MS., Nov 12, 1863.
[81] *Diary* of Gilbert Benedict, MS., Oct 8 & 14, 1864.
[82] W. A. Clark in *Contr. His. Soc. Mont.*, Vol. II, p. 51.
[83] Cornelius Hedges in *Contr. His. Soc. Mont.*, Vol. II, p. 112.
[84] *Owyhee Avalanche*, Nov 4, 1865.

thoughtful address by Hon. W. F. Sanders, himself a leader and founder. His subject was "The Pioneers": "From far away Oregon, through solemn forests, by the Pend d' Oreille Lake, by the Mullan Road, by the Nez Percés Trail, by the Boise Basin, they [the Pioneers] journeyed to the hidden springs of the Missouri and Columbia. From the golden shores of shining California with appetites whetted by the pursuit of this patrician industry, they crossed forbidden deserts and over trackless wastes to the newly discovered Treasure House of the Nation. From recently occupied Colorado, by the Cache Le Poudre, by the Laramies, by Bitter Creek, they came to the Shining Mountains, finding a promising field for mining activity. From all the states bordering on the Great River that we give to the valley which is the Nation's heart, came an onrushing tide of eager, confident immigrants as they swept up the Platte across the mountains and over the Lander Road and Snake River or down the Big Horn to the famed Beaver Head country. Another contribution of sturdy men and women daunted at no obstacle and intent on conquest over forbidden difficulties came from distant Minnesota by Forts Totten, Abercrombie and Union north of the Missouri River and first located in this valley. * * * Brought face to face with each other they [these peoples] were confronted with the newness of the land, with ignorance of its geography, topography, resources, climate and above and beyond all with the fact that they were strangers each to the others. In coming hither they outran law. They found here no pre-extinct civilization. In the raw they brought it with them, and its secure planting was at first an awkward and imperious duty. Opinions clashed. There was no tribunal to settle differences; they had to be argued out to ultimate results without artificial or extraneous aid. Unique characters with strange and sometimes unknown history and weird experiences abounded. Social life and economic life boiled. Industry was a tumultuous struggle, the turmoil was active and the process of unification was slow. No houses, no highways, no fences, no titles; verily, the world was all before them where to choose."[85]

---

[85] *Contr. His Soc. Mont.*, Vol. IV, 122-148.

Their choice was in part guided by information derived from white "waifs of civilization," who had identified themselves with the Indians. There were also "discards of civilization," the highwaymen and free booters, not romantic creatures, but "ugly facts of flesh and blood."

"Events in those early times, profoundly affecting our situation here moved swiftly. The creation of the new Territory of Montana, the establishment of governmental mails July 1, 1864, with its consequent regular stage transportation from Salt Lake City, the installation of governmental officers, the election and action of our first legislative assembly, the construction of a telegraphic line, the permission of the government to have newspapers transmitted in the mails, the building of the Union Pacific Railroad, were events which deeply affected the material and social interests of these communities."

Conditions similar to those of Montana existed in the other regions populated by the mining advance. Because of this advance which we have surveyed in the preceding chapters, as we have seen, a new British colony was formed, and there came into being two new American territories. The act forming the territory of Idaho was approved March 3rd, 1863, and that forming Montana May 26, 1864.

In the following chapters I shall next attempt to discuss special economic and social phases of the mining advance, particularly keeping in view comparisons between British Columbia and the American territories.

PART II

ECONOMIC ASPECTS OF THE MINING ADVANCE

CHAPTER VI

METHODS OF PRODUCTION AND ORGANIZATION OF INDUSTRY

In the development of a gold field from its first discovery by prospecting up to the complicated methods of extraction of quartz, cooperation is necessary. I mention this important point in the beginning of this discussion, because it is basic in the consideration of the industry and of society founded upon this industry, and because in common conception the individualism of placer mining and society is often greatly exaggerated. The "lone prospector" in the period we are considering was largely a myth.

Prospecting was carried on, as a general thing, in small organized parties, consisting of five or six up to perhaps fifty men.[1] Careful preparations were made, particularly with respect to providing horses, food, arms, and mining utensils. The latter would consist of picks, shovels, and always "pans"—vessels of iron or tin six or eight inches deep and a foot or more in diameter at the bottom, useful not only in "panning out" gold, but also for mixing bread. These companies were composed of experienced miners, generally "Californians." Immigrants from Missouri, Minnesota, the "States," or England did comparatively little prospecting. It is interesting to notice, however, the presence of Georgians in Cariboo, Alder Gulch, and at Last Chance.[2] For weeks and months an expedition might range over hundreds of miles of mountains, valleys and cañons, studying the geology of the country, prospecting wherever indications were good, and

---
[1] In later times often only two men might go prospecting, when danger from Indians was lessened. Remarks of Judge W. Y. Pemberton.
[2] The gold mines of Georgia do not seem to have had the attention which their importance warrants in the mining history of the United States.

once in a while fighting Indians. Often failure resulted, but sometimes came one of the most thrilling and exhilerating experiences in the whole gamut of human endeavor, when the "color" was found, and the scales assured two dollars and forty cents per pan—twelve dollars and thirty cents from three pans —one hundred and fifty dollars for a single day's work![3]

When diggings affording such prospects were discovered, the next step was to stake claims. One should not think of a placer claim as approaching in size an agricultural claim. Conceive a gulch (such as Grizzly, back of Helena) nine miles long, the flat portion one hundred or more feet wide between hilly or mountainous sides. Claims in such a gulch would generally extend from hill to hill and be in width one hundred feet. The claims were numbered up and down the gulch from the "Discovery" claim. Discoverers were entitled to one claim by preemption and one by discovery. Later comers were entitled only to a preemption claim. As a general thing a man could purchase in addition one claim, but sometimes, when a camp was quite thoroughly worked, more than one. If the flat was wide, claims would be from 100 feet square to 250 feet square, dependent on the district laws. The British Columbia code allowed only 100 feet square, while in the American territories there seems to have been a tendency to expand the size of the claims.[4] A man could hold claims such as the above in more than one district, and besides he could hold claims on different kinds of placer ground. The claims on Alder Gulch were bar and creek; in British Columbia there were bar, creek or ravine, and hill claims.[5]

---

[3] These are actual figures from Alder Gulch. "A more happy lot of boys it would be hard to find, though covered with seedy clothes."—*Journal of Henry Edgar, Contr. His. Soc. Mont.*, Vol. III, p. 139.

[4] Governor Douglas at first required very small claims, in dry diggings 25 by 30 ft. unless otherwise established by a by-law; but the regular size was later 100 feet square. See *Rules and Regulations for the Working of Gold Mines, Issued in Conformity with the Gold Fields Act*, 1859; also Park, Joseph, a *Practical View of the Mining Laws of British Columbia* (1864), pp. 13 & 14. See also as to decided tendency to larger claims in American territory, Angelo's *Idaho*, pp. 25-6. Claims at Oro Fino were held 150 feet front by 250 feet across the stream, San Francisco *Daily Bulletin*, Aug. 2, 1861.

[5] *Original agreement* of Wm. Fairweather, et al., with other prospectors. MS; Park, Joseph, *Practical View of Mining Laws of British Columbia*. The latter defines bar diggings as "that portion of the banks of a river over which the river

It should be carefully noticed here that the plan of a mining camp corresponded more nearly to that of a town than to that of a country district. While the camps themselves were scattered and isolated, within each camp the structure was comparatively concentrated. Hence, again, we see that combination, co-operation, and organization are basic factors in mining life. Having staked their claims, the discoverers of new fields from lack of supplies or fear of the natives were generally compelled to return to some camp or trading centre. There the news invariably leaked out (a man surely must tell his friends, for whom he had already probably staked out claims), and a local rush ensued. Day laborers, who constituted four-fifths of the population of mining-camps, late-comers, who came in crowds into every large camp, and claim-owners who were not making topnotch figures would drop every employment, put up every dollar for outfit (or go without), and plunge for the new diggings. The great *desideratum* was to be the first on the ground. Merchants and packers, also, would press forward their trains eagerly, for the man who got a well-laden train into a new mining community would make a good-sized fortune.

A vivid picture of the fever of a rush is furnished from Oro Fino when the news of the Salmon River diggings reached the town: "On Friday morning last, when the news of the new diggings had been promulgated, the store of Miner and Arnold was literally besieged. As the news radiated—and it was not long in spreading—picks and shovels were thrown down, claims deserted and turn your eye where you would, you would see droves of people coming in 'hot haste' to town, some packing one thing on their backs and some another, all intent on scaling the mountains through frost and snow, and taking up a claim in the new El Dorado. In the town there was a perfect jam—a mass of human infatuation, jostling, shoving and elbowing each other, whilst the question, 'Did you hear the news about Salmon River?', 'Are you going to Salmon River?', 'Have you got a

---

in its most flooded state extends"; a creek claim as "a parcel of ground taken up on the alluvial banks, or flats, which lie on each side of a river or stream"; and hill claims as "situated on the side or rise of the hills or banks which run along the side of the creek."—pp. 13-14.

Cayuse?', 'How much grub are you going to take?', etc., were put to one another, whilst the most exaggerated statements were made relative to the claims already taken up...... Cayuse horses that the day before would have sold for about $25 sold readily now for $50 to $75, and some went as high as $100. Flour, bacon, beans, tea, coffee, sugar, frying pans, coffee pots and mining utensils, etc., were instantly in demand. The stores were thronged to excess. Pack trains were employed, and the amount of merchandise that has been packed off from this town to the Salmon river diggings since yesterday morning is really astonishing.'"[6]

When an ardent crowd like this reached a gulch or basin, and when successive crowds from farther camps and towns began pouring in, the available mining ground was soon occupied. Before much work was done, however, a miners' meeting was held, and the district was organized by electing a miners' judge, a sheriff, and a recorder and by passing the rules of the camp. Men who had been schooled in California camps not only had learned to mine skillfully, but turned spontaneously to that form of local political organization which had been evolved in California.[7] This was true not only in the American territories, but also in the British; along Fraser River and in Kootenai steps were taken in organization prior to the arrival of the British officials, and the success of these officials in maintaining law was due in very considerable degree to the orderly instincts and methods of the California miners.[8]

One of the most important of the district rules was that concerned with representation. Representation meant the time required for work in holding a claim. Ordinarily one day out of seven was required during the working season, although, sometimes, as in Bivens Gulch (Montana) two days at first were neces-

---

[6] Letter to The Portland *Advertiser*, October 29, 1861, in San Francisco *Daily Bulletin*, Nov. 2, 1861.

[7] A vivid account of the organization of California camps is found in Davis, Hon. John F., *Historical Sketch of Mining Law* in *California* (From *History of Bench and Bar* in *Cal*) pp. 16-33. Shinn, C. H., *Mining Camps*, takes up the subject more elaborately. On the spread of California ideas consult particularly in the latter work Chap XXV on *Effects upon Western Development*.

[8] See Copy of Miners' Resolutions at Fort Yale Bar, Cornwallis, *New Eldorado*, pp. 402-3; also, Report of A. N. Birch, Colonial Secretary to Governor Seymour, Oct. 31, 1864, found in Macfie, *Vancouver Id. and Br Col.*, pp. 255-262.

sary. A man might do the work himself, or have it done. In British Columbia it was required that representation be bona-fide and not colorable, and a claim was considered abandoned if left seventy-two hours. Bona-fide representation, however, included clearing brush for cabin, building cabin, cutting timber away from the claim for works on the claim, and bringing in provisions.[9]

The time when representation was not required or, in other words, when claims were "laid over" was determined in the American territories by district meeting, in British Columbia by the local gold commissioner. Claims were universally laid over during the winter season, but might be laid over temporarily at other times—as for example, during prolonged drouth. The British Columbia method of control seems to have given greater flexibility for adjustment to conditions. When claims were laid over, miners could absent themselves entirely until representation was again required, and no one could legally jump their claims. This arrangement gave miners an opportunity, perhaps, to return to their homes for the winter, if they chanced to live in the Willamette or some Coast community. or at any rate, to go to some town, as Victoria, Portland, Lewiston or Boise, where living was cheaper than in the mines, life more attractive. and the chances for spending all one's money very good. Here, then, is another peculiarity of a mining camp: men seldom thought of creating homes in such a camp, and ownership was based not on residence, as in agricutural homesteads, but on work during a portion of the year.

Still, it would be wrong to think that the camps were wholly deserted during the winter. A very considerable proportion of the miners stayed, and these occupied themselves in sawing lumber, making sluices, etc., and (especially in deep diggings) in digging shafts and drifting. Mining operations in the latter class of diggings could be carried on all winter. Camps often acquired, therefore, more of stability than is commonly thought.

It is time, however, to return to the recently discovered and newly organized district where the miners were ready for their work. Theirs was a busy and laborious life, and it did not con-

---

[9] Park, Joseph, *A Practical View of the Mining Laws of Br. Col.*, pp. 41-43.

sist of picking up golden nuggets out of streams and spending most of their time in hilariousness and adventure. Work, hard physical toil was necessary to development.[10] In the first place there were cabins to build, and in this labor British observers admired the skill of the American axemen—a skillfulness particularly noticeable in Missourians, or those recently from the "States." Ditches were to be dug and sluices and flumes constructed. Lumber had to be obtained by the laborious process of whip-sawing, and good whip-sawyers could always make high wages until the inevitable small sawmill arrived.[11]

The processes of placer mining were somewhat varied. The simplest, after the pan, was the use of the rocker, which was an affair constructed somewhat like a child's old fashioned cradle, having at one end a perforated sheet of iron. The rocker was placed by the side of a stream and one man rocked and poured water, while another dug and carried dirt. This of course was a slow process, and a next step was the use of the sluice.[12] Boxes ten or twelve feet long, twelve inches wide and eleven inches deep, were arranged in "strings" in such manner as to allow a current of water from a ditch to be run through the boxes. In working such a sluice a number of men could be utilized—some to strip sod, some to dig and wheel, one to throw out pebbles and boulders with a sluice-fork and one to throw away tailings. Transverse cleats were nailed to the bottom of both rocker and sluice-box, and quick silver was poured into the mixture of dirt and water in order by amalgamation to secure a larger percentage of gold than would otherwise be possible. A farther modification of the sluice was the use of hydraulic power, in the shape of a powerful stream of water from a hose, instead of picks and shovels.[13]

---

[10] Intensity of work was increased in districts where water could be secured only for a short season. Night shifts were often used then. It took real patriotism at such a time for a man to volunteer on an expedition against marauding Indians. One gets an idea of the steady, plodding labor necessary to develop a claim from the diary of J. F. Morley where day after day is the entry, "At work in the shaft."

[11] Three things were indispensable to a placer miner—water, lumber, and quick-silver.

[12] The "tom" was a simple form of sluice, consisting of but one trough.

[13] Good descriptions of processes may be found in Goulder, W. A. *Reminiscences of a Pioneer*, pp. 211–214; Macfie, *Van. Id. & B. C.*, pp. 266–279; *Mineral Resources*, 1867, pp. 16–23.

The pay dirt lay next to the bed-rock and in shallow diggings could be got at simply by stripping; but in a number of rich fields (Cariboo and Last Chance, for examples) the pay stratum or lead was buried under twenty to sixty feet of stream detritus, and then shafts and drifting had to be resorted to. Drifting of course meant digging out around from the bottom of the shaft. This was work only for an expert miner, and a good drifter was always in demand at wages three or four dollars a day higher than those paid for ordinary labor. The use of shafts and drifts required timber for supports and the rigging of windlasses. Water and boulders often bothered greatly, especially the former. Sometimes pumps were made, but often a bed rock flume was resorted to. In its construction a miner opened up a ditch on the bed rock from a point low enough to drain his claim.

In carrying on these various forms of mining labor, the skill of old Californians was pre-eminent, and everywhere from Cariboo to Owyhee the methods and opinions of Californians were given great respect. In camps where there were many "pilgrims" from the states higher wages were generally paid to old miners. The Californians, indeed, were apt to be a bit supercilious with regard to noviates; at Oro Fino, for example, they complained that the Willamette farmers in the mines did not know how to secure gold properly from the dirt—to which the others might have replied that neither were they so expert in gambling it away after it was secured.[14] The scorn of the expert for the unskilled is somewhat amusingly revealed in a letter from Last Chance, where, the writer says, the gulches were "mostly taken up by Pilgrims, who know more about raising wheat or cranberries, or handling logs, than using pick and shovel.

"Just watch them handle a pick. A good miner has a pick drawn to a fine, sharp point; he works underneath the pay dirt on the bed rock; you know, Mr. Editor, when you knock away a man's underpinning he is easily brought down; and so it is with gravel—get under it with a good long, sharp pick, and it is easily

---

[14] San Francisco *Daily Bulletin*, August 21, 1861; Bristow, *Reencounters*, MS.

brought down. It cannot stand on nothing; but a green horn has a short, thick, stubbed pick; he stands on the top, like a chicken on a grain pile; gets out one rock and finds he has another below it requiring the same labor.'"[15]

Yet there was good demand in every thriving camp for many kinds of labor, so that men turned easily to that employment in which they had had previous training.

Notwithstanding the comparative skillfulness of the Californians, however, the placer mining of this period was wasteful, and unconscious of conservation. This for two reasons: In the first place men were in the mines simply to make as much money as they could and get away in the shortest possible time. This was particularly true, of course, with regard to residents of the Willamette or of Missouri, to many of whom a trip to the mines was of the nature of an excursion, designed to make a little money or pay off a mortgage. In the case of the habitual miner there was no possible way by which he could be constrained to work old ground carefully, when he could make large sums by hasty working and then hie to some other field. A man certainly could not be expected to work carefully a claim that did not pay more than wages. In the second place, the expenses necessarily attendant upon opening a new and remote placer field by the modes of transportation which then obtained, were so great a charge upon the mines that only the very richest gravel could be profitably worked. These placer mines had to pay for establishing routes of transportation and for nurturing civilization under unfavorable conditions.[16] Whatever the reason, at any rate, the mines were skimmed, and the wastage was enormous. Mr. J. Ross Browne, who had spent years in the mining regions and who had opportunity to know the situation better than anyone else in the United States, in his report of 1868 [though he does not mention his authorities] says that, "At a moderate calculation, there has been an unnecessary loss of

---

[15] Montana *Post*, April 29, 1865. A very important workman in each mining locality was the blacksmith. The worth of a mining field was estimated in part at times by the number of blacksmiths employed in it.

[16] Moreover, the lack of the "blue lead" beds of ancient rivers in Montana and Idaho contributed to early exhaustion, compared with California; Carmany, *Review of 1866*, p 9.

precious metals since the discovery of our mines of more than $300,000,000, scarcely a fraction of which can ever be recovered. This is a serious consideration. The question arises whether it is not the duty of government to prevent, as far as may be consistent with individual rights, this waste of a common heritage, in which not only ourselves but our posterity are interested.'"[17]

It was true that waste was to a considerable degree relieved by the incoming of the patient Chinese into every camp after the cream had been taken by the whites, by the introduction in some cases of hydraulic processes by which low grade ground could be profitably worked, and by more careful methods of whites who were content to labor on after the flush times were over.[18] But it remained a fact, and a fact of importance in sociological study of early mining society, that mining communities economically based on placer mines were wasteful and unstable.

In order to overcome this instability, everywhere the more substantial miners, business men, and statesmen turned their attention to quartz. In all mining regions, therefore, whether in British Columbia, Idaho, Oregon, or Montana, quartz lodes were eagerly located and attempts, more or less elaborate and successful, were made at development.[19]

The simplest machinery for working quartz was the arrastra (or arrastre), originally a Mexican invention. This consisted of a circular area paved with stones, in the middle a post and to this post attached a sweep to which a mule or horse was hitched. A block of granite, fastened to the sweep, was dragged around over the quartz distributed within the circle. The remains of these old arrastras may be found in many gulches today. Their

---

[17] *Mineral Resources of the United States,* 1868, p. 9.

[18] More work was carried on than is commonly thought, after the crowds of adventurers had vanished and newspaper notices become sparse. This was true of such places as Cariboo, Oro Fino and Warrens, but not so with regard to Salmon River, Auburn, and Kootenai.

[19] In British Columbia the following bonuses were offered:
1. £500 to the person who should be first in the colony successfully to work quartz, gold or silver by machinery.
2. £500 for discovery of a good coal mine.
3. £500 for building the first vessel in the Colony of not less than 500 tons
4. £500 for discovery of new alluvial diggings capable of giving employment to 500 men. [Notice how the government here takes the initiative in a way that it never did in the territories to the south.] *Government Gazette,* Jan. 7, 1865.

use "required neither capital nor a number of laborers. The owner of the arrastra could dig out his own rock one day, and reduce it the next."[20]

The enterprise of Americans, however, forbade contentment with such rude machinery, and they at once set to work, in spite of enormous obstacles, to construct mills. The first mill in Montana is thus described by one of the pioneers in quartz: "An overshot wheel, twenty feet in diameter, is placed on a shaft 18 feet long, with large pins in the shaft for the purpose of raising the stamps. These stamps are fourteen feet long and 8 inches square, and strapped with iron on the bottom, which work into a box that is lined on the sides with copper plate galvanized with quicksilver, so as to catch the gold as the quartz is crushed and clashed up the sides of the box. Then we have an opening on one side of the box, with a fine screen in it, through which the fine quartz and fine gold pass, and run over a table covered with copper."[21]

More elaborate mills, of course, were constructed, as outside capital was enlisted, and these mills represented what may be called a second stage in quartz development. The study of the reduction of gold and silver in such a mill was fascinating. The quartz was first broken into fragments the size of apples by sledge hammers and then shoveled into feeders, which brought it under large iron stamps, weighing three hundred to eight hundred pounds, and which "rising and falling sixty times per minute with thunder and clatter," made the building tremble, as they crushed the rock to wet powder.

"Quiet, silent workmen run the pulp through the settling tanks, amalgamating pans, agitators and separators, refuse material passing away, and quicksilver collecting the precious metal into a mass of shining amalgam, soft as putty. This goes into the fire retort where it leaves the quicksilver behind and finally into molds whence it comes forth in bars of precious metals."[22]

---

[20] *Mineral Resources,* 1867, p. 21.
[21] Letter of J. F. Allen in Campbell, J. L., *Six Months in the New Gold Diggings,* p. 35. This mill was near Bannack and used the ore from the Dakotah ledge.
[22] Richardson, Albert D., *Beyond the Mississippi,* p. 501. This mill was in Owyhee.

The building of such mills and the working of quartz claims required the use of capital and corporate methods. *The most significant development in the mining industry during the decade 1860-70 was the supercession of surface placer mining methods, wherein the individual working in informal combination had free play, by quartz mining and corporate working of deep placer diggings, wherein individualism began to be submerged and capital became uppermost.*

The necessity of this process is clearly apparent when we look at the position of an ordinary miner who had discovered and perhaps tested a good quartz lode. He could with some trouble get his claim duly recorded and, with more trouble, do or have done the assessment work required. But what then? He did not have money with which to work his claim, and he could not pay his expenses of living as he could from a placer claim. Hence, if he was to realize on his claim, he must inevitably sooner or later call in capital. It is true that some few placer miners saved enough to equip small mills and that there was some evidence of cooperative organization among the men, but in general there was a great call from the mining fields for the application of capital.[23]

Accordingly, we find effort on the part of local claim owners to interest outside capital. Portland capitalists invested at Powder River and Owyhee. There was some connection, also, with San Francisco. But New York was the place towards which effort turned most yearningly. Hardly had the Owyhee quartz been discovered, when Gen. McCarver started east to interest New York capitalists.[24] The Avalanche had among its advertisements the Agency of Geo. L. Curry for selling feet in New York, and the local conditions are suggested by the declaration of an editorial that "There should be less ledges and more New Yorks."[25] The participation of New York (and of some other

---

[23] A notable case of coöperative working of a quartz mine was that of the Oro Fino, in Owyhee, in which case the workmen, on the failure of the firm, assumed the indebtedness and operated the mine successfully. U. S. Commissioner Browne commented on this as follows: "It is singular that so few mines are worked by companies of operative miners, especially when we see how successful such companies usually are."

[24] San Francisco *Daily Bulletin*, Dec. 2, 1864.

[25] Owyhee *Avalanche*, Sept. 9, 1865.

capitalistic centers) in quartz development in Montana is shown in charters granted by the first legislature. Among these we may mention The Montana Gold and Silver Mining Company, whose office was in New York; The Rocky Mountain Gold and Silver Mining Company, whose stockholders lived in Bannack, St. Louis, and New York; and The American Gold and Silver Mining Company, whose stockholders were in London, New York, Philadelphia, St. Louis and in Montana.[26] Concerning British Columbia a thoughtful observer wrote, "Labor has hitherto chiefly performed what has been done, but the performance has been limited, slow and imperfect. Capital must finally develop the resources of the country. Its aid is essential to their full development, but to attract capital it must have free scope, and a reasonable amount of legal protection and encouragement, or, in other words, as much protection as will encourage its introduction."[27] The shaping of laws to encourage capital is mentioned, also, in the first message of Governor Lyon, of Idaho: "All legislation should be carefully molded to invite capital, and the greater the inducement held out, the more rapidly will our population be increased and the greater the peoples' prosperity."[28] This, then, was the situation: development in these mining communities by means of the labour of individuals, who had little capital and organization, soon reached its limit; society stretched forth to the centers of capitalism for aid and was willing so to modify its legislation as to favor the introduction of capital.

This movement towards capitalism and corporate methods was tremendously accelerated by the development of the Comstock lode in Nevada. "The chief gold mines of California," wrote Commissioner Browne, "high as their product is, are small affairs when compared with the vast works of the chief silver companies of Nevada." "A strip of land six hundred yards wide and three miles long yields $12,000,000 annually. There is no parallel to that in ancient or modern times."[29] With this

---
[26] *Laws of Montana*, 1864–5, pp. 558–658.
[27] London *Times*, Aug. 26, 1863.
[28] Hailey, *His. of Idaho*, p. 114.
[29] *Mineral Resources*, 1867, p. 72.

magnificent yield came decisive resort to corporate methods. "Nothing more strikingly illustrates the difference between the miners of California and those of Western Utah," said the Maryville, (California) Appeal, "than the frequent formation in the latter of incorporated companies with a great amount of capital stock."[30] This development in Nevada promptly affected California. In an editorial on *The System of Extensive Mining Corporations in Washoe*, the *Bulletin* said: "The clear tendency of things throughout the entire mining region of California is to this end [i. e., combination]. Those who are the possessors of quartz or 'hydraulic claims' must call in the aid of capital and science, if they hope to make their possessions profitable."[31]

These great achievements in Washoe aroused the capitalists of San Francisco—who up to 1860 had been quite indifferent to mining investments—to active participation in the process of combination.[32] This participation, however, was not altogether healthful, for "it was reserved for Washoe to transfer the most active operations from the fields of actual labor to the pavement and shops of Montgomery street."[33] Then followed a period of riotous speculation. Two hundred and ten companies were formed in 1861 and 1862, with capital stock of $230.000,000.[34] Men and women of all degrees made haste to invest their savings in mining stock of companies, most of whose holdings were worthless. In 1864 came a great panic in these stocks and the "name of Washoe, which had once been blessed, was now accursed by the multitude, though still a source of profit to the few."[35] The mines of the northern interior, however, were not greatly affected by this excess of speculation or its reaction, except that development was somewhat retarded by the latter.

This tendency towards employment of capital in combinations. which is discernible in these remote mining communities which we are studying, was apparent in Australia also and, indeed, in

---

[30] In San Francisco *Daily Bulletin,* Nov. 20, 1860.
[31] *Ibid.*
[32] *Mining & Scientific Press,* Jan. 7, 1865, p. 8.
[33] San Francisco *Daily Bulletin,* July 6, 1864.
[34] Id. Jan. 6, 1863. *Mineral Resources,* (p. 30) places the whole number of companies at 3,000, with a capital stock of $1,000,000,000.
[35] *Mineral Resources,* 1867, p. 31.

all Anglo-Saxon mining localities.[36] Moreover, the period of the Civil War was marked in the eastern United States by the combining of capital and the forming of corporations on a scale before unachieved.[37] The development of mining methods in the camps of the Inland Empire, therefore, in their progression from the simple and hasty methods of the placer miner to the complicated and stable processes of the capitalist and the scientist, shared in the evolution going on in Washoe, California, Australia, and the whole United States.

---

[36] See on this wide change in the precious metal industry an interesting article on *Gold Mining and the Gold Discoveries made since 1851*, in *The Mining and Smelting Magazine*, (London), Vol. I, pp. 392–401.

[37] Fite, *Social and Industrial Conditions During the Civil War*, Chap. VI.

CHAPTER VII

THE PRODUCT AND ITS UTILIZATION

In considering the product of the labor and capital expended in the Mining Advance, one naturally inquires what was the amount of the total product.

This question is one extremely difficult to answer at all and, indeed, impossible to answer with entirely satisfactory precision. In British Columbia with its more ordered administration we can feel more sure of arriving at nearer approximation to accuracy than in the territories to the south, where, until 1867, there was no governmental attempt to gather statistics. Of course one meets all sorts of statements in the literature of the time, given with great confidence; but such statements often originated with parties interested in exaggerating yields—claim owners desirous of selling out, local editors who wished for larger subscription lists, merchants, packers, steamboat men, and even express companies.[1] The last, and especially Wells, Fargo & Company, were, however, a source of information considered fairly reliable. There were earnest efforts made, it is true, to arrive at right estimates, and of these special value attaches to the careful annual reviews of the San Francisco *Bulletin;* but here again vagueness arises from the fact that much of the dust shipped to California was merged in statistics with the California product, and that very considerable amounts were shipped out of the northern regions by way of Salt Lake and the Missouri River of which the *Bulletin* made little account. Moreover, in estimating product,

---

[1] "The seeker of truth will not easily find a more thankless field of investigation than a mining country. For it verily appears that however truthful men have previously been, self-interest seems to make them systematic liars as soon as they become interested in gold mines." Letter from Pike's Peak Region, San Francisco *Daily Bulletin*, Oct. 1, 1860. In support of the untrustworthiness of mining statistics, see Del Mar, *History of the Precious Metals*, pp. 401–406. For other side see *Mineral Resources*, 1868, p. 5.

variation in the value of gold dust must be taken into the account, a variation ranging from gold of Owyhee worth twelve dollars per ounce to that from Kootenai worth eighteen. Again, there was not a little counterfeiting of gold dust, against which laws were enacted in the Colony and the Territories. The Chinese were charged with adeptness in this practice in British Columbia; and in southern Idaho the matter became so serious as to impair the welfare of laborers and lead to meetings of merchants for fixing prices of debased dust. Hence, many factors must be taken into account and many sources drawn upon, in order to arrive at an approach to accuracy in estimating the product of the mining regions which we are studying.

We have, however, two series of estimates, which, after study of various reviews and collecting of fugitive notices, I have come to believe well within the truth. The one for British Columbia is by Mr. George M. Dawson, who was helped in his compilation by the Provincial Department of Mines; the other by Mr. J. Ross Browne, United States Commissioner for the mining regions west of the Rocky Mountains, who drew from a great number of assistants and informants. Mr. Dawson's estimate for British Columbia is as follows:

1858	$705,000
1859	1,615,000
1860	2,228,000
1861	2,666,000
1862	2,856,000
1863	3,913,000
1864	3,735,000
1865	3,491,000
1866	2,622,000
1867	2,480,000
Total	$26,110,000[1]

Mr. Browne summarized the yields in the American fields from the beginning of their working to the close of 1867 as follows:

Washington	$10,000,000
Oregon	20,000,000
Idaho	45,000,000
Montana	65,000,000
Total	$140,000,000[2]

[1] *Geol. Sur. of Can* 1887, 1888. Rpt., p. 23 R.
[2] *Mineral Resources*, 1868, p. 6.

Part of the Oregon yield, however, belongs to western Oregon, but it would probably be safe to credit eastern Oregon with $10,000,000. Deducting this amount from the total, we have $130,000,000. Adding now, the yield of British Columbia we have a grand total of $156,111,000 as the product of these northern interior mines in a decade, the average being at least $15,000,000 per annum.[4]

Rightly to value this production, moreover, one should consider that it was nearly all surplus. In agricultural communities, especially in their earlier stages, a very large proportion of the product is consumed by the producer or his family, and comparatively little, particularly at first, left as surplus; and it is mainly the surplus, of course, that brings into being trade and means of transportation and most of the instruments and appurtenances of civilization. In mining communities it is evident that the product must necessarily be practically all surplus, and a surplus, moreover, in such form as to be readily transmutable into the various commodities and activities of civilized life. Gold dust circulated as money. Each merchant had his scales and every miner carried his pouch, from the contents of which he bought his food, clothing, tools, newspaper, and drink; paid his postage, express charges and fares; attended the theatre or the hurdy-gurdy, perchance gambled, remunerated his lawyer in litigation, paid his taxes, or bestowed his contributions at church.[5] Civilization sprang forth full-panoplied. Merchants came rushing in; buildings were erected and towns sprang up; newspapers were established; lawyers, dentists, and doctors

---

[4] It seems to the writer that these gentlemen, in reaction against exaggeration, arrived at estimates somewhat too low. In support of this criticism it may be noticed that Mr. O'Reilly, Commissioner at Cariboo, a very careful and reliable observer, places the yield of that district, north of Quesnelle River, for 1863 at $3,904,000, (Supra, p. 42), whereas Mr. Dawson's estimate for the whole of British Columbia for that year is $3,913,563; surely the aggregate yield of the numerous scattered bars and camps of British Columbia, outside of Cariboo, was for that year more than $9,563. Cf. also totals of $2,500,000, shipped from Portland in 1861, practically all from the Nez Perces Mines, *Or. His. Quar.* Sept. 1908, pp. 289–90.

[5] While it is true that gold dust readily circulated as money, still there was considerable loss in exchange, and some cheating. Consequently, there was a distinct demand for coin. Transmission to San Francisco, however, was attended by heavy charges; and so in British Columbia Governor Douglas ordered coinage of ten and twenty dollar gold pieces, and in the Territories there was insistent demand for local mint, which was finally established at Boise.

hung out their signs; churches and schools were projected and in many cases erected; transportation thrilled from the pack trail, the stagecoach, the steamboat, through the railroads of the east and the ocean routes of the west, clear to New York and London. It is this aspect of the mining advance (often overlooked now-a-days as we look back over the slow progress of mining communities after the first flush years) which gives it an intensity, a vitality, a compellingness out of all proportion to the actual numbers of population participating. This conception of radiating economic intensity is basic in the just gauging in history of a great mining movement, or in understanding society built upon such a movement.

A comparison with the amount of surplus product of some agricultural regions will help us to understand the true significance of an average annual surplus of $15,000,000 in the first decade of civilized occupation of the Inland Empire. Kentucky in 1832, two generations after its settlement, produced an estimated surplus of $5,250,000, Ohio, about 1834, $10,000,000 and Tennessee in the same year, $6,120,000. The surplus of the whole Mississippi-Ohio valley was estimated in the latter year at $30,000,000.[6] The two states, accordingly, which produced a surplus available for stimulation of commerce approximately equal in amount to the average annual surplus of the Inland Empire, 1858–1867, (viz., Ohio and Kentucky) had in 1830 a combined population of over a million and a half; the entire population of the Inland Empire, white and Chinese, in 1867 was less than 100,000.[7] The comparatively small population of a mining region, therefore, because of the availability of its product as surplus may produce an effect on commerce and transportation, for the time being, equal to that of a much greater agricultural population.[8]

The production of so large a surplus, of immediate availability by so small a population, helps us to understand the largeness of

---

[6] These figures are from Pitkin, *Statistics for 1835*, p. 534, 536.

[7] Ohio, 937 + thousand, Kentucky, 687 + thousand, *Rpt. of Twelfth Census.* Pop Vol. I; British Columbia, 13800. (1866), Despatch of Governor Seymour, Feb. 17, 1866, in Churchill and Cooper, *Br. Col. & Van Id.*, Idaho, 21725, *Mineral Resources*, 1868, p. 512; Montana about 32,000, *Id.*, p. 487; counties of eastern Wash. 4170, *id.* p. 565–7; counties of eastern Oregon not over 10,000, *id.* 576–7.

[8] Mining society, moreover, becomes highly functionalized more quickly than that of agricultural regions.

immigration to the mining regions from the eastern states, from Canada, and from England. A man's *chances* were better in the mining regions. When common labor in the East was paid $1 to $1.25 per day in depreciated greenbacks, $5 to $10 a day in gold—and the chance of making much more—loomed large. There was at this period great labor discontent in the East due to the high prices of commodities, paid in paper currency, such prices unaccompanied by proportionate increase of wages.[9] Even in California a skilled miner could make not more than $3.50 to $4 per day.[10] Men at a distance (particularly if unacquainted with mining localities) overlooked the high prices and discomforts of mining camps—a fact peculiarly true of the general run of immigrants from England. After all, moreover, the average annual earnings may not have been so high as they seemed. Dawson computes that the average annual earnings of miners in British Columbia (1858–68) was slightly under $700, but his computation does not take account of the exchange of product for labor in the mines.[11] But mainly it was the chance at the great prizes, the chance to make a fortune in a few months, that drew men feverishly on. There were many cases where men within a year or two cleared from $2,000 to $100,000, and, when we reflect on how such sums now are regarded by the average laboring or professional man, we can see what it meant to the ordinary man in the sixties. To the poor man the mines held out the hope of a competency.

If we inquire, however, what were the total net profits in the production of the surplus above discussed, after the deduction of money brought into the country, that is a question impossible to answer. The charge was often made, with regard to any particular mining community (a charge oftenest made by some older community which was losing population) that there really was no net profit, or a positive loss. We may observe, however, that even if this were true, the stimulus to business and the impulse to various forms of social activity were not therefore the less intense, although, perhaps, accompanied with loss to many indi-

---

[9] Fite, *Social and Industrial Conditions during the Civil War*, Chap. VII.
[10] Wages in 1867 were $2–$3.50 per day; *Mineral Resources*, 1867, p. 21.
[11] *Geol. Survey of Canada*, 1887–8, Rpt. p. 23R.

viduals. Moreover, besides investments in mining improvements directly, as ditches, mills etc., much both of the money brought into a country and of the surplus produced was invested in various permanent forms of capital, such as the opening up of farms, the building up of towns and communities, and the capitilization of trade and transportation.[12]

One of the most important permanent improvements, attributable largely to the precious metal product, was the development of agriculture. Prices for all sorts of provisions were very high in the mines, and at the towns and stations on the way thither, and this was particularly true with regard to butter, milk, fresh vegetables, etc.—after a man had lived for weeks on bacon, bread and coffee, he would give almost any price for the tonic of butter and vegetables. The economic inducement of high prices was needed in order to settle remote valleys, which, but for the mines, would have waited long for settlers. As it was, agricultural activity was conspicuous both north and south of the Line.[13]

In the mining regions south of the Line the most noticeable agricultural activity occurred in the Walla Walla, Grande Ronde, Payette, Boise, and Gallatin valleys. Cattlemen and farmers had begun to enter the Walla Walla valley before 1860, and the census of that year showed a population in the county of 1,318. In 1866 it was estimated by *The Statesman* that 555,000 bushels of wheat had been raised in that year and 250,000 bushels of oats; flour was beginning to be exported from Walla Walla to San Francisco (there were six mills in the valley), and in June 1867

---

[12] The charge that "more money and labor has been spent to get out the gold than it was worth" was especially prominent in the case of British Columbia immediately after the Fraser River rush. In meeting it a defender of the Colony specified the following valuations, although less than a year had elapsed since the beginning of the rush:

Stock of goods on hand Nov. 1, 1858, ... $250,000.
Real estate in Victoria, one thousand town lots at $100 each, cost price, ... 100,000.
Two hundred more valuable lots together with all the property sold here or at Esquimault, present value, $200,000........................ 500,000.
Wharves, new buildings and other improvements in Victoria, ... 400,000.
Buildings in the interior, all other improvements having been made at government expense .... 50,000.

Waddington, Alfred, *Fraser Mines Vindicated*, pp. 4 & 5.

[13] In localities of scanty rainfall it was an easy transition from miners ditches to irrigation ditches.

five hundred tons were shipped out.[14] The settlement of the Grande Ronde valley started in 1861, and by 1866 it was producing almost as much as Walla Walla.[15] In Boise City visitors were astonished at the fine vegetables that came from the Boise valley and from the Payette. The settlement of the Gallatin valley, which began in 1863 and in which John M. Bozeman was prominent, was of unique importance in that it led to the attempt to open a celebrated road, the Bozeman cut-off, through the heart of the Sioux hunting grounds to Ft. Laramie.[16] In other valleys, also,—as the Powder River, the Bitter Root, and the Colville,—agriculture was enabled to get a secure foothold. Consequently, when the trying time of decline of placer mining came, the territories were enabled to live through, and commodities were furnished for outward transportation.

The stock business flourished even more than farming. While stock raising had long been pursued in the Willamette valley and had begun in the upper country a few years before the mining period, nevertheless, it is from this time that the stock raising in both regions begins as a distinctly important business.[17] Many cattle, sheep, and horses were shipped from Oregon to British Columbia; in 1861 there were imported into Victoria alone 7,081 head of cattle valued at $313,797, most of them from Oregon.[18] The deputy collector of customs at Little Dalles, on the Columbia, reported that in 1866 there had been shipped through that point from Oregon and Washington Territories 2,754 head of sheep, 2,265 beef cattle, 483 horses, 43 mules, 1,132 pack animals, and 264 saddle horses,—the total valuation being $348,292.[19] The

---

[14] *Mineral Resources*, 1868, p. 580.

[15] Jas Veazey wrote from Walla Walla to the *Oregonian*, Aug 31, 1861, that there was room for 1,200 good farmers in the Grande Ronde and added in characteristic American fashion: "I want a claim there and I am going to have one, for its the prettiest country I ever saw." A few weeks later 15 emigrant families began making homes there. *Oregonian*, Sept 28, 1861. See also Idaho *World*, Oct 13, 1866.

[16] *Historical Sketch of Bozeman, Gallatin Valley and Bozeman Pass*, by Peter Koch, *Contr. His. Soc. Mont.*, Vol. II, pp. 126–139.

[17] I am confirmed in this view by the observations of Hon. C B. Bagley, of Seattle.

[18] Barret-Lennard, *Travels in British Columbia*, p. 282.

[19] *Mineral Resources* 1868, p. 559. These figures are probably exceptional for this point since in 1866 the movement to the Upper Columbia was in progress, but they may be taken as fairly representative of numbers generally crossing the border.

mines in the interior south of the Line furnished a market not only for the stockmen of Walla Walla, but also of the Willamette. Some idea of the importance of the stock business in the Walla Walla valley may be derived from the estimate that 5,000 head of cattle were driven to the mines in 1866 and that stockmen still held 6,500 head; in addition 1,500 horses were sold to persons enroute to the mines and 6,000 mules were used in packing and freighting.[20] In 1868, from March 1st to July 15th there were shipped on steamboats from Portland to The Dalles, 12,191 head of cattle and horses, 6,283 head of sheep and 1,594 head of hogs, and it was thought that an equal number during the summer had been driven across the Cascade Mountains.[21] This stimulation of the cattle business contributed to agricultural settlement; for stockmen soon began to turn to the vast bunch-grass plateaus, and from the stock business the transition was made in the seventies and eighties to the great wheat production of the present day.

The beginnings of agriculture in British Columbia in connection with the mining advance present some interesting features. Here too, all along the roads leading to the mines, particularly in the upper country, farms were opened up.[22] This development was noted with great interest in England, where it was thought that the climate and soil of British Columbia were such as to make that colony peculiarly fit for immigration of the poorer population of the mother country. One of the things that is distinctly noticeable in the books published in England during this period concerning British Columbia is the background of distress at home and the desire to relieve this distress. All of these books, therefore, (and they were quite numerous) devote considerable space to the discussion of the agricultural possibilities of British Columbia and the advisability of people from Britain emigrating thither.

Perhaps the most interesting aspect of the starting of agricul-

---

[20] Walla Walla *Statesman,* quoted in Idaho *World,* Dec. 15, 1866.
[21] *Mineral Resources,* 1868, p. 580.
[22] Mr Davidson, near Pavillon, had 175 acres under cultivation. Another farmer drove thirty head of milch cows into Cariboo and netted $75.00 per day from them for four months. Packers wintered their stock in the valleys of the Thompson and Bonaparte. Macfie, *Van. Id. and Br. Col.,* pp. 284-292.

ture in British Columbia, however, from the point of view of our study, is the method of the disposal of the public lands. In working out a method there were some comparisons instituted with other English colonies, particularly with Canada, but the *most decisive formative influence was competition with and imitation of the land system of the United States.*[23] At first in British Columbia there was a disposition on the part of the government to hold land at comparatively high prices, to sell it at auction, and to require that only surveyed lands be sold. Lytton believed in a high upset price, "but", he wrote, "your course must in some degree be guided by the price at which such land is selling in neighboring American communities."[24] The price was set at first at ten shillings ($2.50) per acre, and "squatting" was not to be tolerated—it was outside of law and not British.[25] The same policy, in general, was followed in Vancouver Island.

Against this policy discontent and opposition began to develop. The petition of a public meeting held at Victoria, July 2, 1859, reads as follows: [The petitioners] "having viewed with alarm the departure of many of Her Majesty's loyal subjects and others from this colony to the neighboring republic; and having learned that their departure has been induced by the difficulty of obtaining agricultural lands at once, on application, and by not being obtainable on such terms as would afford equal encouragement to actual settlers in this colony as are offered in the neighboring republic; believing that we shall lose many more, and that except the land system of the colony is materially modified, the prosperity and settlement of the country will be seriously retarded, petition:

a. That Crown lands of this Colony may be opened at once to actual settlers;

b. That a preference may be given to them in the choice of the public lands, surveyed or unsurveyed, over capitalists;

---

[23] It will not be overlooked that the public lands in the colony of British Columbia, unlike those of the United States, were under the control of the government of the colony and were not administered by the Imperial government.

[24] *Papers relating to British Columbia*, I, 49.

[25] O. T. Travaillot was appointed Assistant Commissioner of Crown Lands in 1858, "for protecting the Crown Lands of the Couteau and Fraser River Districts from encroachment, intrusion and trespass."—Douglas, *Miscl. Letters*, MS. July 13, 1858.

c. That they may be secured in a preemptive right;

d. That the highest price to actual settlers may not exceed $1.25 per acre, or such price as will barely cover the expenses of survey."[26] Another meeting at Victoria on Aug. 22, 1859, placed among its resolutions the following clause: "That the practice of making the public lands a source of revenue is unwise and impolitic; that instead of attracting to, it repels population from the country; and that the better policy, grounded on the experience of new countries, is to donate the public domain to bona fide settlers rather than exact a high price with a view to revenue; that the taxable property of a country whose land system is liberal so rapidly increases that it soon yields a revenue which far exceeds the proceeds of the sale of land at any price."[27]

The attitude of Governor Douglas, perhaps because of the pressure brought to bear upon him, underwent a change in the two years from 1858–60. At first on application for preemptions he refused them, quite properly, on the ground of lack of authority.[28] Later (in 1858) he allowed town lots to be leased at Yale, Hope, and Port Douglas, under the conditions of right of resumption by the Crown, a rental of $10 per month (payable in advance), and with a preemption right in the lessee at an upset price of $100, the monthly rent to be reckoned as part of the purchase money.[29] A letter of the Governor from Ft. Hope in the fall of 1859 forecasts a general preemption law: he wrote that there was a very general inquiry for rural lands and that the general impression had gotten abroad, "which I am altogether at a loss to account for", that the Government was not willing to sell land; he caused the registry of applications for 1,500 acres and proposed to "authorize applicants to enter on land without de-

---

[26] McDonald, *British Columbia and Van. Id.* P. 217. This meeting may have been inspired partially by hostility to Governor Douglas. McDonald himself was a bitter critic of Douglas. On the other hand, he shows great perspicuity in the discussion of the land system and reveals thorough acquaintance with the land systems of the United States and of Canada. In commenting on that of the United States he says that "it has done more towards the promotion of settlements and the development of their agricultural resources, than all other causes combined." (p. 58) He noted also the passage of the American homestead law. His book was published in 1863.

[27] *Id.*, p. 349.

[28] *Diary of Gold Discovery on Fraser's River*, MS. May 24, 1858.

[29] Douglas to Moody, *Miscl. Letters*, I, MS. p. 222.

lay and make improvements"; payments of land, where surveyed, were to be at the rate of ten shillings per acre.[30]

Finally, on Jan. 4, 1860, came the preemption proclamation. According to its terms British subjects and aliens who took the oath of allegiance could "acquire unoccupied, and unreserved, and unsurveyed Crown land in British Columbia, (not being the site of an existent or proposed town, or auriferous land available for mining purposes, or an Indian Reserve or settlement), in fee simple." The conditions were that the claim be of 160 acres, of rectangular form, that it be marked by four posts and that it should be recorded; that the occupation of the land be continuous and that improvements to the value of ten shillings per acre be made; and that road, mineral, and ditch rights be reserved.[31] The price was not to be in excess of ten shillings per acre, this statement showing the liberalizing advance over the attitude of a few months previous. As a matter of fact the price was finally set at 4s. 2d per acre.[32] Thus we see that in the first stage of the administration of the lands of British Columbia the land system was perforce conformed to that of the United States.

Another permanent form in which the mining surplus manifested itself was in the upbuilding of towns and communities.

In the interior of the American territories there were founded in five years Walla Walla, Lewiston, Boise, Virgina City, Helena, and a score of smaller centers. The Dalles became a thriving entrepot.[33] In British Columbia there were Hope, Yale, Douglas, Lillooet, Lytton, Barkerville, and others of less importance.[34] The population of these towns, in numbers varying from a few score to perhaps ten thousand as the extreme limit in flush times, appears, in comparison with that of eastern towns, of little importance. But anyone familiar with frontier conditions knows

---

[30] Douglas to Moody, *Correspondence Book*, MS. Sept. 20, 1859.
[31] McDonald, *Van Id. and Br. Col.*, pp. 205–209.
[32] *Id.* p. 214.
[33] The Dalles, "key to the upper country", in 1862 had about 1000 population. San Francisco *Daily Bulletin*, Nov. 13, 1862.
[34] Concerning Lytton Douglas wrote to Travaillot that the town "lately founded at the Forks of Thompson River should be named after the present Secretary of State for the Colonies, a gentleman distinguished alike as a brilliant writer, a profound statesman, and a warm and energetic friend of British Columbia". *Misol. Letters*, MS. I, 35, Nov. 10, 1858.

that such outposts of civilization are of many fold more consequence than villages of like size in the East. They became outfitting posts for vast regions and their trade was out of all proportion to their size; from them went forth prospectors, merchants, packers, stock men, travelers—all the assailants and viewers of the wilderness—and to them from time to time they returned. Such frontier towns were ganglia of civilization, comparable to Roman colonies. Moreover, in the period to come, when railroads were to be projected and built, the existence of such communities was of very considerable moment.[35]

Of the Coast communities, the towns of Puget Sound were less directly in the path of the mining advance than were those of the Fraser and Columbia; consequently the Sound region was of relatively lesser importance during the mining decade. Nevertheless, it was greatly interested in the mining advance and drew from it a measure of prosperity. Governmentally, in particular, as the mining regions developed before the formation of Idaho, the Sound regions of Washington began to fear that they would be outvoted in the legislature by the representatives from the eastern parts of the States. But in material prosperity, also, the effects of the mining advance were plainly in evidence. The Fraser River movement especially benefited the Sound. "The gold excitement has not been without a good result," said the *Puget Sound Herald*, "so far as the Territory at large is concerned. If we may judge of other towns and counties by our own [Steilacoom], there must certainly have been, in the aggregate, a large accession of wealth and population— we mean a permanent, not a transient accession. . . . A few short months ago no mechanical business of any kind, save carpentering and blacksmithing, was carried on here, now there are some half dozen workshops. Six months ago there was not a single light pleasure vehicle of any description. although our roads are of the best. Now there are six or eight, together with a couple of express wagons recently purchased in Victoria."[36] Not only many miners who came during the Fraser River rush, but also

---

[35] On this point consult Smalley, E. V., *History of the Northern Pacific Railroad*, p. 181.

[36] *Puget Sound Herald*, Sept. 24th, 1858

some who from time to time arrived during the after course of the mining advance, took a liking to the Sound country, settled down and became valuable citizens.[37] Thus in general effect a mining rush in a way, like an exposition, served to make a region known and to bring in settlers.[38]

New Westminster, the capital of British Columbia was founded by governmental fiat in 1859, and emerged rapidly from the great primeval forest into a busy town on a noble site. In 1861 its imports amounted to $1,414,000, in 1862, $2,800,000. and in 1863, $2,109,000.[39] Still, New Westminster was by no means content. She felt that the commercial element in Victoria was fattening on British Columbia trade which belonged rightfully to her. Other measures and grievances were thus formulated by the *British Columbian:* (a) A resident governor and responsible government; (b) Improvement in the navigation of the Fraser River; (c) Early survey of the public lands; (d) A system by which miners could make local laws; (e) An export duty on gold.[40] The latter measure was especially desired in order to decrease the tariff duties, with a view to eliminating Victoria as much as possible. Another measure with the same end in view, which was passed when British Columbia obtained a governor separate from Vancouver Island, was to levy tariff duties on the value of goods at the port of export. As a third step in this policy, New Westminster wanted direct steam communication with San Francisco.[41] But it remained for a future city on Burrard Inlet, Vancouver, to accomplish in part what New Westminster meditated.

At that time, however, Victoria was clearly in the lead. Here was a remarkable example of a thriving city whose growth and prosperity depended little upon its near surroundings, but almost entirely upon mines hundreds of miles away in the distant interior of the mainland. One of the most interesting phases of

---

[37] Hon. C. B. Bagley, of Seattle, emphasized the point presented in the text in a reminiscent conversation.

[38] It is worth noticing that the University of Washington was founded in the period of the mining advance, Jan. 28, 1861.

[39] Macfie, *Van. Id. and Br. Col.*, p. 217.

[40] *British Columbian*, Feb. 13, 1861. The bar at the mouth of the Fraser was a hindrance to the entrance of ocean ships.

[41] *Id.* Aug. 15, 1861.

the history of Victoria, however, in the period of our study, was the way in which the city was regarded in English books and papers of the time. She was to be the Liverpool of the Pacific. It was admitted that her own harbour was somewhat shallow, but near at hand was the magnificent harbour of Esquimault.[42] With such an harbour and in so commanding a portion on the Pacific, Victoria surely would become a great emporium for trade. In accordance with this ideal the city's revenue laws were shaped; money was collected from direct taxation, and Victoria was made a free port, like Singapore and Hong Kong.[43]

The Willamette Valley, as we have before noted, looked somewhat askance upon the movement to the mines for the reason that they took from the valley laborers and farmers. This resentfulness is somewhat humourously revealed by a correspondent of the *San Francisco Bulletin,* who writes from Portland as follows: "While our venture-loving population are hurrying on the backs of spare-rib Cayuses to the new found Dorado, the plowshare will rust in the weedy furrow, the sickle hang idly from the deserted roof tree, and the obstreperous old sow and her nine small squeakers will root maintenance out of the neglected garden. Next fall those who survive disease, vagrancy and corn juice will come back moneyless to winter. With arable land enough to feed the Pacific Coast, many of us will be compelled to swap old Pied, that nursed us across the plains, for California and States flour.''[44] Such dismal prognostications, however, were dissipated by the higher prices for wheat and the greater market for cattle which the mines furnished.[45]

In the prosperity of the mining advance Portland emerged from a mere village to the promise of the city it has since become. Forces generated in that period have profoundly affected the city's development. We have before noted the beginnings of capitalization of the city in the debt of the Indian war of 1856,

---

[42] Esquimault was an important rendezvous for the British fleet.
[43] This policy of a free port was one of the reasons why union of Vancouver Island with British Columbia was difficult.
[44] May 9, 1862.
[45] From Portland there were shipped in Feb., Mch., and April, 1861, 6,032 sacks of flour up the Columbia, 25,418 to Victoria, and 63,097 to San Francisco. *Oregonian,* May 4, 1861.

but it was during the period from 1861 to 1865 when the successive waves of migration and trade swept through the city and up the Columbia to Oro Fino, Salmon River, Boise and Alder Gulch, that decisive growth came. By 1862 the population had doubled, wharves were built, steamboats puffed busily on the Willamette, and hotels, eating houses, stores, and saloons were thronged. Long lines of drays unloaded their goods at the wharves.[46] Gas and water mains were laid. The firemen were well organized, numbered a large proportion of the male population, and were influential in politics.[47] A board of stock brokers was formed which included such growing capitalists as R. R. Thompson (President), J. C. Ainsworth, and D. F. Bradford, men who were then developing the Oregon Steam Navigation Company and speculating in the mines.[48] Miners liked to return to Portland to winter. The portion of the surplus from the placer mines, which was expended in Portland, seems to have been quite well distributed in all kinds of business, but it was noticed that, as the placer mines passed their zenith, "the quartz mines, controlled by capital send their product abroad through narrow channels, so that little reaches the general public."[49] Still, the city had received such a marked accession of population, business, and wealth as to insure permanent and steady growth.[50]

But the emporium of the northern mining movement, as she was the metropolis of that movement, was San Francisco. "Three-fourths of the great trains penetrating these gloomy forests," said the Idaho *World*, "and skirting the dreary deserts

---

[46] "I remember in 1861 when the drays were loaded going to the boats of the Oregon Steam Navigation Co. and stood in line it seems to me half a mile long; unloading at night so as to go on in the morning up the river." Deady, *His. of the Progress of Oregon after 1845*, MS. p. 87.

[47] San Francisco *Daily Bulletin*, Sept. 3, 1862. The firemen's organizations were important also at The Dalles and at Virginia City.

[48] *Id.*, April 8, 1864.

[49] *Id.* June 8, 1865.

[50] In 1866 a careful census estimated the permanent population at 6000. *Mineral Resources*, 1868, p. 581.

There was considerable rivalry between Portland and Victoria with regard to the trade of the interior, but Portland had decidedly the advantage because of better routes, particularly in the matter of grass. Victoria never succeeded in getting trade south of the line in the interior, while Portland sent goods far into British Columbia. On this see an editorial of Victoria *Gazette* in S. F. *Daily Bulletin*, Sept. 9, 1860.

with the rising sun in their eyes, are Californians."[51] San Francisco had a trade with Victoria far exceeding that of England with the latter city; in the interior of British Columbia her goods were everywhere to be found; in Boise Basin her hold, though not undisputed by Chicago and St. Louis, was uppermost; and on the far confines of her commercial domains, at Virginia City and Helena, she did battle with St. Joseph and St. Louis.[52] The quality of her goods was of the best and the goods were well adapted to the miners; her woolens and mining machinery were particularly in demand. In accordance with this demand, we may note that in 1867 the Pacific Rolling Mills were established at a cost of $1,000,000 and that the Pacific Woolen Mills turned out annually a product worth $500,000. The growth of the trade with the northern mining region was noted with satisfaction and its importance clearly seen.

In the matter of mining machinery San Francisco had some clear advantage over competitors. Machinery shipped from that city arrived at its destination much earlier in the season than than shipped across the plains. Of greatest advantage, however, was the fact that her machinists were personally familiar with mines and that improvements which were demonstrated successes could be much more quickly adopted there than in the East. San Francisco machinery, therefore, had little to fear from eastern competition in Idaho, but in Montana the great advantage of freight shipments by the Missouri gave her rivals, Chicago and St. Louis, the lead.[53]

We perceive, therefore, that the product of the mines of the northern interior was very important in the upbuilding of wide trade and of many communities on the Pacific Coast. Let us

---

[51] Oct. 14, 1865.
[52] The imports into Victoria from San Francisco in 1861 were valued at $1,151,000 as against $457,000 from Great Britain; in 1862 the amounts were respectively, $2,887,000 and $703,000; in 1863, $1,940,000 and $1,294,000. Macfie, *Van Id. and Br. Col.*, pp. 106-7. The direct trade with the mother country was on the increase, but for these three years the totals were, respectively, $5,478,000 and $2,454,000.

San Francisco goods could compete in the early spring and late fall to advantage in Montana, but when the heavily laden steamers arrived competition was restricted to woolens, teas, and a few other articles. See thoughtful letter from Helena to the Idaho *World*, Feb. 3, 1866.

[53] Ibid; also, Richardson, *Beyond the Mississippi*, p. 507.

now inquire the national significance to the United States of this product and movement.

Of the wide effect of the development of these mining regions upon transportation I shall treat in the next chapter. It is a fact certainly worthy of attention, also, that during the progress of so great a struggle as that of the Civil War, vigorous new communities should have come into existence under the control of the Federal Government.

But I wish now especially to consider the significance of the treasure production upon the national welfare.[54] The opening up of new treasure fields was looked to with very great interest at the time, because their product was regarded as aiding the credit of the nation, helping to restore a specie basis, and, possibly, as directly contributing to the payment of the national debt. "The production of gold and silver in the United States", said the Banker's Magazine, "is one of the important financial and social questions of the day. We look to California and other states of the Pacific to yield, for some years to come, an abundant supply of these metals, with which to restore the country to a specie basis in its commerce with other portions of the world."[55] We can commence our calculations advantageously in the year 1861, when receipts of treasure in San Francisco from the mines of the northern interior began to be appreciable, and we can continue them through 1867, the year in which the United States Mining Commissioner, J. Ross Browne, aggregated estimates. The following table will give a general idea of the yields:

---

[54] I am conscious of the danger that a student of sectional history may overrate the importance of the section that he is studying. Not only may he be somewhat influenced in his judgments by the bias of special investigation, but also, possibly, by an unconscious promotive tendency. While this sort of study helps to bring into needed relief the history of sections, it nevertheless may over accentuate them. It may be, therefore, that after our American history has been sufficiently worked out by special sections and in special periods, re-valuation will be necessary by comprehensive historians.

[55] Vol. XX. 1865-6, p. 606. A thoughtful financier wrote that it was impracticable for the United States to carry on international exchanges when its money was depreciated currency, and suggested that one of the ways in which the United States was trying to overcome the evils of its currency in relation to foreign trade was by continuous augmentation of tariff rates, letter from Robert J. Walker, *Mineral Resources*, 1868, p 664.

Year	Total Gold Product of U. S.	Gold Product of California	Silver Product of U. S.	Total Bullion Product of U. S.
1861	$43,000,000	$40,000,000	$2,000,000	$45,000,000
1862	39,200,000	34,700,000	4,500,000	43,700,000
1863	40,000,000	30,000,000	8,500,000	48,500,000
1864	46,100,000	26,600,000	11,000,000	57,100,000
1865	53,225,000	28,500,000	11,250,000	64,475,000
1866	53,500,000	25,500,000	10,000,000	63,500,000
1867	51,725,000	25,000,000	13,500,000	65,225,000
Total	$326,750,000	$210,300,000	$60,750,000	$387,500,000[56]

Now, as we have seen, the total bullion product of the mining regions which we are studying, to the close of 1867, with some confidence may be estimated at $156,111,000. In comparing this amount with the total product of the United States, however, some deductions must be made. British Columbia produced previous to 1861, $4,648,000; moreover, not quite all of the British Columbia product was manifested through San Francisco although far the greater part was.[57] We have then, a total accretion of $151,463,000 as the contribution of these mines to the national stock of bullion out of a total increase of $387,500,000. That is, they produced in the years when the nation most needed increase of treasure production, not quite 40 per cent. of the total increase. Furthermore, this percentage is still higher, when gold alone is considered. Far the larger part of the increase in silver came from the phenomenal output of Nevada, and question was already being raised as to the effect upon values. But the product of the Inland Empire in these years, with the exception of the silver of Owyhee, was amost entirely gold; and the silver of Owyhee probably did not amount to over $1,500,000, since much of the quartz was gold. We are reasonably safe, therefore, in saying that somewhat over 40 per cent. of the total gold product of the United States, at a trying financial period, came from the mining regions which we are studying.[58]

---

[56] These figures are from *Mineral Resources*, 1874, pp. 543 & 4, by R. W. Raymond. He says that they are compiled from various sources and that the "aggregates are believed to be approximately correct". Some further figures from the same report in regard to silver production are startling: From 1848–1861 the U. S. produced silver to the value of $800,000; from 1868 to 1873, inclusive, $124,500,000. In the latter year the silver production lacked only $250,000 of being equal to that of gold.

[57] There is no way to arrive at the exact amount of this deduction, and to that extent allowance should be made in our conclusions.

[58] It is significant, moreover, that this product came as reinforcement at a time when California's yield was steadily and markedly decreasing. See table above.

CHAPTER VIII

TRANSPORTATION

The subject of transportation might well have been treated under the heading of the preceding chapter, because the establishment of means of transportation and the capitalization of transportation were among the most important permanent forms in the utilization of the mining product. However, the subject is so large as to demand a separate chapter.

That the building up of transportation lines was a part of the permanent production of the mines is apparent when we consider that trade rushed to mining centres not because of high prices, but because of difference of price levels; and that the cost of transportation represented a large part of this difference. For example, a moderate difference is disclosed between Portland and Oro Fino in 1861 in the following figures:

	Portland	Oro Fino
Bacon	8–9c	35–40c
Flour	$3.75–4.50	$16–18
Tea	50c–$1	$1.25
Candles	28–30c	$1.00
Nails	5½–6c	33–37c
Beans	6c	25c
Sugar	11c	40c
Coffee	20–25c	45–50c[1]

The larger share of such difference in prices between Portland and the upper country, paid for out of the treasure product, fell to the principal intermediary, the Oregon Steam Navigation Company, and helped to capitalize that important instrument of transportation.

To remote places the charges for transportation were enormous. For example, the statement is made that a trader in 1862 took to the mines of Cariboo goods costing in Victoria about $15,000,

---

[1] *Oregonian*, June 29, 1861.

upon which the customary and unavoidable charges before they reached their destination amounted to $70,000. The charges from San Francisco to Cariboo, excluding customs duties, merchants' commissions, and retailers' profits, it was said, cost in 1863 $1628 per ton, of which $1440 was for land transport.[2] In view of such charges it was a wise policy in the British Columbia government to collect heavy revenues and to spend large sums on the roads. When the great trunk road from Yale to Cariboo was opened in 1864, freight fell from 60 cents to 30 cents per pound and in the next year to 15 cents.[3] These figures give some conception of the heavy charges paid from the product of the mines.

With such returns in the transportation business, it is easy to understand that an army of packers, freighters, and stagecoach men were needed to carry passengers and goods from the heads of steamboat navigation to the widely scattered mines. Into the most remote localities and over trails of all grades and conditions came the pack animals with the tinkle of their bells and the shouts of their Mexican drivers.[4] Packing was a trade, which required skill and strength. To swing a heavy pack upon an animal's back and to make it stay there was no light accomplishment.[5] The pack animals were generally wintered in the lower and warmer valleys.[6] It was not at all unusual for packers, as their business declined, to become stockmen and farmers. This business always weakened, when the improvement of roads,

---

[2] London *Times*, Aug. 8, 1863.
[3] Harvey, Arthur, *A Statistical Account of British Columbia*, p. 11.
[4] Trains were generally owned by Americans; but Mexicans, because of special skill, were generally, though not always, the packers.
[5] "I must plead guilty to a sneaking admiration of 'packers' (muleteers) and teamsters. These men are wondrous results of the law of demand and supply; for the work demanded they have become thoroughly capable and that work demands strength, skill, daring, endurance and trustworthiness * * * Having to lift heavy weights sheer from the ground on to the pack saddle, 'packers' are very muscular men, with grand chests and shoulders. They have also many savage accomplishments; are good farriers, can accomplish marvels with the axe, a screw key and a young sapling for a lever. But they are a godless race both actively and passively. They earn considerable wages, and after a few years settle down in some of our beautiful valleys, surrounded by an Indian clientele." Report of Rev. James Reynard, *Occasional Papers of Columbian Mission*, 1869, pp. 63-4.
[6] A good idea of Walla Walla as a packing centre may be got from Schafer, *History of the Pacific Northwest*, pp. 258-60.

bridges, and ferries permitted the use of freight teams.[7] The tinkle of the bells was replaced by the gee-haw of the "bullwhackers" and the cracks of the teamsters' whips. From Yale to Cariboo, from Ft. Benton to Helena and Virginia City, from Umatilla or Wallula to Boise Basin long trains of slow-moving, heavily laden wagons were to be seen, carrying to the camps the wares of civilization.[8]

As to passenger movement, many of the miners walked from the heads of steamboat navigation to the mines. Others clubbed together and bought a horse to carry their impedimenta, while still others provided themselves with a horse for each individual. In other cases passengers were carried by saddle train, and this sometimes became an important business. The owners of a saddle train would furnish riding horses, carry a small amount of baggage, and provide provisions.[9] Stage coaches, of course, came rapidly into use on all the most travelled thoroughfares. The main stagelines were those from Salt Lake City to Virginia City and Helena, from Salt Lake via Boise and Walla Walla to Wallula, and from Yale to Barkerville. Ben Holladay in Idaho and Montana, as elsewhere in the west, was dominant, having a clear advantage because of his contract for carrying the United States mails. We get a glimpse of the spirit of the times in the *Song of the Overland Stage*, written by Nat Steen, one of the employes of Holladay's Company:

"It's thus you're safely carried throughout the mighty West, Where chances to make fortunes are ever of the best;
And thus the precious pouches of mail are brought to hand, Through the ready hearts that center on the jolly Overland.''

---

[7] The coming in of freighters, between Umatilla and Boise Basin reduced slow freight from ten and twelve cents per pound to six and eight cents, Hailey, *His. of Idaho*, p. 99

[8] One gets a suggestion of the amount of goods transported by teams into mining regions from the advertisement of a wholesale firm in Virginia City, Baume, Angevine and Merry, who in 1864 advertised for sale 500 boxes of tobacco, 250 bbls. of liquor, 1500 sacks of flour, 500 lbs. of ham, 10,000 lbs. of bacon, 400 cans of lard, 50 bags of coffee and 100 kegs of nails; Montana *Post*, Sept. 24, 1864.

[9] For a good description of this phase of transportation, as well as running a stage line, one should not fail to read chapter XII, XIX and XXV of Hailey's *History of Idaho*. These chapters are based on experience and show intimate knowledge.

Chorus.

"Statesmen and warriors, traders and the rest,
May boast of their profession, and think it is the best;
Their state I'll never envy, I'll have you understand,
Long as I can be a driver on the jolly Overland."

But Holladay was not without competition. A. J. Oliver and Company started the first stage from Virginia City to Bannack,— "A weekly affair, not much good, but a long way ahead of nothing."[10] This line was extended to Helena, and, when Holladay came on the scene, the rivalry was intense. For awhile the fare between the two places was one dollar, and the distance, one hundred and ten miles, was made in twelve hours or less, the horses being kept at a hard gallop.[11] Some of the best staging in the United States was done between Virginia City and Helena.[12] There was competition, also, on the southern route, where Ish and Hailey carried on a careful and prosperous line between Boise and Umatilla.[13]

One of the most interesting and important aspects of transportation in the mining regions was the express business. Into every most remote camp, months before the mail was established, pushed hardy carriers bearing with them the longed for news of the war and the letters "from the dear ones in the distant homes—letters in which the kisses are yet warm and the heart beats yet audible."[14] The life of the expressman was particularly hard in the winter time, when, guiding himself often by compass, risking snow blindness, often camping for the night in the snow, he made his way with the utmost fidelity to the lone

---
[10] Remarks of Judge W. Y. Pemberton, of Helena.
[11] Ibid.
[12] "The best staging in the United States", Richardson, *Our New States and Territories*, p 70.
[13] Other local lines were those of Greathouse & Co. from Boise City to Idaho City and of Hill Beachy from Boise City to Silver City. Later a stage was run from Silver City to Virginia City, Nevada, and another (by Capt. John Mullan) from Silver City to Red Bluffs, California. There was a good deal of effort to get a feasible direct connection between Idaho and California, and it was partially successful
[14] Goulder, *Reminiscences of a Pioneer*, p. 216.

camps. Such a man was David D. Chamberlain, who carried letters at a dollar apiece from Walla Walla to East Bannack during the winter of 1863-4.[15] Another was Joaquin Miller, afterwards to become famous as poet, who rode express from Walla Walla to Salmon River.[16] This business was soon taken up by companies. There were a number of small concerns such as that of Ballou in British Columbia.[17] But the great company, whose offices were to be found in every large town, whose messengers travelled on almost every steamer, or sat by the driver on almost every stage, was Wells, Fargo and Company. They were ubiquitous in the mining regions, both north and south of the Line, and a very large proportion of the treasure reached the outer world through them.[18]

For the mail, of course, there was very great urgency. Petitions from territorial legislatures for establishment of new mail routes as new camps were formed, were very numerous. The government of British Columbia was more tardy in responding to the need for mail facilities than were the United States authorities.[19] But in both regions the mail served to tie the new communities to the old seats of civilization. A thousand tendrils ran back to friends, relatives, and sweethearts in the East and in Britain and kept alive sentiments in danger of being blurred in the new life. The over-emphasis upon the adventurous, rough, romantic side of the miners' lives has neglected this very strong influence; one who reads some of the letters to the miners telling the little nothings of neighborhood doings, or sometimes bringing solemn announcement of death of loved ones

---

[16] *Sketches of Early Settlers in Montana* by Col. W. F. Sanders, MS

[15] For the experiences of Miller see a *Pioneer Pony Express Rider*, Chap X of *Illustrated History of Montana*, published by Lewis Pub. Co. The first part of this book was written by him.

[17] Ballou's *Adventures* are found in MS in the Bancroft Library. They may be fairly trustworthy as to the express business, but in other matters they are evidently gasconade.

[18] The student of history longs to get at the records of Wells, Fargo & Co. Its history would make excellent material for a monograph.

[19] There were eight post offices in British Columbia, Dec. 31, 1863 The total expenditure was 3291 pounds and the total income 749 pounds. One half of the mail carried was that of the Government. The Post Master General wanted a monopoly in the Government in order to restrain private carriage; Report of Post Master General, *Govt. Gazette*, Feb. 5, 1864.

back home, gets a finer conception of the real life of the miners than that typified by the six-shooter. There was demand, also, for the telegraph, and before 1870 the principal towns both north and south of the line were connected with the outer world by this means. Thus the constant tendency in these far-away communities was towards better facilities of communication.

For land transportation of every species roads, ferries, and bridges were very necessary. We who are so accustomed to such conveniences now can scarcely imagine under what difficulties the pioneers labored in trying to provide them in a country of great distances, swift streams, and mountainous grades. We have noted how manfully and successfully Governor Douglas attacked the great problem of roads to Cariboo. In British Columbia there was less resort to private parties, with special charters, than there was in the territories to the south. Every legislature in these territories was besieged for special charters for roads, bridges, and ferries, and they were granted in large numbers. Men who obtained a monopoly of ferriage over a stream otherwise impassable, and on the main road to a large mining camp, were sure of making money.[20] On the other hand, as on old pioneer expressed it to me, "We had to have roads and bridges and ferries, we had no money, and how were we to get them?"[21] The construction of roads and trails was often very expensive and the season for heavy travel short.[22] Still, the aggregate of toll charges was a serious expense. For example, the tolls for the round trip from Umatilla to Boise cost ten dollars for each animal.[23] Governor Ashley, of Montana, said in his message of 1869 that the tolls from Helena to Corinne, Utah, were forty dollars for each team.[24]

Important as was the land transportation, however, it had not the significance of the steamboat navigation. Steamboating entered upon a new phase in its efforts to serve the wants of the

---

[20] At Craig's Ferry at Lewiston in 1662, Mrs. Schultze found waiting "500 men, much freight, and hundreds of mules and horses."—*Anecdotes of Early Settlement of northern Idaho.* MS. p. 2.
[21] Remark of Judge W. Y. Pemberton.
[22] Hailey, *His. of Idaho,* p. 30.
[23] *Id* p. 62.
[24] *Contributions to His. Soc. of Mont.* Vol. VI, p. 279.

mines of the Inland Empire. Never before in history had steamboats penetrated so far from lands of settled habitation, nor encountered such risks, as they did on the long stretch of the upper Missouri, with its bare and tortuous channels, or on the swift waters of the Columbia and the Fraser, with their snags and rapids.

Let us consider separately the navigation on each of these streams.

On the last named, navigation may be said to have extended from Victoria to Yale.[25] A steamboat was also placed upon the upper Fraser from Quesnelmouth to Soda Creek. Men were charmed then as they are now by the beauty of the scenery—the islands of the Gulf of Georgia, Mount Baker towering in the distance, the thickly wooded banks of the lower Fraser, and the increasing majesty of the bluffs further up. Still more beautiful was the trip up Harrison Lake. So matter-of-fact a man as J. C. Ainsworth, chief organizer of the Oregon Steam Navigation Co., wrote concerning the first steamboat trip into this lake: "We were running along just at dusk of a warm day in July—it must have been nine o'clock in the evening—when all at once we opened into this great lake twenty-four miles long and four or five miles wide, surrounded by those beautiful mountains and the full moon was rising right from the lake. Well, I never saw men so affected by excitement in my life.[26] They were greatly affected by the grandeur of the scene. Well, it would have excited anybody I partook of some of the excitement myself."[27] As captain and owner of the vessel, however, he prudently restrained himself and ran this first passage cautiously.

It was Americans, indeed, who owned and ran most of the Fraser River steamboats. The Hudson's Bay Company at the commencement of the mining advance had two small steamers, which ran to Hope; but they were dirty, and the meals were poor.[28] It was an American steamer, the Umatilla, that first dared to encounter the swift current between Hope and Yale. The

---
[25] Also up Harrison River and Lake.
[26] There were seventy miners aboard.
[27] *Statement of Capt. J. C. Ainsworth*, MS. p. 16.
[28] San Francisco *Daily Bulletin*, Feb. 6, 1861.

strength of the current in this stretch of about fifteen miles is revealed by the fact that it took six hours to go up, and half an hour to come down.[29] British travelers marveled at the recklessness of the Americans. The vessel on which Mr. Macfie journeyed from Hope to Yale, although the steam pressure was way beyond that allowed by law, for twenty minutes at one place appeared to make no progress; the captain and other Americans on board made bets as to the issue and coolly discussed the chances of an explosion.[30] The characteristic indifference of Americans with regard to human life came out in a conversation shared by Mr. Macfie, when the inquiry was put to a Yankee as to the safety of a certain steamer: "She may do very well for passengers," was the reply, "but I wouldn't trust treasure in her."[31] On the other hand, the British admired the cleanliness of the American boats, the abundance and goodness of the provisions, the superiority of the service, and the comfort of the cabins.[32]

The history of steamboat navigation on the Columbia River during the period of the mining advance is the history of the Oregon Steam Navigation Company. And the history of this company is of a peculiar interest and importance both from the point of view of the development of the great mining area whose transportation it controlled, and as a concrete and simplified example of monopolistic methods; but the details of its history have been so adequately presented elsewhere, that I shall attempt to touch only salient features.[33] The *sine qua non* of the company was the control of the portages at the Cascades and the Dalles. At first various individuals and groups owned what facilities there were at these places and also the steamboats be-

---

[29] Macfie, *Van Id. and Br. Col.*, p. 232.
[30] *Id.*
[31] *Id.*
[32] Hazlitt, *Cariboo*, p. 78. A noted American boat was the Wilson G. Hunt, which had before seen service on the Sacramento and was later transferred to the Columbia. The steamer on which Ainsworth went into Lake Harrison had been built on the Columbia above the Cascades, but by misadventure had gone over. Ainsworth bought an interest in her and took her to British Columbia. *Statement*, p. 14.
[33] Poppleton, Irene Lincoln. *Oregon's First Monopoly, Quarterly of the Or. His. Soc.* Sept. 1908, Vol. IX, No. 3, pp 274-304. A bibliography is appended, to which may be added the *Statement of Capt. J. C. Ainsworth*, MS. in the Bancroft Collection and item in *Mineral Resources*, 1868, pp. 579,-80.

low, above, and between. Far sighted individuals emerged from these contending groups, who by patience, tact, and pressure brought about consolidation into one company. Then we have clearly the characteristics of monopolistic control: deft, though not clearly blameworthy, handling of legislatures; extremely high rates, all that the traffic would bear; strong attempt at competition, and obnoxious methods of stifling it; popular resentment and distrust; swift aggregation of capital, as civilized society took possession of the vast tributary area; prudent and skillful management, notable efficiency and enterprise:—in fact, real industrial leadership. Steamboat navigation of the time reached its highest point in the powerful boats, nicely responsive to the steersman's touch, which surmounted the rapids of the Columbia and the Snake.[34] The appointments of the boats were first class, the meals good, and everything was clean and neat. The enterprise of the company is shown in the way in which it put boats on remote navigable stretches. On the upper Columbia it owned the Forty Nine; on the Clark's Fork of the Columbia and Lake Pend d' Oreille it had the Mary Moody and two other boats; on the upper Snake in southern Idaho it built the Shoshone at an expense of $100,000, in order to try to get some of the Salt Lake trade.[35] Far-reaching enterprise, efficiency, and monopolistic grasp were, therefore, the outstanding characteristics of the Oregon Steam Navigation Company.

There could be no such monopoly in the steamboat navigation which served the mining regions by way of the upper Missouri. Starting with the Chippewa in 1859, from two to eight boats ascended the river each year from 1860 to 1865 (except 1861); then the Sioux hostilities on the Bozeman Road from 1866 to 1868, coinciding with much industrial activity in western Mon-

---

[34] A Trip from Portland to Boise, S. F. *Daily Bulletin*, June, 23, 1864, gives some interesting facts about these steamers and their work.

[35] *Statement of Ainsworth*, p. 24

The Mary Moody was built in 1865. In four months from the time the first tree was felled for her, she was launched. "She was 108 feet in length, 20 feet beams, and was 85 tons burden and constructed entirely of whipsawed lumber" Sketch by Judge Frank H. Moody, *Contr. His. Soc. Mont.* Vol. II, p. 104. This attempt to navigate the Upper Snake failed, and the Shoshone ran the frightful cañons to Lewiston. In the history of steamboating in the United States it would be hard to parallel this perilous feat.

tana, suddenly raised the number to thirty-one in 1866, thirty-nine in 1867, thirty-five in 1868 and twenty-four in 1869.[36] These years marked the high tide of the river traffic, for it swiftly sank as the Union Pacific arrived at competing distance. Some idea of its dimensions are gained from statistics. In 1867, 8061 tons of freight were carried to Ft. Benton and some 10,000 pasengers. As the latter paid $150 fare each, the total for passenger transport alone amounted to $1,500,000.[37] The profits were so great as to more than make up for high rates of insurance and the occasional loss of a steamer—Captain La Barge in the Octavia is reported to have cleared $40,000 from one trip in 1867 and the profits of other vessels in the previous year are reported at from $16,000 to $65,000.[38] The dangers and trials of the steamboat men, however, were many and various. From St. Louis to Ft. Benton the distance was 2300 miles, and there stretched from the verge of the settlements (near Ft. Randall) over 1300 miles of little known river.[39] Snags forbade running at night, except at great risk; numerous bars had to be "grasshoppered" over by sparring; wood was hard to get and very expensive; boilers and pilot houses had to be bulwarked; constant guard had to be kept against Indian attacks; there were dangerous and trying delays due to falling water. Sometimes throngs of buffalo crossing the river caused a halt.[40]

The destination to which these steamboats struggled was a straggling village near the old adobe fort of the American Fur Company, Ft. Benton. On the crowded levee of this village (called, also, Ft. Benton) was piled a mass of varied merchan-

---

[36] *Contr. Mont. His. Soc.* Vol. 1, 317–325. An excellent account of the Sioux war along the Bozeman Road is found in Paxson, the *Last American Frontier*, Chap. XVI.

[37] *Report* of Capt. C. W. Howell, Ex. Doc., House Rep. 3d. Sess. 40th Cong., Report Sec'y. War, p. 622 ff; reprinted in N. Dak. *State His. Soc. Collections*, Vol. II, pp. 379–91.

[38] Chittenden, H. M. *History* of *Early Steamboat Navigation on the Missouri River*, Vol. II, pp. 275–6.

[39] Hanson, *The Conquest of the Missouri*, p. 64. Chap. IX of this work is particularly commendable.

[40] Journal of Capt. C. W. Howell, Ex Doc. H. R. 3d. Sess. 40th Cong., pp. 634–54; reprinted in N. D. *His. Soc. Col.* Vol. 11, pp. 392–415. To the authorities on the navigation of the upper Missouri, which have been mentioned in our text should be added logs of various steamers, found in N. Dak. *His. Soc. Col.*, Vol. II, pp. 267–371.

dise. For the interior points there were boxes of drygoods and clothing, barrels of liquor, sacks of provisions, cases of mining tools, and quartz mills; for the down trade there were buffalo hides and peltries of all sorts. Every warehouse was jammed with goods, and private dwellings were used as warehouses. The safes of the town were taxed to their utmost capacity to store gold dust as it was brought in, and precious packages were sometimes carelessly left in stores. One steamer bore away $1,250,000 in gold. In the streets of the town was a throng of varied and picturesque humanity: lumbermen from Minnesota and farmers from many parts of the great valley; confederate sympathizers from Missouri and Union men from the Western Reserve; miners from the Pacific Coast and "fur-traders and hunters of the vanishing Northwestern wilderness", Indians of many tribes; desperadoes and lovers of order; miners, traders, clergymen, speculators, land-seekers, government officials—all the exuberant array of the American frontier. Freight wagons, consisting of two or three wagons coupled together, and drawn by a dozen or more oxen or mules, rumbled ceaselessly through the streets. Not less than six hundred outfits participated in this traffic. The area to which it ministered was extensive; not only did the Ft. Benton trade supply the wide semicircle of the camps of Western Montana, but in its outer limits it touched British Columbia, Calgary, and Edmonton.

Another interesting phase of the business of Ft. Benton, the mackinaw fleet, is described by an able writer as follows:—"The steamboat season over and the freight distributed, the mackinaw season set in. At all seasons of the year when the river was open mackinaws were to be found descending it; but it was in September that the great rush commenced. Then, as winter approached, the successful miners who had accumulated wealth and the unsuccessful who were discouraged and disheartened bestirred themselves to escape from the country. Thronging to Ft. Benton they rendered the levee the scene of renewed activity. Scores of rough boats sprang into existence and day after day they would push off with a crew of from half a dozen to thirty and forty souls, sometimes single, sometimes in flotillas, and drop down the river to various points from Sioux City to Saint Louis..

"In the neighborhood of 200 boats and 1200 passengers would thus sail from Benton annually. These boats were usually broad, flat-bottomed crafts, with square sterns and roughly built, to be sold as lumber or abandoned at the end of the voyage. They were supplied with oars and sometimes sails, but the rapid current of the river was relied upon for the main progress * * * Under favorable circumstances a hundred miles a day was accomplished in these vessels. Frequent running aground, danger from Indians and occasional shipwrecks were among the incidents of the voyage, and the party was fortunate that got through without any mishap."[41]

In addition to the emigrants who went to the mining regions from the East on the Missouri steamboats, there was a very large movement by the overland trails: "It was estimated that the migration in 1864 from the one town of Omaha amounted to 75,000 people, 22,500 tons of freight, 30,000 horses and mules, and 75,000 cattle, while all authorities seem to agree that the total migration from all the Missouri River towns, through Kansas and Nebraska by all routes, equaled 150,000 people."[42] Of this number certainly a very considerable proportion was destined for the northwest mines. Rev. Jonathan Blanchard thought that two-thirds of the twenty-four thousand immigrants who had preceded him in 1864 on the trail to Laramie were bound for Idaho.[43] While thus the old Oregon trail, because of its

---

[41] Bradley, Lieut. Jas. H., *Effects at Ft. Benton of the Gold Excitement in Montana*, MS. Besides this article, I have used for the last two paragraphs, Hanson, *The Conquest of the Missouri*, Chap X and Ferguson, H A. V., *Ft. Benton Memories*, MS. Mention should also be made of Chittenden, H. M., *The Ancient Town of Ft. Benton in Montana*. See also Campbell, J. S.; *Six Months in the New Gold Diggings*, who says, "During the past season (1864) an immense emigration, precendented by none save the early rush to the Eldorado of the Pacific, has swelled the mountain gorges and valleys of Montana." It was thought that between 75.000 and 100,000 persons visited Virginia City in 1864, of whom probably four-fifths returned to the States. (pp. 4 & 5) The advertisements in Campbell give an idea of the far-reaching stimulus to eastern commercial ganglia and to railroads which the mining regions gave. Merchants of Council Bluffs, Omaha, St. Joseph, St. Louis and Chicago advertise their facilities for outfitting or for furnishing manufactures; while the Hannibal and St. Joseph, the Chicago and St. Louis, the Michigan Central and the Pennsylvania Lines call attention to the advantage of making the first part of the trip to the mines over their routes.

[42] Fite, *Social and Industrial Conditions in the North during the Civil War*, p. 39.

[43] *Id.*, p. 38.

good grass and comparatively easy grades, maintained a clear supremacy among the overland routes, two other routes are of special interest from the point of view of this study. These are the northern route to Montana and the route to British Columbia.[44]

It was the Salmon River excitement of 1861-2 that first started migration by the northern route from Minnesota. In that year two large parties made their way over the plains from rendezvous on the Red River of the north. The first started from St. Joseph (now Walhalla, N. D.), and the other from Ft. Abercrombie; both went by way of Ft. Union.[45] The second was under the command of Capt. Jas. L. Fisk, to whom this duty was assigned by the Secretary of War, and one of Fisk's assistants was N. P. Langford.[46] Fisk's work was of the same nature as that performed by Capt. Medoram Crawford in the same year on the southern route: "To afford protection to these emigrants, and at the same time test the practicability of this northern route for future emigration", were stated to be the objects of the expedition. It consisted of 140 persons, most of whom were Minnesota frontiersmen. In constructing bridges these expert lumbermen would swim the streams, hats on head and pipes in mouth, in order to float the logs to place, and handled the axe and the spade-like playthings. The numbers of buffalo seen on the way were prodigious, Fisk estimating the number seen in one day at 100,000. The party arrived safely at Ft. Benton, but instead of proceeding to Salmon River scattered to the newly discovered diggings of western Idaho.[47]

In spite of the Sioux outbreak of 1862 another successful expedition under Capt. Fisk was made in 1863.[48] The expedition of 1864, however, failed to go through, being attacked by Indians in the Bad Lands, from whom it was rescued by troops of General Sully. Another under Fisk, unsupported by the govern-

---

[44] The Bozeman road may be regarded as a branch of the Oregon trail.
[45] For account of the first see N. Dak. *His. Soc. Collections*, Vol. II, pp. 75-78.
[46] Author of *Vigilante Days and Ways* and important promoter of Yellowstone Park, now a resident of St. Paul. *The World Today*, May, 1911, pp. 598-99, gives an account of Mr. Langford's personality and work.
[47] A reprint of Fisk's report (Ex. Doc. No. 80, 37th Cong., third Sess.) is in N. Dak. *His Soc. Col.* Vol. II, App. pp. 34-72.
[48] *Id.*, App pp. 78-83.

ment, took the shape of an imposing scheme for the promotion of town-building and mining on the Upper Yellowstone, but this expedition failed to materialize. The last of Fisk's expeditions, that of 1866, "was different from any of the preceding in its larger size, in the absence of government aid and from the fact that for many it was a commercial venture, not a gold hunting trip."[49]

In all of these expeditions St. Paul took an active interest. Indeed, from the very beginning of the mining rushes the business men of this city planned for overland routes, for connection with the Red River of the North, and for development of trade with the Selkirk settlements and the regions beyond. The Chamber of Commerce of St. Paul "declared that the city's whole commercial future was projected with the far Northwest in view."[50]

When we consider the overland route to British Columbia, we come likewise upon large conceptions and the beginnings of great things. Immediately upon the organization of British Columbia, Sir Edward Bulwer Lytton "proclaimed in the name of the government, the policy of continuous colonies from Lake Superior to the Pacific and a highway across British America as the most direct route from London to Pekin or Jeddo."[51] From this time onward there was constant discussion in British Columbia, Canada, and Great Britian concerning the Great Inter-oceanic Railway.[52] Attention was called to the possession of fine ports at either end of the line—Halifax and Esquimault—and to great coal deposits near them. At least one man, however, with remarkable prescience, thought that Burrard's Inlet, the present

---

[49] *Id.*, p. 450 Original documents concerning the last three expeditions are found in works cited, pp. 442–461. In addition to the desire to hunt gold, immigrants from Minnesota were impelled by general discontent of the border counties in the years following the Sioux outbreaks and the Civil War On this aspect consult Hilger, David, *Overland Trail, Con. His. Soc. Mont.*, Vol. VII, pp 257–270

[50] Fite, *Social and Industrial Conditions during the Civil War*, p. 69. See also Puget Sound *Herald*, Sept. 10, 1858.

[51] *Relations between the United States and N. W. British America*, Ex. Doc, 37th Cong, 3d Ses, Exhibit D, St. Paul, April 17, 1861, p. 27.

[52] The titles of two books of the time are suggestive: Rawling's *America from the Atlantic to the Pacific* and Milton and Cheadle, *The Northwest Passage by Land*.

location of Vancouver, was destined to be the great port of the Pacific, rather than Victoria.[53] Rivalry with the United States in the building of a transcontinental line was a conspicuous motive, and mention was made of the desirability of the railroad in case of war with the United States. The designs of France in Mexico, also, were regarded with suspicion and it was suggested that one object of the French Emperor in acquiring Mexico was to bid for the Oriental trade by building a railroad from Vera Cruz to Acapulco and putting on a line of steamers from the latter port to China and Japan.[54] The importance of the Red River settlements and of the great country westward from them was dilated upon, and Lytton wanted to erect these into an independent colony; but the Hudson's Bay Company possessed these lands by charter (not by license to trade, as in the case of British Columbia), and the Company naturally was slow to fall in with changes which might interfere with the fur trade.[55] A project more generally favored than that of making the Selkirk settlements a Crown colony was that of incorporating them into a union of all the British North American possessions. All of these plans received fresh impulse when, in 1862, the magnificent Cariboo field put British Columbia finally on its feet, and the announcement was made of the discovery of gold on the upper Saskatchewan. British Columbia was to be another California and the Saskatchewan field another Colorado. It is important for the student of the history of these movements to realize in addition to the really remarkable achievements of the period, the glamour and enticement of the seemingly roseate immediate future.

While full fruition of these aspirations was to be postponed for another generation, some interesting and important steps

---

[53] "I have more than once discussed the feasibility of this grand scheme with Colonel Moody, of the Royal Engineers—a question in which he felt great interest. His fixed idea always was that Burrard's Inlet, from its situation, depth of water, and other natural advantages, was destined to be the great emporium of commerce on the Pacific, at the terminus of the railway." Barret-Lennard, *Travels in British Columbia*, pp. 181-2.

[54] Macfie, *Van Id. and Br. Col.* pp. 367-8

[55] Report of Sir Edmund Head, Governor of the Company, Macfie, *Van. Id and Br. Col.* pp. 54-55. The company, however, shipped wire to the Selkirk settlement for a telegraph line to British Columbia.

were taken in the decade following the founding of British Columbia. The year 1859 witnessed the beginnings of steamboat transportation on the Red River of the North, when a steamboat was brought across from the upper waters of the Mississippi and launched in Red River as the Anson Northrup. In the same year the Hudson's Bay Company established a town on the Minnesota side about fifteen miles north of the present Fargo, North Dakota, and named the new town Georgetown in honor of Sir George Simpson, then Governor of Rupert's Land. A stage line was put on by Burbank & Company between Georgetown and St. Paul. A second boat, The International, was built at Georgetown and launched in 1862. Its motto was "Germinaverunt speciosa deserti," and on its first trip it took 150 miners enroute for Cariboo.[56]

For the organization of the overland route two interesting companies were promoted and chartered. The one, whose chief projector was Mr. W. M. Dawson, was called The Northwest Transportation Company. Its mainspring was in Canada, where there was eager desire for participation in the traffic with British Columbia.[57] This company proposed to establish steam communication with Ft. William, at the head of Lake Superior, and then to place half-a-dozen small river steamers on the chain of rivers and lakes which run from that to the foot of the Rocky Mountains with a few easily surmounted portages.[58] The last phase suggests the inadequacy of the conceptions with regard to the new regions which was even more conspicuous in the English plans of the time than in the Canadian. In England there was largeness and elaborateness of projection in regard to the new countries and the ways of getting there, but also a certain fumbling incapability of execution or of grasping real conditions, which was in marked contrast to the straightforward, quickly adjustable enterprise of Americans. It was simply the difference, of course,

---

[56] The foregoing data are from a *Sketch of the Northwest of America* by Mgr. Tache, Bishop of St. Boniface in 1868. We should not over rate the part of the mining country in bringing about these beginnings of transportation because the time had about arrived; anyhow, when the Selkirk settlements had to have better communications with St. Paul

[57] Canadian *News*, Mar. 20, 1862, quoted in Hazlitt's *Cariboo*, pp. 92-3.

[58] Hazlitt's *Cariboo*, pp. 105-6.

between those who were familiar with conditions and those who were not. This characteristic was well illustrated in the *British Columbia Overland Transit Company, Ltd*, which was organized in London with a proposed capital of half a million pounds and an imposing directorate of "eminent" and "respectable" names. The object was "to establish a transport system for mails and passengers by carts and relays of horses" to British Columbia. The route was to be by Montreal, St. Paul, Pembina, Carlton House, and Edmonton. The time from England to the gold diggings was to be about five weeks. In regard to this time a correspondent of the Times, "Canada West", wrote that the shortest time would be three months, more likely four or five, and perhaps all winter. To this Secretary Henson, of the company, replied that " 'Canada West' proves that his calculations are based on thorough ignorance. For instance, he gives ten days from St. Paul to Red River; whereas two days is the time now occupied by the steamers which run on the Red River from Georgetown to Ft. Garry." [The Secretary seemed to think the distance from St. Paul to Georgetown negligible.] "Canada West" replied that last season he had journeyed from St. Paul to Georgetown, that the trip occupied four days, and that thence to Ft. Garry by steamer took three or four days more. Still another correspondent sent a letter from his brother stating that he had made the trip from Red River to Victoria, but that it had taken seven months and that he had nearly starved to death on the road.[59] Several parties of considerable size did go through to Cariboo from St. Paul by the overland route, most with success, but some with death and suffering. The Victoria Colonist, however, summarized the route by saying that the way was easy to the Rockies, but extremely difficult thence to Cariboo, and that there was a tendency to go down the Columbia via Colville and Portland.[60] The Overland Transit Company seems to have vanished without accomplishing anything. The signifi-

---

[59] These letters are republished in *McDonald, Br. Col. and Van. Id* pp. 403–417. Their details seem unimportant, but they illustrate the interest taken in England in the projected route.

[60] Barret-Lennard, *Travels in British Columbia*, pp 187–198; London *Times*, Jan. 1, 1863; San Francisco *Daily Bulletin*, Aug. 1, 1863; McNaughton, Margaret, *Overland to Cariboo*, (a journey of 1862).

cance of all these attempts and aspirations lies in their realization in the great railway system which, in a unified Canada, stretches from the Atlantic to the Pacific,—the only complete interoceanic railway.

There remains to be considered the ocean routes by which immigrants went from England to British Columbia. Most of the many books published in the mother country at this time concerning the new colony discuss the routes thither, compare cost of passage and give detailed directions.[61] In this respect they were like the numerous emigrants' guides in the United States. The two routes most favorably mentioned were the one by way of St. Thomas, Panama, and San Francisco, which was held to be the shorter, but the more expensive; and the other around the Horn, which was thought to be the cheaper and more suitable, therefore, for families. Alternative routes were to go to New York and thence to Aspinwall, or to proceed from the former city across the continent. The whole transportation business from Panama to San Francisco and from there to Victoria was controlled by Americans—a fact deplored in the British Colonies, particularly with respect to the mails.[62]

The effects of the mining advance into the Inland Empire, it may be safely asserted, were widely distributed among agencies of trade and transportation. Perhaps the movement in this respect might be likened to an immense spider's web, throwing out from a central area of intense activity far reaching cords.

---

[61] For example, Macfie, *Van. Id. and Br Col.* pp. 519-26; Rattray, *Van Id. and Br. Col.* pp. 177-82.

[62] The cost of transportation to British Columbia was greater than to any other British Colony. Passage from London to New Zealand or Cape of Good Hope cost £20 and to Australia £16, whereas to Victoria, via the Horn it cost £30 and via Panama £77; colonization circular issued by Her Majesty's Emigration Commissioners, in McDonald, *Br Col. and Van. Id.*, p. 469.

PART III

SOCIAL ASPECTS OF THE MINING ADVANCE

CHAPTER IX

COMPONENTS AND CHARACTERISTICS OF SOCIETY

The elements of population which composed the mining advance will be the first subject of inquiry in this chapter.

One fact stands out prominently, and that is that the population was very heterogeneous. In addition to an original basis of French half-breeds and of mountain-men, representatives from all parts of the United States and from every quarter of the globe were to be found,—Americans, Canadians, Englishmen, Germans, Frenchmen, Italians, Spanish, Chinese, Mexicans, Chilanos, Australians, Hawaiians. One observer of the throngs wrote: "Within a few hours, I have met in the streets of Victoria persons who had respectively crossed the Andes, ascended Mont Blanc, fought in the Crimea, explored the Northwest passage, seen Pekin, ransacked Mexican antiquities, lived on the coast of Africa, revelled in the luxuries of India, witnessed Sepoys blown from British guns, wintered in Petersburg, and engaged in buffalo hunts on the great prairies of North America."[1] In estimating the intelligence of the mining population account should be taken of the extensiveness of the miners' travels and of the diversities of their contacts.

As to the proportions of the different elements in the population we may gain some general ideas, but we can arrive at no precise figures. When the first steamer from San Francisco arrived at Victoria in the Fraser River rush, she had on board 400 men enroute for the mines; of this number there were about sixty British subjects, with an equal number of native-born Americans, the rest being chiefly Germans, with a smaller proportion of Frenchmen and Italians.[2] *The Victoria Gazette* stated

---
[1] Macfie, *Van. Id and Br Col.*, p. 412.
[2] Despatch of Gov Douglas, Cornwallis, *New Eldorado,* p 357.

that, of the whole number of passengers carried up to July, 1858, by the Surprise—the principal steamer then running up Fraser River—nearly one-half were Irish and a large proportion Italian and French, but added that in July more Americans were coming. The proportion of Irishmen was particularly noticeable, also, in southern Idaho. The population at The Dalles (which was an index to that of the upper country) was said to have been composed of "Saxon, Celt, Teuton, Gaul, Greaser, Celestial and Indian".[3] Statistics from Port Douglas, in British Columbia, give the following data for a population numbering 206.

```
Coloured men ................................. 8
Mexicans and Spaniards ......................29
Chinese .......................................37
French and Italians ..........................16
Central Europe ............................... 4
Northern Europe .............................. 4
Citizens of the United States.................73
British subjects ............................35[4]
```

A census of Ft. Hope in 1861 showed 55 British subjects and 111 foreigners. It is certain that in British Columbia during the mining period the British element in the population was greatly in the minority, and that the largest single ingredient of population was furnished by citizens of the United States.[5] Moreover, a very large proportion of the men engaged in the mining rushes—possibly not far from one-half—were not Americans or Britons; and, furthermore, of those styled Californians, (and hence Americans) a very large proportion were of other than Anglo-Saxon nativity. If these facts be true, then we may fairly raise the question whether the enterprise, adventurousness, and adaptability which were characteristics of the mining population—and, especially the spontaneity which was shown

---

[3] San Francisco *Bulletin*, Nov. 13, 1862.
[4] Paper by Rev. Mr. Gammage quoted by McDonald, *Br. Col. and Van Id.*, p. 166.
[5] "Our American friends especially are our pioneer miners, our principal traders and our chief packers" *Colonist*, Jan. 2, 1862. "The tone of society has become decidedly more British since 1859; but still, as then the American element prevails" Macfie, *Van. Id. & Br. Col*, p 379.

in working out the laws of the mining camps,—were quite so peculiarly Anglo-Saxon as has been thought.[6]

While the mining camps were very heterogeneous in population, still, certain elements are more conspicuous in some places than elsewhere. In British Columbia, after the opening of Cariboo, English, Cornish, Scotch and Welch were to be met with more numerously than in other parts of the mining areas. So, too, Oregonians (and men from the Sound) were distinguished in the Nez Percés mines, Missourians and Pike's Peakers in Boise Basin, and people from Minnesota in Montana. This does not mean, of course, that other elements were not present in all these camps. In the Montana camps, in particular, there was a curious mingling of eastern "tenderfeet" and western "yon-siders", who were amused at each others' lingo; the tapaderas of the latter were to the former toe-fenders—machiers, saddle-scabbards—cantinas, handy-bags.[7] But whatever elements of population prevailed in one or the other place, there was one everywhere present, everywhere respected, everywhere vital—the Californian. To Fraser River, Cariboo, Kootenay; John Day, Boise, Alder Gulch, Helena, went the adopted sons of California—youngest begetter of colonies,—carrying with them the methods, the customs, and the ideas of the mother region, and retaining for it not a little of love and veneration. "Idaho", said the *World*, "is but the colony of California. What England is to the world, what the New England states have been to the West, California has been and still is to the country west of the Great Plains. Her people have swept in successive waves over every adjacent district from Durango to the Yellowstone. She is the mother of these Pacific States and Territories."[8]

---

[6] It seems to the author that, while the British people have shown marked efficiency in seizing new lands for colonies and in governing them, they have shown no special aptitude as colonists From 1660 onward the immigration to the colonies now forming the United States was largely continental; and the American frontiersman was not an Englishman, although often of English antecedents The western Canada of today would lack much in its population, if the American pioneers were not there.

[7] *Owyhee Avalanche*, Nov. 11, 1865.

[8] Idaho *World*, July 15 and Oct. 14, 1865. The career of Henry Comstock, who gave his name to perhaps the greatest lode known in history, was typical in wanderings of that of many Californians; though, we may hope, not typical in its ill-fortune. Comstock in 1862 struck a quartz lead at John Day (S. F.

Another element of population represented everywhere, but often entirely overlooked in characterizing the mining population, was that of the women—and we mean here respectable women. It is true that a large majority of the population was made up of men, especially at the beginning of a rush, but always some women began soon to arrive and formed in many districts an appreciable element. Some of the women were survivors of the fur-trading regime and were to be found at the old posts; as a general thing, also, there were pretty sure to be women at the road houses and stopping places. So, early in the winter of 1862-3, in the region now known as Montana, out of a total listed population of 670, 59 were respectable females; and in the years immediately succeeding numbers of the most venerated of the pioneer women of Montana came.[9] Southern Idaho, as has been mentioned before, was conspicuous for the number of families residing there, many of which had left Missouri because of war troubles. In the Grande Ronde Valley and at Auburn a young single man had quite good chances of getting a wife from immigrant girls At Victoria, besides ladies in the families of citizens, a cargo or two of young women, according to the custom of new colonies, was brought from England. Even in far-away Cariboo there was a kindly Mrs. Lee to extend help to the minister's wife in her time of greatest need, and ever and anon on his travels the minister found it pleasant to see a "sonsie" Scotchwoman beaming a welcome and to hear her Scots tongue.[10] Another indication of the presence of women was that a good many divorces were granted by legislatures; but, on the other hand, that in all the papers almost from their first issues were notices of marriages It is true, however, that most

---

Daily Bulletin, Aug 29, 1862); at Christmas he was in Auburn (*Id.* Jan. 2, 1863); the next fall found him at Alturas, near Boise, where he was running five arastras and a saw mill (*Id.* Aug. 30, 1864.) In 1868 he resided in Butte City, his intellect darkened, but his hand still skilful and his heart sympathetic for the poor. He worked a small claim, but imagined that he still owned the Comstock lode (*Mineral Resources,* 1868, p 505) At last, 1870, he shot himself at Bozeman, and his body was found in a hole back of the jail, not a cent in his pocket He was buried at the county expense (Anaconda *Standard,* Dec. 16, 1900).

[9] *Contributions Historical Society of Montana,* Vol I, pp 334-54

[10] *Occasional Papers,* Columbian Mission, Report for 1869, pp. 64 and 69

ladies were to be found in the families of professional men, merchants, and farmers, because the miners themselves were too roving to get married, but there were some exceptions. At any rate, it seems worth calling attention to the fact that the dearth of good women in the mining regions was not so complete as is often assumed.

There are two classes of the population, the negroes and the Chinese, to which I wish to give separate treatment; to the one a brief statement, to the other more extended discussion.

The negroes were seldom, if ever, found in the mining camps, but about four hundred of them came early in the mining movement to Vancouver Island and British Columbia, the majority of them settling in Victoria. They came from California, and their purposes as explained by one of themselves, were as follows:

(1) To better their political conditions, since in California they were disfranchised and without legal protection of life and property.
(2) Not to seek "particular associations", but to "enjoy those common rights which civilized, enlightened and well-regulated communities guarantee to all their members."
(3) To make this country the land of adoption for themselves and their children.[11]

By working at draying and like employments and investing their savings in land, many of these colored people became well-to-do. Clergymen fresh from England or Canada, took high philanthropic and religious grounds toward them, although the Bishop noted that the negroes found it difficult to get used to the ways of the Church of England, since they had been reared Baptists and Methodists. But trouble arose with the white Americans, notwithstanding that most of these in British Columbia were, during the war, ardent supporters of the Union; and there was a serious riot in a theatre. The whites remonstrated, also, at admitting colored people to the churches, and, when one zealous divine took up the cause of Africa and coloured people flocked to him, the whites left—promptly to be followed by the negroes, in

[11] Letter of J. J. Moore, *British Colonist*, Feb. 5, 1859.

order to be in a more fashionable church.[12] But the latter were treated by the English officials as any other citizens were treated.

The Chinese were a very important economic part of the mining advance, but not of it socially. Sooner or later they were found in every town, along every trail, in every mining camp. Debarred from the camps so long as claims paid "wages" or better, they were welcomed later to buy the claims, once washed, which no white miner would consent to touch. There was great hostility to them because of their lowering wages and living hardly, but the time was sure to come when the miners' meeting of every district would admit these patient, quiet, laborious men, clothed in cheap garments. It was seldom that the Chinaman worked for the white man, but he often paid large sums for his claim—as high in some cases as $8,000—and he paid in cash, or the white owner of the claim took out of the sluice boxes each Saturday night a certain amount until paid. The Chinese were not so skillful as the Americans in the use of machinery, but their industry enabled them to extract much gold from the abandoned claims. Undoubtedly America owes considerable to them for saving treasure which might otherwise have been wasted. Of their numbers it is hard to get a just estimate. In Montana they were thought to number 800 in 1869, and in British Columbia in 1866 they numbered 1800 out of a total population of 13,800 and in Vancouver Island 200.[13] As camps waxed old in the American territories, the Chinamen generally outnumbered the whites. A pioneer states that twelve hundred of them came into Warren's Diggings, when they were allowed to come.[14]

Many of them came direct from China, but many also from California. They were generally brought in droves by some Chinese contractor; for example, forty Chinese were sent to Idaho from Virginia City, Nevada, at one time by Yong Wo and Company.[15] The men sometimes were contracted, sometimes bought, and sometimes kidnapped.[16] The masters provided the

---

[12] Macfie, *Van. Id. and Br. Col.*, pp. 388–392.
[13] *Mineral Resources*, 1869, p. 140. Despatch of Gov. Seymour Feb. 17, 1866 in Churchill and Cooper, *British Columbia and Van. Id* p. 21.
[14] Hofen, Leo, *His. of Idaho County*, MS., p. 4.
[15] San Francisco *Daily Bulletin*, May 19, 1865.
[16] McDonald, *Van. Id. and Br. Col.*, pp 299–300.

outfit and required both repayment of expenses and profits for themselves.[17] Not all, however, were coolies, for there were not a few fine looking and independent men. Numbers of the Chinese, as usual, engaged in the laundry business, and some in other forms of business or in farming. A flourishing colony of them congregated on Pandora Street, Victoria. A good many of them everywhere became well-to-do and some wealthy, but others lost fortunes gambling after the fashion of the whites.[18]

In the treatment accorded them by the whites there was a fair measure of equality before the law. In British Columbia, of course, the Chinaman was treated with perfect civic equality, and in American territories there are records of white men being brought to trial and convicted for assaulting or killing them.[19] But in the matter of taxation there was a decided difference: in British Columbia a Chinese miner paid the same tax as any other miner, while in the American territories he was singled out for exceptional and heavy taxation. In Idaho a law was passed (styled a law for taxing foreign miners and copied directly from the California law) which required every Mongolian to pay a tax of $5.00 per month; if the tax were not paid, the property could be sold on three hours notice.[20] Moreover, the law included as foreign miners all Mongolians, whatever their occupations,—a provision, however, later declared invalid by the courts.[21] Yet the Chinese miners were forced to pay the exceptional tax and, moreover, were sometimes robbed by officials under guise of "watchmen" and "collectors."[22] For the regular tax, on the other hand, there was some justification, from the fact that Chinamen acquired comparatively little property which could be reached by ordinary taxation. In Montana Chinamen were taxed by a law compelling all *male* persons engaged in the laundry business to pay a tax of fifteen dollars per quarter; "It is admitted," said Gov. Ashley, "that this section is oppressive and was intended to compel the Chinaman to pay an unjust tax."[23]

[17] London *Times*, March 25, 1862
[18] *Reminiscences of Harvey, A Chinaman at Yale*, MS
[19] Idaho *World*, Nov. 18, 1865.
[20] Goulder, *Reminiscences*, Chap. 49; Idaho *World*, Feb. 3, 1866.
[21] Idaho *World*, March 24, 1866.
[22] Knapp, *Statement of Events in Idaho*, MS, p. 6.
[23] *Contr. His Soc. Mon.*, Vol. 6, p. 267.

The white miners always looked on the Chinamen as inferiors. When the latter were admitted into the John Day diggings, the Dalles Mountaineer said: "It is to be hoped that by another year each honest miner in this country will have his dozen coolies delving in his claims. There is an eminent fitness in this relation of the races."[24] Indeed "foreigners" to the miners did not mean the "unnaturalized Russian, Greek, Finn, Frenchman, or Irishman," but the Mongolian.[25] In Montana it was thought that the public was undemonstrative either for or against them; although, occasionally "we hear of outrages inflicted upon some one of them in the same manner, and perhaps as frequently, as dogs or cattle are maltreated."[26] From the first contact with the Mongolian in the mining regions, therefore, whether justly or unjustly, there has been a feeling with regard to him on the part of the whites, different to that held toward other races. But that his part in the economic development of those regions was an important one admits of no doubt.[27]

Having now considered the various elements of the population, let us next see how the white portion of it lived.

The characteristic abode in the mining regions was a log cabin, roofed with shakes or (particularly in Montana) with dirt. In storms the latter roof leaked, much to the distress of lady housekeepers. Green cow-skins were often nailed on the floor in lieu of carpets. A cabin of one of the bachelor miners, as it appeared at the beginning of winter is thus sketched: "To the left of the stage road leading to Idaho City, stands a log cabin, ten by twelve feet in size, the roof extending eight feet from the main building, a pile of pitch wood to the left of the door; over the wood hangs a fore and hind quarter of a beef. Under the same porch is seen a hand sleigh used for sledding wood and articles from town. We open the door and go in. Description is almost

---

[24] Article in *Mining and Scientific Press*, Vol. 12, 1866, p. 239.
[25] Goulder, *Reminiscences*, p. 354.
[26] *Mineral Resources*, 1869, p. 40.
[27] A fine field for investigation lies in the history of the Chinese on the Pacific Coast, particularly if one could get at Chinese sources. A still wider field presents itself in the activity of this race in all the mining regions of the Pacific. "The number of Chinese to be met with all over the world", says Barret-Leonard, "wherever gold has been discovered, is a singular and characteristic fact."— *Van Id. and British Col.*, pp. 147–148.

impossible, but I will endeavor to depict the scene. On the left of the room is stored any amount of provisions, over which are fixed two bunks one above the other. To the right of the fireplace stands a small table on which are piled books, papers, and many other small articles too numerous to mention; and still to the right is a goods box nailed to the wall for a cupboard, which is filled with all kinds of cooking traps. On the right hand side of the room is the window, one pane of glass constitutes the size, under which is placed the dining table. The right-hand side of the room is ornamented with a large mirror and pictures: among them are seen Abraham Lincoln and his secretaries, generals, forts, battles, etc."[27a] In respect to these latter ornaments, it may be observed, many miners would probably have preferred pictures of Jefferson Davis and of Southern generals; but the description is fairly characteristic of the ordinary miner's cabin in the winter time.

Places of business, also, were for the most part of logs, although in the first stages of towns tents were often used; as a town prospered, substantial buildings of sawed lumber or of stone were usually erected. Owners of general stores often built cellars as warehouses for storing goods, a precaution against the fires which many times swept mining towns. Frequently several firms carrying on different lines of mercantile business occupied the same store, which very likely served also as office for some doctor or lawyer; and at night the various occupants (with probably a guest or two) quite generally used the scene of their day-time endeavor as sleeping quarters.[28] The appearance of one such store, thus used, reminded an English traveler in the interior of British Columbia of the robber's cave in the *Arabian Nights*.

The staple foods were bread, bacon, beans, coffee, and (in British Columbia) tea. In the towns, of course, there was greater variety; but a man, by paying a good price, could generally get such luxuries as eggs and butter. Fresh meat was usually obtainable at reasonable prices in the summer time, when

---

[27a] Mullan, John, *Miners' and Travelers' Guide*, pp. 126–128; cf. also, description of cabin in *Diary* of J. H. Morley MS, May 22, 1863.

[28] Sanders, Col W. F., *Sketches of Early Settlers in Montana*, MS

drovers brought cattle and sheep on foot to the camps. Fish, also, were often used, there being fine trout in Montana and salmon on the west side of the mountains; but miners who could make $5.00 per day or more could not profitably spend much time in fishing or hunting. Still, prospecting parties, in particular, found game useful. Fresh vegetables and potatoes were much sought, in order to avoid the terrible scurvy. Miners at Oro Fino in the winter of 1861–2 packed potatoes on their backs fifteen or twenty miles through deep snow, in order to stay the ravages of this disease. "Uncooked potatoes sliced up and soaked in vinegar were far from affording a very appetizing dish, but it proved a sovereign remedy for the scurvy."[29] Far the greater portion of the food stuffs were imported from outside the mining regions—from California, the Willamette Valley, Utah, and the States. Consequently, when insufficient supplies were laid in, and winter snows blocked the trails, miners in lone camps were sometimes reduced to boiling ferns, or oats, or the inner bark of trees in order to stave off starvation; while merchants in town often ran flour up to monopolistic prices, $1.50 per lb. or higher,—a procedure which generally produced flour riots.[30] There were many restaurants and hotels in the town and roadhouses along the trails, but except when traveling (and often then) experienced miners did their own cooking.

Amusements and companionships the miner had to have, and, in reaction from the hard labor on the claim, he generally sought eagerly those forms of amusement offered to him in the towns. He was bound of course, to be attracted by horse-racing and prize-fighting; there were always men around who wanted to match their favorite colts, or to aspire to pugilistic honors. Saloons abounded in all towns, and generally sold villainous concoctions; but they were the only places where a man could freely find companionship, and "some of them were kept by men of intelligence whose general impulses were excellent."[31] Other saloonkeepers were like the one at Yale, who when the miners

---

[29] Goulder, *Reminiscences*, p. 233.
[30] It was considered very creditable to the Hudson's Bay Company, when American speculators at Victoria had cornered the market, that the Company broke the corner and refused to profit by the miners' necessities.
[31] *Sketches of Early Settlers in Montana*, Col. W F. Sanders, MS.

were well "slewed", would dispense with the scales and take goodly pinches of gold from the extended pouches.[32] Nearly everybody drank, and getting drunk was a venal transgression: the members of the Philipsburg, (Mont.) Pioneer Association—composed of "those who have assisted in opening up for settlement and civilization" California, Idaho, and Montana—in their resolutions "Reserve the right to get decently drunk." Liquor was generally taken straight and at one gulp. Vigorous men with the health of pure mountain air surging within them could drink safely an amount of liquor that would have crazed an office denizen. On the other hand, the ill effects of drink were by no means escaped: the "Miners' Ten Commandments" speaks of men broiling in the sun, or emerging half drowned from prospect holes and ditches, of gold dust and the comforts it might have purchased lying at the bottom of a damaged stomach, and of "all the unholy catalogue of evils," that follow in the train of excess.[33] Some of the men who played heroic and conspicuous parts in the ranks of the Vigilantes of Montana afterwards went to pieces through drink. Billiard tables were to be found in almost every saloon, and were much patronized—British travelers wondered at the numbers of these tables in Victoria.

Gambling was exceedingly common and open. In almost every town could be heard the cry that brought back to Californians the times of '49: "Make your game, gentlemen, make your game—all down—no more—game's made." The men who ran the gambling houses were not all the sleek, lizard-eyed villians which occasional writers portray, but some of them conducted their business with fairness and would tolerate no crooked work. As a class they were brave, virile, and generous-hearted. A man knew when he went into the game that there was a percentage in favor of the house. Still, a number of games regarded as legally unfair are enumerated in a law of Montana which forbade "three card monte, strap game, thimble-rig game, patent safe game, black and red, any dice game, two card box at faro." Undoubtedly much of the terrible wastage that left many of the miners

---

[32] *Reminiscences of Wilham Stout of Yale*, MS

[33] The "Miners' Ten Commandments" is a somewhat ludicrous portrayal of the miner's life, but should be read by one who wishes to know many of the failings and of the aspirations of that life; a copy is printed in Macfie, *Van. Id. and Br. Col.*, pp 418-422.

exposed to an impecunious old age was produced by the gaming table.[34]

An innocent form of diversion was the theaters, one or more of which were to be found in every town of any importance. Troupes of players, male and female, were often encountered by travelers, making the long journeys from town to town. A glimpse of a theater at Walla Walla is given by a newspaper correspondent. The room was a dismanteled barroom, and the platform was flanked by blankets. Mrs. Leighton and a troupe presented the play "Naval Engagements" to the "highly marine population of Walla Walla. Thirty-five ladies graced the dress circle and 162 gentlemen laughed with delight on board benches at the expense of one dollar each."[35]

The hurdy-gurdy or dance houses were features of every center. One of them is described as follows: "At one end of a long hall a well stocked bar and a monte bank in full blast; at the other a platform on which were three musicians. After each dance there was a drink at the bar. The house was open from 9 P. M. until day-light. Every dance was $1.00—half to the woman and half to the proprietor. Publicly, decorum was preserved; and to many miners, who had not seen a feminine face for six months, these poor women represented vaguely something of the tenderness and sacredness of their sex."[36] Most of the hurdies were German women, who followed the business for gain—the majority homely enough, but some good dancers. It is a mistake to confuse these dance halls with houses of prostitution; seldom did one of these women become a prostitute, and some of them settled down in the country and became good wives.[38] The lighter side of the dancing was sung in Cariboo Rhymes:

"Bonnie are the hurdies O!
The German Hurdie-Gurdies O!
The daftest hour that e'er I spent
Was dancing wi'the hurdies O!"[39]

---

[34] Montana *Post*, Jan 21, 1865
[35] San Francisco *Daily Bulletin*, June 25, 1864.
[36] Richardson, *Beyond the Mississippi*, p 480
[38] A very much respected pioneer told me that he had known a number of these women and had been acquainted with their later careers, and that all had turned out well
[39] *Jeames' Letters to Saunie*, quoted in Bancroft, *His. Pac States*, Vol. XXVII, p. 519.

The other side was presented by the Montana Post, which asserted that the hurdy-gurdy houses exercised a most pernicious influence, particularly in that they helped to pauperize labourers; too often they were scenes of quarreling, violence, and drunkenness. There seemed to be a "desire to run everything in the shape of amusements beyond all safe limits."[40]

There were houses of prostitution in practically all towns, and vice flaunted itself more openly than in older communities. "A bespangled and flounced woman of costly garments" was not infrequently seen on the streets, while on the trails might occasionally be met small companies of "things calling themselves women", dressed in men's clothing and with revolvers strapped to their waists, and some of these even dared the rugged trails to Cariboo.[41]

For the steady part of the population there were gathering places seldom taken into account in the history of mining communities. Quiet citizens would gather in some store, as that of George Chrissman at Bannack City and of Pfouts at Virginia City,—and there, seated on stools, benches, and boxes, would tell strange experiences or discuss grave questions. But generally the talk fell naturally on mines; for, to "find mines, to plant mining communities occupied industrial attention."[42] There were halls where fraternal organizations might gather, or a neighborhood dance be held. Miners of studious tastes might form public libraries, as at Helena.[42a] Church buildings, also, were early erected in most of the larger towns, and in them Sunday schools were carried on, more or less regular preaching services held, and occasional special meetings called.

In trying to find out the characteristics of the population, at whose amusements we have glanced, two extremes are to be avoided: The one is the view of those superficial writers who,

---

[40] Montana *Post*, Jan. 14, 1865.
[41] *Pilgrimage of W. S. Haskell and Family to the gold regions in 1864*, MS. entry May 4; San Francisco *Daily Bulletin*, July 18, 1863.
[42] *Sketches of Early Settlers in Montana*, Col. W. F. Sanders, MS.
[42a] *Contr. His. Soc. Mont.*, Vol. VII, p. 187 The Historical Society of Montana was incorporated in 1865 by H. S. Hosmer, C. P. Higgins, John Owen, James Stuart, W. F. Sanders, Malcolm Clark, F. M. Thompson, William Graham, Granville Stuart, W. W. DeLacy, C. E. Irvine, and Charles Buggs.—*Contr. His. Soc. Mont.*, Vol. II, p. 19.

seizing on the unusual, unconventional, or abnormal features of the life of the mining communities, and especially regarding the exploits of desperadoes, conclude that ruffianism and violence were the normal qualities of these communities; the other (and the more forgiveable) is that of some of the pioneers who, looking back through mellowing years, and remembering the good and true men who formed the majority of the mining populace, forget some of the undeniably bad blots upon the society of the time.

In truth, for the observer wishing to be impartial, a great deal depends upon one's point of view. If he undertakes to apply to mining communities the conventional standards of conduct which ruled in the sixties in quiet villages of the East, he will find sufficient transgressions to shock him; and these standards were precisely those that were applied by some of the writers of the time. They inferred that, since miners generally were profane and reckless and did not keep the Sabbath, often gambled and drank, and wore weapons habitually, therefore they were violent, ignorant, and depraved, ready for any depth of sin or crime. Moreover, the impressions given by such witnesses are sometimes confirmed by some of the pioneers themselves who, finding the outrageous side of life most eagerly listened to, put to the fore in their accounts murders, robberies, and brawls. On the other hand, the impartial student, without in the least denying or seeking to palliate what was ugly, will not overlook essential traits of manhood, but will remember that most of the mining populace were young men, far from the restraints of home; that they had come, many of them, from the less exhilarating atmosphere of lower altitudes, to the splendid invigoration of mountain air and outdoor life, and, consequently, effervesced with energy; that their excesses were often reactions against the monotony of their toil; and that many of them earned large sums of money quickly and, feeling certain that they could replace them easily in the apparently endless succession of new fields, spent their treasure prodigally. Above all, he who seeks a just estimate of mining populations, as of any other, will make general statements cautiously.

Perhaps the best way of approaching the matter is to start with the observation of a careful and experienced participant in the mining advance, who wrote that "Society was divided into two classes—the good and the bad "[43] This observation is, of course, true of society in general, but to that of mining camps it is particularly apropos, since ties of friendship and associations, in the absence often of more defined regulations of society, were peculiarly close.

The "bad" classes were represented in some camps by an inferior lot of hangers-on who were lazy and unenterprising; but a lazy man stood a good chance of starving, and the hobo class was conspicuously absent.[44] It took a *man* to face the long journeys to the mines and the vicissitudes of life there. There were also some mere rowdies who might participate in a riot at times, but who were easily cowed by Judge Begbie in British Columbia or by the mere mention of a vigilante committee in the territories.[45] But the really bad class, the class that did so much to give a bad name to mining communities, were the desperadoes. These were often brave men gone wrong, who had formed criminal tendencies and associations in California, and who continued their evil associations in the various camps of the northern interior, until finally they were graduated into very bad, overbearing, and dangerous criminals. Many of the murders so often mentioned in characterizations of mining communities, were simply killings of one or the other of these men by another of the same class; but not infrequently, allured by large amounts of treasure carried by travelers, or by a rancher's scattered horses (both a form of plunder not hard to dispose of), and emboldened by the unorganized and unprotected condition of society, these villains banded themselves together for most atrocious rapine and murder, directed against quiet citizens. The numbers of this class, however, were very small compared to the whole population.

One of the most noticeable characteristics of the miners as a class, on the other hand, was that they were law-abiding and orderly. The very nature of their occupations made them that. Men who were seriously working rich claims, or making large

---
[43] Butler, *Life and Times in Idaho*, MS., p. 9.
[44] Conversation with Judge W. Y. Pemberton, of Helena.
[45] Pemberton. J. D., *Van. Id. and Br. Col*, pp. 130–1.

wages, could not afford to commit crimes, if they wanted to. Most of the miners, moreover, were men of good antecedents, a fact as true of the large foreign element as of the Anglo-Saxon. The Germans and Frenchmen who came to the mining regions were not gutter spawn, but often younger sons of good families, or peasants; and they were well trained to obedience to law. Moreover, the men who came from California had had good training in participating in the evolution of customs and laws of the mining camps; and, besides, being now older than when they had first gone to California, they were the more inclined to ways of steadiness.[46] The testimony of the sources in regard to the law-abiding instincts of the miners is clear and practically unanimous, and this is especially true of the sources dealing with British Columbia. Although the officials there had been warned that these men were the ragtags and off-scourings of the universe, they were surprised to find, like Judge Begbie, that the miners "manifested a great desire to see justice fairly done and great patience with the difficulties which the magistrates and the judiciary have had to contend with."[47] Again, the same distinguished judge observed, "There was on all sides a submission to authority, a recognition of the right, which, looking to the mixed nature of the population, and the very large predominance of the Californian element, I confess I had not expected to meet."[48] The proportion of the law-abiding element in the American territories is probably fairly expressed by Mr. Hailey, who says, "I think I may truthfully say that ninety-five per cent of these people were good, industrious, honorable and enterprising, and to all appearances desired to make money in a legitimate way."[49]

The law-abiding instincts of the miners—and as well another chief characteristic, their virility,—are interestingly brought out in a letter, tinged perhaps with idealism, to *The London Times:*

---

[46] These considerations with respect to the foreign element, were earnestly presented to me by Dr. James S. Helmcken, son-in-law of Sir James Douglas and Speaker of the first Assembly of Vancouver Island. He had every opportunity to observe the miners closely and had no reason to be prejudiced in their favor

[47] Quoted from Judge Begbie in Pemberton, J. D., *Van Id. and Br Col.,* p. 130-1.

[48] *Journal of the Royal Geographical Society,* Vol. XXXI, p. 247.

[49] *His. of Idaho,* p 91.

"All who come to British Columbia, be they gentle, be they simple, whatever their class or previous calling, must be men,— true men, resolute, persevering, cheerful, temperate men, men of dauntless character. They need not be strong men, particularly, but if not strong in body, nor particularly inured to hardship as to constitution, they must be hardy in mind. They must be of the stuff on which England's glory is founded. If they are puny, or complaining, or talkative, imaginative fellows, they had better stay at home where they are. In a state of society more or less artificial they may find a living, but not here They will die, and scarcely, if at all, be regretted by anybody. Here we revert to first principles in all things; and I am happy to say the miners of British Columbia as a body are the very finest fellows I ever came across—hardy fellows, heroes, in a kind of way. Of course there are exceptions, but I speak of the mass, and I make no distinction of nation. We have British subjects, English, Scotch, Irish, Welsh, Canadian, Australian, New Zealand, French, German, Dane, Swede, Norwegian, Spaniard, Italian, Mexican, United States, Confederate States—in fact bone and sinew, life and energy, skimmed as the cream from the manliness of all nations. That is my opinion of the miners of British Columbia, and I would wish it to be openly declared as against all who may gainsay it; don't let anybody believe they are a people unsafe to live among I mention this because absurd tales are told (and I am sorry to say the foolish practice among them of carrying revolvers gives a sort of color to it) of the wild recklessness and violence of the miners. If a person will mind his own business, keep a civil tongue in his head, look straight into a man's eye, and fear nobody, he will lead as quiet a life as he can desire. As a body the miners are above average intelligence, and fully recognize the value of law and order, and are always ready to maintain it."[50] The virile qualities of the miners are emphasized, also, by another English observer, as follows: "Intent on speedy gain they are ready to brave every risk, face every hardship and privation. Dauntless, fearless, and restless, they will brook no opposition nor restraint, but with a wild self-de-

---

[50] The London *Times*, Jan. 30th, 1862

pendence of character plunge wherever gold attracts them, defying everything, and surmounting all obstacles."[51]

Besides being law-abiding and virile, the average miner was intelligent. In a population "coming from all parts of the world, drawn from every social grade, animated by the most diverse ideas and principles, differing in every essential particular necessary to social or moral organization", the abrasions of society were themselves educative.[52] Not a few of the miners were men of education. Books, magazines, or newspapers were found commonly in the cabins, and were often conned to good advantage in winter. One of the first things that Morley did on settling down at Bannack (Montana) was to order magazines from Salt Lake; Goulder at Oro Fino (Idaho) in the long winter evenings read Scott's novels to his comrades, in British Columbia the Bishop found miners at Cariboo possessing copies of Gibbon, Macaulay, Shakspeare, and Plutarch.[53] Since the miners, however, were rough in appearance, travelers sometimes misjudged them. Mrs. Leighton, journeying on the upper Columbia in the '49, looked with suspicion on the miners aboard, but found them interesting on acquaintance: one of a company collected for a wagon trip "looked like a brigand with his dark hair and eyes"; but when—in addition to showing thorough knowledge of the country through which they were passing—he talked about the "soft Spanish names of places in California", and of "the primitive forms in which minerals crystallized", and told of the gallantry of the miners when the "Central America" was wrecked, she concluded that he would have been "interesting anywhere."[54] The Bishop of Columbia thought that his congregations at Victoria contained a "larger proportion of shrewd, thinking, intelligent educated gentlemen than any in England out of London."[54a]

The characteristic most dwelt upon, however, by participants in the mining rushes was enterprise. This characteristic is em-

---

[51] Cornwallis, *The New El Dorado*, p 10.
[52] The *Oregonian*, June 28, 1861.
[53] Morley, J. H., *Diary*, MS., Sept 21, 1862; Goulder, W. A, *Reminiscences*, p. 221-2; *Extracts from the Journal of the Bishop of British Columbia*, 1862-3
[54] Leighton, Caroline C, *Life at Puget Sound, with Sketches of Travel*, pp. 93-99
[54a] *Columbian Mission, Occasional Papers*, 1862, p 7.

phasized, rather naively, in a few lines of rhyme from Idaho City:

> "I'm standing now upon the hill
> That looks down on the town.
> I'm thinking of that mighty will
> Which never can bow down;
> I mean the will of Enterprise
> That made our nation grow,
> And from these Indian wilds built up
> The town of Idaho."[55]

Enterprise is placed foremost by the *Montana Post* in an estimate of the mining population—an estimate which mentions, also, some other interesting characteristics. "The great features of our people," it said, "are enterprise, restless activity and contempt of danger or privation. Hospitality is general and unaffected. There is a sort of rough, though genuine courtesy much in vogue among mountaineers, that makes them excellent companions in danger or hardship. Men of education may meet their fellows here. Majors, colonels, judges, and doctors include about one-third of the adult males, but the reverence usually accorded to those high-sounding cognomens is left at home; and in the gulch Major Blank wheels, while Colonel Carat fills."[56]

Nicknames were often used, "extemporized from some personal eccentricity, some notable expression, or event of experience." If a man seemed educated, he might be called "doc" or "cap", a large man would be called Big Bill or Big Jim. Frequent reference to place whence he had come might result in "Rattlesnake Jack" or "Oregon Bob". One man who was fond of displaying an array of initials and titles was called "Alphabet McD—". These designations were sometimes especially handy, in cases where an individual had some delicacy about his real name.[57]

---

[55] Boise *News*, Aug. 20, 1864.
[56] Montana *Post*, June 28, 1865.
[57] Material for this paragraph is found mostly in Macfie, *Van Id. and Br Col*, p. 414. This author makes another observation which I have not come across elsewhere, when he says that the "intense pitch to which the feelings of people are strung in a gold-producing country is a frequent cause for insanity", p. 410.

The mining population was one extremely nomadic—often disastrously so to the individual. The old wander-lust stirred the blood mightily, and especially so in the spring. The call of new and rich diggings, even though deceptive, was seldom resisted. "What a clover-field is to a steer," wrote the *Oregonian* with somewhat crude humor, "the sky to the lark—a mudhole to a hog, such are new diggings to a miner. Feed him on a succession of new diggings, and his youth would be perennial."[58] Forgotten were rheumatism, toil, and disappointments when reports of big strikes circulated. An old miner on being asked by the Bishop of Columbia why the old-time miners had not realized fortunes, answered that they were "always agitated by news of rich diggings" and that they gave up good paying claims on hear-say reports, and often came back impoverished. "I myself," he added, "if I hear of anything better cannot keep quiet; I must be off."[59]

That humor lightened many of the troubles of the miners and played over and through their experiences, is suggested by a few specimens that glimmer through our sources. The humor was sometimes irreverent and grotesque; as, for example, concerning a supposedly conceited nominee for the Legislature, an unfriendly critic remarked, "If that chap is elected to the Legislature, God 'O mighty's overcoat wouldn't make a vest pattern for him". It was generally picturesque, descriptive, and full of slang, as "two squaw-power," concerning two Indian women paddling a canoe; "Boston jackasses," applied to men labouring under packs to Salmon River; "jawbone" (signifying credit) and "gumticklers" and "flashes of lightning"—different kinds of liquors. Sometimes the humor was grim; as talk of a vigilante organization for a "mid-air dance", or, on rumor of the assertion of Indian titles to miners' claims, the remark that the Indians would need to be "armor-plated." A pun might crop out; as in commenting on lack of interest in education on the part of a quartz community, it was remarked that "a large majority of the fathers prefer the development of *feet* to the head." A more subtle form appeared in the case of a miner who by re-

---
[58] *Oregonian*, July 12, 1862.
[59] *Journal of Bishop of Columbia*, p. 15.

peated experiences having found an acquaintance of no account, characterized the unfortunate by saying, "I have panned him out clear down to bed rock, but I couldn't raise the color."

The profanity of the miners was omnipresent, exuberant, "diabolical", and habitual. Men were not unlikely to swear unconsciously when their thoughts were really of higher things. One miner was over-heard by the Bishop of Columbia swearing roundly as he defended the Church; "What would society be without it?" he asked with an oath, "I tell you it has a refining influence."[60]

Lack of observance of Sunday was everywhere prevalent. On that day the miner, (if he discontinued usual labor) washed and patched his clothing, cooked up food for the next week, mended broken tools; or he went to town to get his pick sharpened, get the mail, settle his accounts, meet his fellows, and have a good time. Sunday, indeed, in the towns was generally the liveliest day of the week. Dance halls, saloons, and gambling houses ran full blast, and usually there was a horse-race or prize-fight. Business places were all open. The rector at Cariboo had hard work getting church officers from among the business men, because any one accepting an office would be expected to close his store on Sunday and would thus be at a disadvantage. An Idaho law which forbade court procedures on Sunday had to be modified so as to permit taxation of packers who waited until Sunday to bring in their trains, and to allow issuance of attachments on that day, in order to stop absconding of debtors.[61] In extenuation of this Sabbath-breaking, it may be said that the men really had few, except reminiscent, motives for observing the day, and that in the mining season it was necessary to push all work hard; another reason for Sunday work appealed to steady men like J. H. Morley, who writes, "Thinking of loved ones at home, it seems no sin in this savage country to exert oneself on their behalf, on the Sabbath."[62]

In addition to what has been said in preceding pages in regard to the relations of miners to women, two or three other phases

---

[60] *Journal*, p. 45.
[61] *Occasional Papers, Columbian Mission*, 1869, p. 66; Idaho *World*, Jan. 6, 1866.
[62] *Diary*, July 19, 1863.

need to be presented. In the American territories there seems to have been a clearly marked antipathy to miscegenation, while in British Columbia this feeling was less clear. In Idaho, the legislature passed a law forbidding cohabitation with Indians, Chinese, or Negroes. In British Columbia, if we are to believe the reports of the clergy, there was noticeable resort to concubinage with Indian squaws, or "klootchmen," as they were there called. "In all these settlements," writes the Rev. James Reynard on a trip in the interior, "the great, the crying evils are Indian concubinage, and the poor neglected half-breed families." Again, as he comments on the degradation, which the Indian connection at last produced, he exclaims, "English mothers and sisters! do you know how your sons and brothers live away from you?"[63] There was, however, little abandonment of Indian families by white fathers. One fact stands out conspicuously through absence of literature of the time, whether north or south of the line: namely, there is no mention, so far as the author's reading extends, of any outrages committed upon white women by men of the mining advance, although, as we have seen, women were present in all mining communities.

Rough society undoubtedly was, and in many respects, unattractive; individuals there were who were sordid, mean, violent, disgraceful. But taken as a whole, for qualities of real manhood—chivalrousness toward women, hardihood, industry, intelligence, enterprise, and submission to law—the mining population was worthy of respect.

Mining society, however, was very heterogeneous and incoherent—a fact which made formal organization difficult; yet there were certain interesting bonds of union.

In the first place, men from a given locality naturally grouped themselves with other men from that locality. Thus Californians, Pike's Peakers, and Minnesotians—especially at the start in any camp—were inclined to act together. These groupings, however, made more difficult the establishment of law and increased the opportunities for the lawless classes to make trouble, since law-abiding citizens were not at first acquainted with the men of like mind from different sections.

---

[63] *Occasional Papers, Columbian Mission*, Report of 1870, pp. 62-3 and 65.

Again, friendship in the mines formed a very real bond of union. In the midst of dangers and trying experiences men were drawn together into peculiarly close and enduring relationships. A man could count on his friends standing by him and he by them through every vicissitude of fortune. In sickness friends nursed a man; if he got lost or was in danger of freezing, they hunted for him and succored him, or buried him; if he was out of money, friends "staked" him. If he, on his part, found a new prospect, he would surely let his friends know of it and stake off claims for them; if a friend got into a fight, he would see that there was fair play; and, if that friend were in great danger, would hazard his own life in his defense. One of the very essentials of manhood was violated if fidelity to friends was lacking. It was the strength of such associations as these that helped to make more difficult the task of establishing law and order; for criminals themselves had their friends, some of whom might be well-intentioned citizens. It took a high degree of daring and determination for leaders on the side of law, in trying to bring criminals to justice, to confront not only the criminal, but his friends. On the other hand, when desperadoes shot down a good citizen, they would have to reckon with the latter's friends; as in the case of Lloyd Magruder, of Lewiston whose murderers were followed from Lewiston to San Francisco by Magruder's friend, Hill Beachy, and brought back to the gallows.[64]

Another tie that tended to unite separated "units of society" was Masonry. Brother Masons soon became known to each other, and lodges were formed in a number of places. T. M. Reed of Florence, elected Speaker of the Assembly of Washington Territory in 1862, was a leading Mason.[65] The claim has been made that Masonry was an active, though quiet, force in bringing about order in Montana, and it is undoubtedly true that many of the leaders in that work were Masons.[66]

[64] For an account of this case, see Hailey, *His. of Idaho*, Chap. 14. Other sources for this paragraph are Cornwallis, *The New El Dorado*, p. 207; *Contr. His. Soc., Mon.*, Vol. I, p. 124; remarks by Judge W. Y. Pemberton. Leaving a friend as narrated by Goulder in the case of some Jew traders, was an exception to usual custom, *Reminiscences*, pp. 224-227.
[65] San Francisco *Daily Bulletin*, Jan. 2, 1863.
[66] *Contr. His. Soc. Mon.*, Vol. VII, p 186; Langford, *Vigilante Days and Ways*,

Of peculiar interest was another organization, which could not exist in British Columbia, but which in the Territories was conspicious and active. This was Fenianism. Local circles of Fenians were formed in many mining towns. The Owyhee circle numbered one hundred; strong organizations existed at Idaho City and Virginia City, and in Helena when, on St. Patrick's Day, 1869, twelve hundred men paraded, Fenian sentiment was rife.[67] These circles were given definite organization, having as officers a Center, Treasurer, Secretary and Committee of Safety. In Idaho there was, also, a territorial organization, of which John M. Murphy was Head Center, and a territorial convention was held in 1866 at Idaho City in the Hall of the Fenian Brotherhood.[68] The Brotherhood in Idaho was affiliated with the national organization; when a rupture occurred in that, however, the territorial Council was instructed "to adopt a line of policy in consonance with our brethern of California."[69] The Territorial Council and Center had entire control of the organization, save for the convention, and could act at any moment.[70] Each local center was to report monthly the number of members, their age, and whether married or single. The object was to be ready to co-operate in the grand simultaneous rising of Irishmen in Canada, England, and Ireland. England was vulnerable to the Fenians of Idaho and Montana, it was thought, in the possible seizure of British Columbia and the Hudson's Bay Company's territories. Strong and brave Irishmen would hew their way through the provinces and cross the sea, while their brethren at home were keeping England busy. Money was collected, and military training was carried on. It was sought to include in the ranks all Irishmen and, also, those who sympathized with their cause; the result of the latter classification being the inclusion of many not Irishmen. Participation in American politics was disavowed, but *The Idaho Statesman* charged that in Idaho Democratic politicians made use of Fenianism.[71] The so-

---

[67] Owyhee *Avalanche*, Jan. 16, 1869; Idaho *World*, June 30, 1866; *Contr. His. Soc., Mont.*, Vol VI, p. 107.
[68] Idaho *World*, May 28, 1866.
[69] *Id*.
[70] *Id*.
[71] Idaho *Weekly Statesman*, April 22, 1866.

cial side was not passed over by this war-like brotherhood; a notable Fenian ball was given on one occasion at Idaho City by the Emmett Life Guards.[72]

In bringing this chapter to a close, it may be profitable to give some special attention to the immigration to British Columbia from Great Britain.

British Columbia, it was asserted, was especially suited to Englishmen. "With respect to the colony", wrote a correspondent of *The London Times,* "I can safely say from some experience in these things in my many years of wandering service and knowledge of several colonies, that of all in the wide range of British empire not one is so well adapted for Englishmen in every respect and to found a family in. All may, with ordinary industry and prudence, gain a comfortable independence at an early period and many may make fortunes. The climate is that of Surrey or Kent—rather earlier and safer in the spring as to agriculture—and always with a thoroughly grain ripening summer.'"[73] The crags and dells of some parts of British Columbia seemed to Scotchmen very like those of their native land, and to English wanderers Christmas at Victoria, much more than at Melbourne or Calcutta, seemed like a Christmas at home. These considerations, intensified by the reports of the marvelous riches of Cariboo and promulgated in the columns of the greatly respected *Times,* produced early in 1862 a furore for migration to this splendid land of promise.[74]

In England at this time, in addition to the usual poverty and misery among the poorer classes, there was the distress caused by the Civil War in the United States. In books on British Columbia written by Englishmen at this period, there constantly recur references to the crowded condition in England, the little chance that there was to rise in the world, and the hopeless outlook for old age. "The subject of emigration," wrote Mr. Macfie, "ought to be regarded by the Government and philanthropists as the most important national question that can engage public attention, for there is none more vitally connected with

---

[72] *Idaho World,* June 30, 1866.
[73] *The London Times,* Jan. 30, 1862.
[74] Johnson, *Very Far West Indeed,* p. 1.

the amelioration of poverty and the reduction of crime. You can have all sorts of societies, etc., but people ought to be taken out of debasing *conditions.*"[75] In the old world, it was asserted, society was overburdened with the numerical strength of the labouring class. In new society conditions were reversed; the laborer there was "welcomed, not repulsed. His strong frame there represents one added unit of production from a boundless and untouched field of wealth which would otherwise be fallow, not an additional supplicant for the alms of society, derived from a circumscribed and over-farmed enclosure.'"[76] "If it were possible," wrote Hazlitt, "to show many of those who are there [at Coventry] in a state of actual distress a high road by which they may secure for their industry and skill a sphere in a new land, by which they may find a home, and a vigorous one, in this distant colony—great good would no doubt be done.'"[77]

In order to enlighten the distressed classes and to assist them to go to the new colony, it was suggested that emigration lecturers should be provided by the Imperial Government for giving instruction in the advantages of colonization. "Young criminals," it was urged, " susceptible of reform, might be sent with the consent of the colonists."[78] Since the Government of British Columbia was straining all its resources to construct roads, it had no money for free and assisted passages (such as were granted by other distant colonies) nor for taking care of immigrants on arrival, and it was felt that the mother country ought to help pay the expenses for these objects; but the Imperial Government was following a policy of economy in the founding of British Columbia, and no aid was given. Private philanthrophy was more generous, and the Columbian Emigration Society was formed as an adjunct of the Columbian Mission. Considerable money was contributed to the cause, among the prominent contributors being Miss Burdett-Coutts, the Hudson's Bay Company, and Cavan, Lubbock, and Company, each of whom gave

---

[75] Macfie, *Van. Id. and Br. Col.*, p. 514.
[76] Johnson, *Very Far West Indeed*, pp 275–6.
[77] Hazlitt, *Cariboo*, p. 80–81.
[78] Macfie, *Van Id. and Br. Col*, p. 516

one hundred pounds. Under the auspices of this society two ship-loads of female emigrants were sent to the colony.[79]

A noticeable feature of the attitude of British philanthropic workers toward emigrants to British Columbia, as revealed in the various books of the time, is paternalism—one might almost say grand-motherliness. Emigrants were to be incited to go, and were to be assisted and directed at every turn. Some of the directions were sufficiently ludicrous; as when one author includes in a long list of "necessaries" eighteen white or printed shirts, six coloured shirts, three dozen collars, and twenty-four pocket handkerchiefs.[80] At the auctions on the street corners in Victoria, one might see put up articles utterly useless to men expecting to face the rough up-country—dress-suits, dressing cases, and even, in one instance, an elaborate wash-stand.[81]. Men who knew conditions, however, advised very simple outfits, such as those used by American frontiersmen.

The large emigration of 1862, while it contained a sprinkling of experienced Welsh and Cornish miners and of veteran colonists from Australia and New Zealand, for the most part was made up of men without capital and utterly unused to manual labor—clerks, impecunious university men, "prodigal sons, and a host of other romantic non-de-scripts who indulged in visions of sudden wealth obtainable with scarcely more exertion than is usually put forth in a pleasure excursion to the continent of Europe."[82] Governor Douglas was besieged by applicants for positions, who bore letters from influential persons in England. Answering a letter of a member of Parliament, who had mentioned two emigrants he wrote as follows: "The number of respectable young men now arriving from England and other parts of the world is very great and many of them I fear will be disappointed, unless they are prepared for the roughs and smooths of Colonial life and have a command of capital sufficient, to embark in farming or in the opening and working of mining claims; either of these pursuits being highly lucrative, and would

---

[79] Hazlitt, *Cariboo*, pp. 80–82; Macfie, *Van. Id. and Br. Col*, pp 493–7; Sir James Douglas, *Correspondence Book*, pp. 64–67, MS.

[80] Hazlitt, *Cariboo*, p 86

[81] Johnson, *Very Far West Indeed*, p. 49–50

[82] Macfie, *Van. Id. and Br Col*, p. 76

afford a profitable return, but without pecuniary resources or the capacity to labor their condition will be deplorable.''[83]

The dreams of these immigrants faded, when, on arrival at Victoria, they found themselves still hundreds of miles from Cariboo, and facing a journey which involved endless privations and discomforts on the way and hard manual labor at the end. Many went part way and turned back, but a few went through and did well. Hundreds of young gentlemen who had arrived at Victoria with jaunty air and much luggage were reduced in the following winter to chopping wood and grubbing stumps to escape starvation. They found that the class distinctions, to which they were accustomed at home, were of no avail in the vigorous and impartial life of the new colony; Oxford or Cambridge men might be found laboring for servants—now prosperous butchers, draymen, or returned miners—on whom they had looked down at home.[84]

Such men, naturally, were bitterly disappointed in the country, and their letters and narratives complained greatly of the privations which they endured in this uncivilized part of the world. In commenting on these complaints, *The London Times* printed a suggestive editorial, part of which read as follows: ''The emigrant to British Columbia would find a soil as fertile and a climate as agreeable as those left behind him. The colony, in fact, was precisely what so many people have sighed for in the struggles of a home career. It was a Britain without competition and without social difficulties, where the land was still unappropriated and men were worth more than money. What might have been done in England before the landing of Julius Caesar might be done in British Columbia at the present day. It could only be done, however, at the same cost and that fact should never be forgotten. When England was all common,

---

[83] Sir James Douglas to Hon. C. Fortesque M. P., *Correspondence Book*, MS, p. 67. A different kind of British participation in the life of the new colony at this period was manifested when British capital began to come into the colony more freely. The Bank of British Columbia was founded by English capitalists and had, besides the main office at Victoria, agencies at Nanaimo, New Westminster, Yale, and Cariboo. *Id.*, p 38; Macfie, *Van. Id. and Br. Col.*, p. 87.

[84] Macfie, *Van. Id. and Br. Col.*, p. 412. This author observes (p 77), that even if the immigration had been of a sort best suited to a new country, "A much larger number came than the country, with a deficient supply of roads was prepared to receive."

and any man might have an estate for the choosing, England was without roads or bridges, or the other adjuncts of civilization. It was just as hard to get from the Thames to the Humber as it is to get from Victoria to Cariboo. Improvements and property came together. No accommodations can be expected on No Man's Land. * * * British Columbia is open to occupiers only because it has never been occupied, and a country which has never been occupied cannot be traversed without difficulty or settled without hardships.[85]

Through trials, indeed, a process of selection was going on. Authors who wrote before 1862 urged immigration indiscriminately, but those who wrote after that time are careful to point out classes which might come and those who should stay at home. It was to be remembered that the problem of life was simplified in the colonies, and that there were no aristocratic middlemen who spring forth from the "luxurious habits and super-abundant wealth of thickly-populated districts.[86] Hence, educated men could not expect patrons. Indeed, "clerks, poor gentlemen of education and breeding in quest of government appointments, governesses, school masters, and adventurers without funds and trained to no particular employment," stood small show for success, for the colony was not far enough advanced for them.[87] But men accustomed to physical labor and strong in will might come, and, particularly, the small farmer. Female domestic servants were in great demand at high wages, and would find good chances for marriage. Small manufacturers and merchants, millers, pitch and resin manufacturers, and fishermen with small capital and pluck would do well. Retired officers of the army and navy would find Victoria a lovely place in which to live, could utilize their land bounties, and could get high rates of interest for their money. Capitalists were especially welcome, for they were needed to develop the resources of the country and "to open the way for the wider and steadier employment of labor".[88] Capitalists would get large returns for the use of their money, and if, through misadventure, they lost it, a fresh start would be easy.

---

[85] Quotation from the London *Times* in the *San Francisco Daily Bulletin*, Dec. 12, 1862.
[86] Johnson, *Very Far West Indeed*, pp. 270-80.
[87] Macfie, *Van. Id. and Br. Col.*, pp. 493-517.
[88] *Id.*

CHAPTER X

EDUCATION AND RELIGION

While, as compared with new agricultural settlements, there were few children in the mining communities, nevertheless families gathered in all well-established camps; and there arose demand for some sort of educational facilities. This demand was voiced both in British Columbia and the American territories, but was responded to in different ways in the two regions.

In the American territories schools sprang quickly and spontaneously from the people, and in simple forms. Private, or subscription schools were usually the first to start; such were those of Professor Dimsdale in Virginia City, of Miss Dunlap in Nevada City, and of Miss Darling in Bannack.[1] The first public school in Montana was started in 1866 in Virginia City, the school-house being the Union church.[2] One of the perplexities of both public and private teachers was the almost amusing diversity of text-books, due to the fact that the parents of the children had come from almost every state in the Union and brought text-books with them. The only text-book which could be bought in Virginia City was Webster's "little blue-backed speller", which cost one dollar each, and the supply was soon exhausted. The interest of the eastern counties of Oregon in education is shown by the fact that in 1864 there were seven school districts in Baker County and six in Umatilla County.[3]

---

[1] Miss Darling was an Ohio lady, a niece of Governor Edgerton, of Montana. An interesting account of the school taught by her, including valuable notes on other schools, may be found in *Contr. His. Soc. Mon.*, Vol. V, pp. 187-197.

[2] *Id.*, pp. 198-9. Mr. W. I. Marshall, afterwards principal of the W. E. Gladstone School in Chicago and well known for his contributions to the Oregon question, was for four years principal of this school.

[3] *House Journal of Oregon*, 1864, Appendix, Report of County School Superintendents.

In Idaho the beginnings of a common school system were almost contemporaneous with the founding of the Territory. At the second session of the legislature an act was passed establishing the system and providing that 5 per cent of all moneys paid into the county treasuries and all moneys from fines should be used for schools.[4] One percentum, also, of the gross incomes of toll roads, bridges, and ferries, was to be applied to school purposes.[5] J. H. Chittenden, an energetic assayer of Silver City, who had been a teacher in his former home, was appointed Territorial Superintendent. His report of 1865 mentions that there were in the Territory 1239 children of school age, that there were three school houses, and that twelve schools had been held. In 1866 there was expended on education in the four leading counties $6,685.[6] These beginnings seem not discreditable to communities just sprung up in the wilderness, but there are many comments in the literature of the time on the indifference shown to education, and there was constant urging to greater efforts.

It is noticeable that in the starting and carrying on of the schools in the American territories religion and religious organizations had little direct part. A bill was reported to the Idaho legislature, it is true, which provided for the "issuance of bonds for $30,000, bearing interest at 10 per cent. and payable to the order of Right Rev. Francis Blanchett, Archbishop of Oregon, out of the proceeds of the sales of certain school lands, to enable his reverence and the Sisters of Mary and Jesus at Portland, Oregon, and the Sisters of Providence, at Vancouver, Washington Territory, to establish and maintain schools within this Territory upon an extensive scale." In advocacy of the measure it was claimed that in Idaho there was a peculiar situation, in that the male population of the mining districts was fluctuating, and that this arrangement would enable the parents to live in the mines and still would allow the children to be educated. The opponents objected that the manner of disposing of the lands de-

---

[4] *Laws of the Territory of Idaho, Second Session*, pp. 377-83.
[5] Report of J. H Chittenden, Supt. of Public Instruction, 1865, Owyhee *Avalanche*, Oct. 28, 1865.
[6] Hailey, *His of Idaho*, p. 134.

pended upon Congress, and that such schools would be aristocratic.[7] The bill failed to pass, and public schools in the American Territories remained free from religious patronage.

In the English Colonies, however, the participation of the church in education was stimulated by the precedence of Roman Catholic schools at Victoria, and by 1863 two collegiate schools of the Episcopal church were in existence there having eight teachers and sixty-one pupils. The desire for schools on the mainland was voiced in a petition from Yale to the Bishop of Columbia, in which the married inhabitants stated that the previous summer they had tried to form a school, but that it "had succumbed to the strife for gold"; that now they hoped for the establishment of schools, as well as churches, in the various townships; and that such institutions would encourage individuals to bring wives and children.[8] The bishop promised a schoolmaster. A like petition came from Hope. An address from New Westminster praised the Bishop's ideas in regard to schools.[9] There was an address also, from the "Clergy, Churchwardens, Members of the Church of England and Inhabitants of Vancouver's Island", which expressed pleasure at the "intention to form and maintain schools for the education of the rising generation and of Indians.[10]

One of the marked features, indeed, of the educational work inaugurated in the British Colonies under the auspices of the church was the inclusion of Indians, and even of Chinese. The addresses, mentioned above, signify the desire for education of Indians, and English rectors formed classes for Chinese.[11] In the American territories, on the other hand, education of Indians was not thought of as a duty on the part of the local popu-

---

[7] *Journals of the Council and House of Representatives of Idaho Territory, Fourth Session*, pp 351-7 In connection with the beginnings of education in the Inland Empire, we may note that, in 1861, Rev. Mr. Eells was at the Old Mission at Walla Walla, worn with teaching, and purposing to form at that place an institution of higher learning; *Oregonian*, Aug. 17, 1861.
[8] *Columbian Mission, Occasional Papers*, 1860, App. I, p. 37-8.
[9] *Id.*, App., II and III, pp 38-41.
[10] *Id*, App, IV, p. 42-3.
[11] A remarkable school and Indian settlement was founded by Wm. Duncan at Metlakkathlah, about twenty miles from Ft. Simpson; on this see *Holcombe, Rev. J. J., Stranger than Fiction*.

lation and the instruction of Chinamen, so far as the author has been able to learn, was not considered.

But the process of establishing public schools in British Columbia lacked the instantaneousness and spontaneity which were exhibited in the American districts. In 1855, indeed, three schools of a semi-public character, the expense of which was met from the colonial treasury, were established on Vancouver Island by the Hudson's Bay Company. These were under the supervision of Rev. E. Cridge, M. A. Early in 1861 need was felt for additional public schools, but it was not until 1865 that the Vancouver Island House of Assembly set aside ten thousand dollars for public school purposes. Mr. A. Waddington became superintendent, and there was an attendance of four hundred pupils. At the union with British Columbia, however, in 1866, these schools were practically defunct, though some were kept open for a year or two longer. After the union a Common School Ordinance was passed in 1869, which was amended in 1870; under this ordinance a few new schools were established, chiefly on the mainland. The system, however, did not provide for absolute free schools, and experience demonstrated that these were necessary. Finally, on entering the confederation, a free Public School Act was passed, under which the public school system of British Columbia has steadily progressed.[12]

The establishment of religious institutions was early put in train both in the colonies and the territories, but, as in the case of education, the process exhibits characteristic differences.

In the American region churches were sometimes initiated by local efforts, but more often at the impulse of representatives of eastern missionary societies. At Silver City a union church building was erected, for the most part from local funds. At a Christmas festival in 1866 it was filled with "the youth and age of both sexes" and many Christmas gifts were exchanged; the local paper said that it was "pride inspiring and a retaste of God's country."[13] At Boise City *The Statesman* mentioned that

---

[12] *First Annual Report of the Public Schools of British Columbia*, John Jessop, Superintendent of Education, Victoria, 1872, p. 2. "There had been a public school in New Westminster from about 1863, supported by fees from the pupils, supplemented by a Government grant."—Note from Judge F. W. Howay.

[13] Owyhee *Avalanche*, Feb. 3, 1866.

three clergymen had held services on one Sunday, and in the Boise Basin Father Paulin was accustomed to hold services in all the important towns.[14] Though there were doubtless in Idaho, as elsewhere among the miners, a good many assertive skeptics, yet respect was paid to such representatives of religion as Bishop Tuttle of the Episcopal Church: "The Bishop was loved and respected by the men of the Basin, no matter what their creed or nationality, and no matter how crowded the streets might be, if the men saw the Bishop coming, the way was cleared and as he passed, hats were lifted and kindly greetings given".[15] Bishop Tuttle labored long, also, in Montana, although ministers of other denominations preceded him. In 1864 there were at work in Montana, Rev. Jonathan Blanchard, D. D., president of Wheaton College, (Illinois), Rev. A. M. Tarbet, Baptist; Rev. George Grantham Smith, Presbyterian, and Rev. A. M. Hough, Methodist.[16] Sometimes, as in the case of Mr. Blanchard and of Mr. Smith, ministers were sent out as exploring missionaries by eastern societies—in mining parlance one might call such, clergymen prospectors. Within a few years following 1864 church buildings of different denominations were erected in all the important towns.

Biographical notes from some of the early preachers in the mining communities give glimpses of the life in these communities.

The Rev. George Grantham Smith arrived in Bannack in June of 1864, and his trunk was eighteen months in following him, "So that I was in my first parish for eighteen months with no book save my small English Bible without note or comment; and I have the most intelligent and wide-awake congregation I have ever ministered unto." On his arrival the sight of his umbrella, in a country of very little rain, brought forth shouts up and down the street of "tenderfoot" and "pilgrim." Since board at the hotel cost one hundred dollars per week in legal tender, Mr. Smith erected a rude cabin and boarded himself. But even then when speculators sent flour to five hundred dollars per barrel

---
[14] Idaho *Weekly Statesman*, Nov 19, 1865; *Idaho World*, April 14, 1862.
[15] Halley, *His. of Idaho*, p. 117.
[16] *Contr. His. Soc. Mont.*, Vol. VI, pp. 292–4.

(legal tender), he had to live on meat straight. He preached in an unused store room, "organized a Sunday School and commenced regular Sabbath services with good and attractive audiences". Later he went over to Virginia City. There the room in which he preached was next door to a big gambling establishment, which had a brass band. When the band struck up, the miners in Mr. Smith's audience began beating time so loudly with their heavy boots, that the minister was compelled to stop; then a "long lank, lean fellow in buckskins called out, 'Boys never mind the music. The elder has the floor. You listen to him. Elder, go on; you shall not be disturbed again'. I was not. The text was 'Godliness is profitable unto all things.' Still my subject was scarcely grave enough to keep me from laughing when I dismissed the congregation, for the seats of the pants of those men, who had not laid aside their American trousers and come into the full-fledged native buckskin, were patched with all the varied brands from flour sacks, such as 'Superfine', 'I X. L.', 'Superior', 'Excelsior' or 'Gilt Edge".[17]

The work of the Episcopal Church in Montana was well begun by Bishop Daniel S. Tuttle, (mentioned above) who preached at Virginia City, Deer Lodge, Missoula, Helena, Butte, Bozeman, and many other places. It was typical of his work in Montana, he wrote, that many people, "who were not churchmen or churchwomen, nevertheless cast their lot with us and heartily, loyally, and generously supported our work " Contributions were comparatively large for new communities; at Virginia City the congregation paid a fixed salary of $2,500, and at Helena $3,000. One singular contribution came, characteristic of miners' ways, when men urged a certain Scotchman, who thought himself a poet, to give a public reading in a hall. They industriously sold tickets and then at the reading guyed the poor fellow unmercifully. The proceeds, $102, were given to the Bishop for the use of the poor. Although living in a rude cabin, the Bishop wrote concerning the first year in Virginia City: "I am loth to lay by my pen in writing of my first year in Montana. My letters to Mrs. Tuttle from the cabin are filled with enthusiastic outbursts over the sunniness and pleasantness of the winter. And

---

[17] *Contr. His. Soc , Mont.,* Vol. VI, pp. 295-299.

that, too, though more than once the thermometer registered into the twenties below zero, and though the winds piled some snow through the crevices of my abode. So, also, spite of the wildness and wickedness with which I knew I was surrounded, and spite, too, of a loneliness which would make itself felt, there were great stretches of sunniness and pleasantness in my Virginia City experiences for which then, and all along after and now, I have thanked God and take courage." At Helena the Bishop helped vigorously in fighting the great fire of February 15, 1869, and marveled at the "buoyancy and pluck" of the people in at once starting rebuilding. His first experience in Butte was described as follows: "Butte was an infant quartz town, struggling with its swathing bands. No church of any kind was there, or minister either. We secured the use of an unfurnished new store on Main street, fitted up a big dry goods box for a pulpit; stretched boards on carpenter's 'horses' for seats, and held our services in the evening. Sleeping quarters were hard to find. Some one gave us two the privilege of betaking ourselves to his cabin. There was no floor. Rolled in our blankets we went to sleep on the soft earth. And we thought ourselves alone. When we awoke next morning eleven fellow sleepers were with us, packed almost like the occupants of a sardine box." Sojourning thus in rough quarters, driving often long distances, the young Bishop through many years performed the kindly ministrations of burial, wedding, baptism, and preaching.[18]

The following notice chronicled the dedication of the first Methodist church in Montana: "Providence permitting, the first Methodist Episcopal Church of Montana Territory in Virginia City, will be dedicated to the worship of God, Sabbath, Nov. 6, 1864 * * * a general attendance of all lovers of Zion is invited.'"[19] The building was made of logs split in two with saws, muslin was used for windows, and there was a dirt roof which gave much trouble. There were thirty members at Virginia City. Of these "Brother Ritchie was a laundryman—class leader, Sunday School superintendent, trustee, chorister, and

---

[18] Tuttle, Bishop Daniel S., *Early History of the Episcopal Church in Montana*, Contr. His. Soc., Mont., Vol V, pp. 289-324.
[19] Montana *Post*, Oct 29, 1864.

sexton." Brother Geo. W. Forbes was "our financier"; he had come in with the first rush, having a few hundred dollars and returned home three years later worth $75,000. Brother J. B. Weeks was a quartz enthusiast, sturdy in frame, who spent most of his time prospecting. Rev. A. M. Hough was the minister. At one time, Mr. Hough, on a trip to Prickly Pear had to stop for a night at Daly's Ranch. All were compelled to stay in the bar-room, where there was gambling, drinking, and "huge profanity." "I confess I was afaid as I saw every man with a large knife and revolver strapped about him. I did not know the character of those rough mountaineers as well then, as I did afterwards." At bed time Mr. Hough read from the Bible aloud and prayed; there was perfect silence, a number knelt in prayer, and profanity ceased. In Prickly Pear Valley he preached once in a saloon, and "everything was done to make it comfortable, by the gentlemanly proprietor." Another saloon-keeper at Nevada City offered the use of his saloon on any evening of the week, but could not afford to let it be used on Sunday. The people were generous in contributions, the collection plates usually being gold pans; "Men drew out their buckskin purses, and either poured out a quantity of gold dust on the plate, or took out a pinch between the thumb and finger, which would be equal to 25-50 cents." "Funerals were sometimes simplified to the last degree. I saw one where the coffin was made of 'shakes,' a wheelbarrow served as a hearse, and the procession consisted of one man." An interesting observation is made by Mr. Hough concerning enforcement of law. "One of the things I could never understand", he says, "was that in communities where the population was ready to rise *en masse* and hang men guilty of great crimes or sustain an organized Vigilance Committee in doing it, a legal conviction and execution will not be sustained."[20]

In the activities of the Roman Catholic Church in Montana the Society of Jesus was conspicuous. This Order had long had well-conducted establishments for the Indians at St. Ignatius, Coeur d' Alene, and St. Mary, though the latter was now aban-

---

[20] Hough, Rev. A. M, *Establishment of our Mission in Montana—Notes from My Diary*, MS.

doned. At these stations white miners were often entertained and, sometimes, in times of danger from the Indians, received shelter. But the Jesuits felt that their first duty was to the Indians, and it was difficult to get priests for the whites—a difficulty increased by the great dearth of clergymen caused by the rapid rise of new communities throughout the West. A chapel for whites was, however, erected in 1863 near Hell's Gate Village, and Father Giorda in the same year visited Virginia City. The first church at that place, All Saints, was dedicated about Christmas time, 1865, and at Helena the next year a church was dedicated to the Sacred Hearts of Jesus and Mary.[21]

It would be a mistake, of course, to think that the mass of the American mining population was composed of men who conformed to the requirements of religion; but it is equally a mistake to think of this population as entirely oblivious of religion, or to think of the agencies of religion as entirely neglected. Indeed, it is surprising that the people of the East, engaged in the Civil War, should have been as active as they were in trying to found institutions of religion in these far-off camps.

In the founding of religious institutions in the British colonies the efforts of the motherland to reproduce the main features of its own society were particularly earnest, conscious, and systematic.

Churches of several denominations were started in Victoria and on the mainland. Congregationalists were assisted by the British Colonial Missionary Society, and Presbyterians by the Presbyterian Church of Ireland. The Jews had a good synagogue in Victoria, presided over by an intelligent and respected rabbi. A minister of the Church of Scotland, also, held services. Methodists were composed largely of Canadians, a fact which may help to explain the early activity of that denomination in Cariboo. The Roman Catholic Church was first in the field, and it possessed at Victoria a "commodious church and extensive schools." A Roman Catholic Bishop in Victoria had served among the Indians nearly thirty years. It was said that a "con-

---

[21] Palladino, Rev. Lawrence, S. J., *Indian and White in the Northwest, A History of Catholicity in Montana*, Part II, Chaps. III-VI.

siderable portion of the means by which that Church is sustained comes from the Propaganda of Lyons."[22]

In the establishment of these various denominations in the British Colonies, there was nothing particularly distinguishable in the process from that which was going on in the American territories; but in the planting of the Church of England there were elements characteristically British.

There was an earnest desire in England that this promising colony should not be the scene of such disorder and bloodshed and cruelty to Indians as, it was reported, had occurred in California, and that the institutions of England should be early reproduced in the Colonies. The Diocese of Columbia, accordingly, was created, and the Rev. George Hill was appointed Bishop. The revenues of the new diocese were large; collections and subscriptions from various congregations in England amounted to £15,220, and Miss Burdett-Coutts gave an endowment of £25,000. In 1862 the contributions from various sources were as follows:

```
Columbian Mission ........................ £4700
Society for the Propagation of the Gospel ....... £1100
Church Missionary Society ................... £300
Congregational efforts ..................... £2000
```

Besides, there was raised in the Diocese itself in the first three years the sum of £6232.[23]

The interest taken in England in the starting of the Mission is shown in the *Report of the Proceedngs at a Public Meeting. Held in the Egyptian Hall, Mansion House,* London, November 16, 1859. The meeting was called at the request of "various Merchants, Bankers and Traders" and The Right Honorable the Lord Mayor was in the chair. In his speech the Lord Mayor

---

[22] If the above report were true, it is interesting to think of a Church being nourished in these distant regions by the ancient community whose Christians in the times of Marcus Aurelius were persecuted.

The account in the paragraph is based for the most part upon Macfie, *Van. Id. and Br. Col.*, pp. 77-90. This author makes a classification of churchmembers in Victoria according to business engaged in: Methodists, he says were small retailers and jobbers; Presbyterians and Congregationalists, jobbers and larger store keepers; Church of England men, whole-salers, bankers, and lawyers. P. 417.

[23] *Columbian Mission, Occasional Papers,* 1860, p. 32; Id. 1863, *Pastoral Addresses,* p 5

said: "By this discovery of gold it appears patent and palpable to me that the Anglo-Saxon race have had opportunities given them of extending themselves yet more widely, and of peopling countries that but a few years ago were mere deserts. But there is something more than that. The Anglo-Saxon race, remembering the religion of their fathers, are anxious to maintain, implant, and support that religion on the distant shores of the other side of the globe." The Bishop of Oxford spoke as follows: "Now, My Lord Mayor, I can hardly conceive a more important matter to be done by a Christian people than that of founding a new colony. (Hear, hear.) England I think, has been for the most part guilty in this matter. She has thrown as it were the seed of men upon this and that part of the earth without any further consideration than that she relieves some temporary press at home, or gets rid of some inconvenient members of the home society. She has seldom contemplated * * * what it was indeed to be the foundress of a nation. Of course the first conditions, My Lord Mayor, of carrying this great work out faithfully must be this: that provision must be made by the founding nation for reproducing itself, in its own characteristic elements and in its own special institutions, in the distant land to which it sends its sons. * * * This great responsibility this nation is now undertaking in the settlement of British Columbia". At this meeting there was announced a contribution from Her Majesty of £250 to the Mission, and from the Marquis of Westminster of £200.[24]

The Bishop landed at Victoria in January of 1860. With him were seven clergymen and three ladies. His diocese comprised both Vancouver Island and British Columbia.

A serious question confronted him at the start. This was whether there should be an attempt to establish in the diocese a State Church. For some time there had been very warm discussion of the subject in the colonies, and Governor Douglas had been bitterly assailed for having given some grants of land on which to erect church buildings and for alleged favoring of a

---

[24] *Columbian Mission, Occasional Papers*, 1860, pp. 17-30.

State Church.[25] It had been anticipated that the Bishop would favor an Establishment, but in his first sermon he distinctly disavowed any such idea.[26]

The Bishop made a number of long journeys on the mainland, on one of which he endured the terrible toil of a trip to Cariboo, when the trails were still unimproved. Brave, energetic, and patient, he adapted himself well to the new strange life, mingled easily with all classes of men, and keenly observed the country and its people. He dedicated a new church at New Westminster (the site for which was cleared by the Royal Engineers), and preached in a saloon at Antler Creek. Communicants were few, but audiences were good and of every religious complexion— "Wesleyans, Presbyterians, Roman Catholics, Socinians; Jews and Deists, Tom Painists, Phrenological Materialists, Atheists." It was remarkable, as an old major of the United States Army commented in Cariboo, "how those brought up in the Episcopal Church retained their affection for it, and how adherence was continued from father to son". There seemed a marked difference in the respect paid to religion by Canadians and those from others of "our colonies", as compared with other miners— not a few of whom were abusive of religion. The Bishop's life in the new world often contrasted strangely with his life in England: "On this my 44th birthday", he wrote in his journal, "I awoke on the floor of a log hut, in the wild and almost inaccessible recesses of the Cascade Mountains, the Frazer (sic) flowing at my feet." But the Bishop rejoiced in the glorious scenery of the Fraser and made no word of complaint. He liked to talk with miners and packers, and admired the enterprise, ingenuity, and versatility of the Americans. To the condition of the Indians he gave sympathetic attention. In his work he had earnest helpers, such as the reverend gentlemen, Brown, Sheepshanks, Reynard, and Knipe. By 1863 there were in the diocese eleven churches, six mission chapels, and eighteen stations, served by fifteen clergymen and three catechists. The work

---

[25] Columbian Mission, 1860, p. 13; A petition to His Grace the Duke of Newcastle, Her Majesty's Principal Secretary of State for the Colonies,—*The British Columbian*, Feb. 28, 1861; Pemberton, J. D., *Van. Id. and Br. Col.*, p. 132.

[26] Macfie, *Van. Id. and Br. Col.*, p 354–5.

was carried on in the towns, the rural districts, and the mines, and among the Indians and in education.[27]

The work in Cariboo, for years "the very heart and center of the whole colony", was especially significant. Rev. Mr. Garrett and others laboured there for a number of summers; but in the summer-time when the water was running, the miners were so intent on their work that they would pay little attention to religious services. By 1866, however, many miners and merchants had come to winter in Cariboo, and the resident population was estimated at 2000. These men were idle during the winter, and then was the opportunity for getting hold of them. It was felt that a resident clergyman was needed. But it was perceived, also, that this field demanded an able man—"active, affable yet self-contained, wise, prudent, patient." "This emphatically", wrote the Rev. Mr. Garrett, "is not the place for an inferior man".

To this difficult field Rev. J. Reynard, Principal of the Indian Mission at Victoria, volunteered to go with his wife and family, and he was assigned the post. When it was known that they proposed to stay the winter in Cariboo, there were emphatic remonstrances: "They will starve," telegraphed Chief-justice Begbie to the Bishop. Nevertheless, Mr. Reynard and his family arrived in Barkerville in August 1867 and settled down in a two-roomed cabin at a rental of $60 per month.

The ideal of this ministry may be given in Mr. Reynard's own words. "I hope," he wrote, "to live amongst my flock the simple, straight-forward life of a 'Country Parson,' exercising a frank and cheerful hospitality; showing to many, sundered by years and thousands of leagues from early influences, that homes do still exist. I purpose to carry to the outlying creeks and lonesome settlements of this wild land the kindly ministrations of religion; to help and direct all innocent amusements, and to afford to the frugal and industrious Chinese some light of schooling and Christian truth."[28] Again at the end of his third year Mr. Reynard wrote as follows: "I look back on the past winter

---

[27] The sources for this paragraph are the *Journals* of Bishop Hill from 1860 and for 1862-3. These are found in *Occasional Papers*, 1860 and 1863; also extracts from that of 1860 in Hazlitt's *Cariboo*, pp. 158-165.

[28] *Occasional Papers*, Report, 1869, p. 56.

with great satisfaction. Every step in advance has been honorably striven for,—won by unstinted unslackening effort. I hope still, with God's help, to go on: reasoning of 'righteousness, temperance and judgment to come', helping on all that is 'honest and of good report', turning to the service of Christ men hard indeed to impress, but so well worth the effort".[29]

The trials of the work were severe. Hardly was Mr. Reynard well settled, when a mining-camp fire swept over the settlement, destroying one hundred houses. The old church by which he hoped to pay for a cottage, was burnt. "Lamps, benches, books, robes"—articles hard to replace in Cariboo—were gone. Most people advised him to leave, "but this I cannot do, dare not, will not think of". There was a good deal of bold and brutal infidelity among the miners; some asserted that "religions are all alike—useless and purposeless". "It has been a cruel time," he wrote, "hopeless and bookless"; but the "old Yorkshire tenacity of purpose" held true. Solace came with the arrival of some books, and once more he felt, in his own words, "totus teres atque rotundus". Soon after, however, came a spell of severe cold when the mercury "at one leap" went to thirty-eight degrees below zero and then froze. The parson, unskilled as most Englishmen in the use of the axe, cut his hand badly. While suffering from this wound, he took his son along to the place where he held meetings, in order to distribute books, and the boy's foot was so badly frozen that the skin peeled off. "And now, my lord, I felt beaten, tyrannous, cold, maimed hand and foot—for the first time incapable of the world's work—my 'hands hung down', and I felt as I think I should had I been another sort of soldier, and, stricken down at the beginning of some great battle, heard my comrades pass on 'shouting' for the victory". In another time of extreme cold, "a fifth little recipient of our Saviour's grace and tender pity was born unto us. We were poor then, my lord, and the cold made life all the harder * * *. What wonder, then, that the mother's maternal 'joy that a man was born into the world was attempered with emotions of pure tenderness, and piteous moans of. 'My poor baby, thou'rt come to a cold world.' " In the bed near the stove the port wine froze.

---

[29] *Occasional Papers*, Report of 1870, p. 58.

But, "We had a true neighbor in Mrs. Lee. My hand was better and we pulled through". "That poor baby, blue with cold", Mr. Reynard wrote the next summer, "is now a great hearty lad all smiles and dimples."

One of the main efforts of Mr. Reynard's work in Cariboo was to keep the young men away from the saloons and dance houses. To this end he organized a "Church Institute" and advertised it in the Cariboo Sentinel. On Monday evening instruction in Latin and English was offered, and on Tuesday evening there was band practice; on Wednesday and Saturday evenings the room was opened for reading, chess, etc., the magazines available being Blackwood, Cornhill, the Edinburg Quarterly, and the Pall Mall Budget; on Thursday evening there were algebra and arithmetic, and on Friday choir practice. An offer, probably often accepted, was that more elementary instruction would be given, if required. Some Chinese studied under Mr. Reynard, among whom were four Tartars "men of remarkable concentration"; the Chinese proper he found full of fun and more simplehearted. Mr. Reynard appears to have been a man of wide culture with a taste for teaching, and with something of genius for music. The classes in music were well attended, and "a good 'hearty, joyful noise' my Cariboo chorus makes." "Often I have felt repaid for all this exertion", he wrote, "when going home I have seen the gleam of a cariboo lantern going up and up the snow-clad hillside, and heard from the distant heights phrases of quaint madrigals or melodious glees. Then the cheery 'good nights' would be heard, as one by one the tenants of the lonely cabins reached home, and the manly bass of the last man having farthest to travel was heard fainter and fainter. 'Music made the winter fly' they said".[30]

A mission journey of some six hundred miles one summer relieved the tedium of Cariboo. The country on the road to Lilloet appeared "most attractive in its varied beauty" after "long experience of the creeks and sombre pine clad mountains of Cariboo". In the course of the journey on one occasion he preached to some sturdy lads about being "good soldiers 'fight-

---

[30] A Cariboo lantern consisted of a bottle with the bottom broken off, inverted, and a candle inside.

ing a good fight', by being brave, honest, simple, pure in heart", and contrasted such with cowards, deserters and traitors; on another he told an Indian beating his wife, "God hates anger * * *. Give the wife good words, and untie her hands; a wife is not a slave." At Clinton he held service in the hotel parlor on Sunday afternoon, "but a party of Oregon horse-dealers having advertised a race only a few attended."

In Cariboo the church service, especially the music, attracted a varied congregation. At one service the minister caught sight of the jack of clubs peeping from a gambler's pocket; and an Even Song Service brought in strangers of "all nations: Europeans, two Chinamen, and a few Indians. In the remotest corner was a Lascar, his dark oriental face, lean figure and gleaming eyes in contrast to the rest." A main purpose of Mr. Reynard in Cariboo was the building of a church "worthy of our system", "a decorous church that can give strength to the parson as well as influence to the people." But in this project he met much discouragement and ridicule. "The Barkerville people at this time grieved me much", he wrote. "Cruel people *du pays!* ready to worship success with mean adulation, ready to think one defeated and then, voe victis." It was only with difficulty that men could be found willing to serve on the Church Committee, this unwillingness arising in part, however, from disinclination to give up Sunday labor. Material for building was expensive, the carriage of glass from Victoria costing $127, which was six times the original cost. But, finally, the following notice appeared in the Cariboo Sentinel of September 24th, 1870: "St. Saviors Church". "Rev. James Reynard formally opened the new church bearing the above name in Barkerville on Sunday last. A larger number of people than usual attended the service, and the completion of the church was the occasion of much congratulation toward Mr. Reynard, who has shown a great deal of patience, energy and industry in the work he undertook."

Mr. Reynard acknowledged that his work in Cariboo was not a great numerical success, but "It has gathered round me the young, the intelligent—the better sort every way: it is an influence to strengthen all that is good, honest, true; to help the wavering by frank companionship, and profference of the solid for the doubtful; an influence to warn the fallen; while it is an undying protest against all that is reckless and wanton".

Mr. Reynard stayed one more winter in Cariboo, and then, his health having failed, he was transferred to Nanaimo. "The loss", said the report of 1871, "is great for Cariboo, and no one has been found to take his place".[31]

It would seem clear, we may say in conclusion, that, though there were characteristic differences in forms of religious action in the colony and in the Territories, the mining advance in both regions was accompanied by early, vigorous, and, in a measure, successful efforts to plant in the new fields the institutions of religion.

[31] The material for this account of the Cariboo mission has been derived from the *Occasional Papers and Reports of the Columbian Mission*, 1868–71. I have not had access to a wider range of sources, which might reveal other aspects.

PART IV

LAW AND GOVERNMENT

CHAPTER XI

THE ESTABLISHMENT OF GOVERNMENT AND LAW IN BRITISH COLUMBIA

In considering the establishment of government and law in British Columbia, we shall limit our study to the period preceding union in 1866 with the Colony of Vancouver Island, and, for the most part, to the administration of Sir James Douglas.[1]

Sir James Douglas stands out as the most significant figure in the history of the mining advance. He had in British Columbia, it is true, able and distinguished coadjutors, and south of the Line there arose in many localities energetic and determined leaders, greatly worthy of respect; but in neither region was there any one person whose life was so broadly, essentially, and commandingly impressed upon his time as was that of the first governor of British Columbia.

Douglas was born on the island of Demarara in the West Indies in 1803. As a lad of seventeen he took service with the North West Fur Company and, on the merging of that company into the Hudson's Bay Company, continued in the employ of the latter, his field of activity being the region west of the Rocky Mountains. A young man of energy and decision, Douglas rose rapidly in the company's ranks until finally he became Chief Factor. In addition to this office, he was appointed in 1851 Governor of the Colony of Vancouver Island, and these two offices he held when in the spring of 1858, as has been narrated in a former chapter, came the great influx of miners which brought about the founding of the Colony of British Columbia.[2]

---

[1] It would be interesting to trace the important process of unification with Vancouver Island and then of confederation in the Dominion, but such study would digress from the purpose of this work.

[2] Chapter III.

For two years before the great movement to the Fraser River, as we have there noted, Mr. Douglas had kept gathering information in regard to the discoveries of gold on the mainland and had transmitted this information to the colonial office and to the officials of the Hudson's Bay Company in London. In his letters to the home authorities there is constant recurrence to the danger to be apprehended from trouble between the Indians and whites, in case of large numbers of the latter coming into the country; to the necessity for keeping order and the need of a military force for that purpose; and to the requirement, consequently, of adequate revenue from some quarter.[3] Even before the coming of the miners in large numbers, on December 28th, 1857, Mr. Douglas issued a proclamation (which he caused to be published in the newspapers of Oregon and Washington), in which he asserted that "by Law all mines of Gold and all Gold in its natural state of deposit within the Districts of Frazer, River, and of Thompson River, commonly known as the Quaatlan, Couteau, or Shewshap countries, whether on the lands of the Queen or any of Her Majesty's subjects, belong to the Crown". All persons were forbidden to search, dig, or take gold without being duly authorized by "Her Majesty's Colonial Government"; such authorization (announced in "Regulations" issued the next day) was to be conferred by license obtainable at Victoria and was dependent upon the payment of twenty-one shillings per month.[4]

In asserting the ownership in the Crown of precious metals whether found in Crown lands or in those privately owned, Mr. Douglas was acting in conformity to English law and precedent, but in contrast to the customs which held sway in the American

---

[3] Copies of a number of these letters are printed in Cornwallis, *The New El Dorado*, pp. 341-368.

[4] *British Columbia Proclamations*, pp. 1-8. So late as May 8, 1858, however, this system had not come into operation. (Dispatch to Right Hon. Henry Labouchere, May 8, 1858). In June, however, the requirements were decisively put in force. At Victoria there was a long line of men at the Fort to obtain licences and H. B. M's steamer Satellite was stationed at the mouth of the Fraser with orders to allow no one to proceed up river without a license. On one occasion some fifty passengers, mostly Irishmen, on board the American steamer Surprise, refused to take out licenses, but were cowed by a file of marines. (Victoria *Gazette*, June 30, 1858). Still, miners who came overland evaded the license, and few paid for more than one month. (De Groot, *Br. Col.,: Its Condition and Prospects*, p. 23.)

territories. The principle on which the American miners acted was expressed by Governor Stevens when, in protesting against the British tax, he wrote: "in the absence of positive law prohibiting such occupation and use, it is believed to be the natural right of every man who enters a totally unoccupied country to cut timber and wood, to consume the fruits of the earth, and gather all the products of the soil, which have not before been appropriated".[5]

The authority of Mr. Douglas for issuing the above proclamation and regulations, indeed, was questionable. The form used in making the proclamation was "By His Excellency James Douglas, Governor and Commander-in-Chief of the Colony of Vancouver's Island and its dependencies, and Vice Admiral of the same, etc." Douglas himself wrote on this point: "My authority for issuing that proclamation, seeing that it refers to certain districts of continental America, which are not strictly speaking within the jurisdiction of this Government, may perhaps be called in question; and I trust that the motives which have influenced me on this occasion, and the fact of my being invested with authority over the premises of the Hudson's Bay Company, and the only authority commissioned by her Majesty's Government within reach, will plead my excuse. Moreover, should her Majesty's Government not deem it advisable to enforce the rights of the Crown, as set forth in the proclamation, it may be allowed to fall to the ground and become a mere dead letter."[6] Her Majesty's Government, however, through Sir E. Bulwer Lytton approved the course of Douglas "in asserting both the dominion of the Crown over this region, and the right of the Crown over the precious metals."[7]

Another proclamation, however, was distinctly disallowed by the home Government, and was bitterly assailed by many persons in the colony and in the American territories. This was the proclamation of May 8, 1858, heretofore discussed, which

---

[5] Letters from Isaac I. Stevens, Congressional Delegate from Washington Territory, to Hon. Lewis Cass, Secretary of State, July 21, 1858, found in Cornwallis, *New El Dorado*, pp. 322-337.

[6] Douglas to Labouchere, Dec. 29, 1857, Cornwallis, *New El Dorado*, p. 348-9.

[7] Secretary Sir E. Bulwer Lytton to Governor Douglas, July 1, 1858, id., p. 366-7.

forbade trade and navigation on the Fraser River except on sufferance of the Hudson's Bay Company. It was claimed that the miners were deprived of supplies badly needed, that the whole mining population was forced to pay toll, that the profits from furnishing supplies from California, Oregon, and Washintgon would be diverted to the coffers of the company, and that trade with London would be stifled.[8] Indeed, the restrictions sought to be imposed were sufficiently rigorous, especially when contrasted with the free-for-all attitude in the American territories. A sufferance for canoes cost six dollars, and for larger vessels twelve; the use of any unoccupied Crown land by the erection of a temporary building or tent for the purpose of carrying on trade, thirty shillings per month, and licenses for selling liquors, one hundred to one hundred twenty pounds per annum. In defense of his course the governor claimed that the Hudson's Bay Company were not accountable for the prohibitions, but the customs-law of Great Britian, in accordance with which all persons not nationals were excluded from trade on the Fraser River.[9]

In fact there was a tangle of interests at this time, and Governor Douglas, standing at the central point of the swift whirl of events and somewhat apprehensive of the American advance, with strong feeling of loyalty to the great company for whose interests he had so long planned and toiled, yet with some promptings of imperialism and with growing ambition for distinction in the Colonial Service,—by no means, indeed, unmindful of the welfare of the miners,—pursued a conservative and tentative course. All legislation for British Columbia up to the formal announcement (in November, 1858) of the annulment of the Hudson's Bay Company's License to Trade and of the establishment of the new government was exigent and temporary. On the whole, British Columbia may be counted fortunate that there was available in her hurried birth throes at the time of a great mining rush a man who knew thoroughly the country, who was intimately acquainted with the Indians and with Indian

---

[8] See Steven's letter to Secretary Cass, Cornwallis, *New El Dorado*, p. 336; also, for various points of view consult id., pp. 392–400.
[9] *British Columbia Proclamations*, p. 7.

habits, and who was trained in a great administrative system—a man masterful and firm (if at times, perhaps, mistakenly so) and at any rate, a man who applied himself with diligence and devotion and thoughtfulness to a great work. The British colonial administration system did not always have at hand men of the calibre of Douglas, and so, in any comparison of the governmental systems north and south of the Line, it is at least fair to make allowance for the happy coincidence, in the case of British Columbia, of a formative time and a superior leader.

The home government was not dilatory in taking the necessary steps for the establishment of government in "certain wild and unoccupied territories on the northwest coast of North America, commonly known by the designation of New Caledonia." The act to provide for the government of British Columbia was passed August 2, 1858. In the preamble it was declared that "it is desirable to make some temporary provision for the civil government of such territories, until permanent settlements shall be thereupon established, and the number of colonists increased". The most important clause was that which empowered Her Majesty by orders in council "to make, ordain and establish, and (subject to such conditions or restrictions as to her shall seem meet) to authorize and empower such officer as she may from time to time appoint as Governor of British Columbia, to make provision for the administration of justice therein, and generally to make, ordain, and establish all such laws, institutions, and ordinances as may be necessary for the peace, order and good government of her Majesty's subjects and others therein", provided that all such orders in council, and all laws and ordinances, "shall be laid before both Houses of Parliament as soon as conveniently may be after the making and enactment thereof respectively." It was to be lawful for her Majesty, whenever she might judge it convenient by an order in council to empower the governor to constitute a legislature to be composed of a Council or Council and Assembly, "to be composed of such and so many persons, and to be appointed or elected in such manner and for such periods, and subject to such regulations, as to her Majesty may seem expedient". Appeals in civil suits might be taken to her Majesty in council in the same manner as suits in Canada, but subject to such further regulations as her Majesty, with the advice of the Privy Council, might enact. No part of the colony of Vancouver Island was to be comprised within the new colony, but on the reception of an address from the two houses of the legislature of Vancouver's Island, her Majesty might annex that colony to British Columbia. The act was to continue in force until the end of the then next session of parliament.[10]

Some interesting features are found in the debates in parliament upon this act. There was very considerable hostility shown towards the Hudson's Bay Company and, therewith, adverse criticism of Governor Douglas. Some members showed comprehension of the trials of a young mining community; as, for example, Mr. Roebuck, who declared his belief that lynch law really might be a beneficial institution. Mr. Gladstone somewhat passionately protested against the mode of founding a colony as outlined in the act, for it allowed too autocratic power, he asserted, to the Crown and to the governor of the colony. Sir E. Bulwer Lytton in defense said that the immediate object was to establish temporary law and order; and added that, besides the promising outlook in gold mining, "more national, if less exciting, hopes of the importance of the colony rest upon its other resources * * * and upon the influence of its magnificent situation upon the ripening grandeur of British North America."[11]

The position of governor was conferred upon Mr. Douglas on strict condition of his giving up all connection with the Hudson's Bay Company; but he still continued to be governor of Vancouver Island. Matthew Bailie Begbie was appointed Judge of the Supreme Court of British Columbia, and other officials were named by the Crown for the positions of Colonial Secretary, Treasurer, Attorney General, Commissioner of Lands and Surveyor General, Collector of Customs, Chief Inspector of Police, Register General and Harbor Master.[12] The new colony was

---

[10] *British State Papers*, 1858-9, pp. 739-42; a copy of the Act is found also in Cornwallis, *New El Dorado*, pp. 317-22.
[11] Hansard, *Parliamentary Debates*, pp. 1096-1121 and 1762-1770.
[12] The London *Times*, March 24, 1859; *British Columbia Proclamations*, p 151.

formally declared at Langley, November 19, 1858. Proclamations were issued at the same time which declared English law in force in British Columbia and which indemnified the governor for previous acts.[13]

Before we proceed to discuss the main features of the administration of Governor Douglas, it may be well to make some inquiry as to his personality. In stature above six feet and well-proportioned, he exhibited in his bearing a certain stateliness, tinged, perhaps, with self consciousness. His face was clear-cut, though at this period weather-beaten, and his features suggested most prominently intellectuality, determination, and quickness of action. His manner was generally austere, but on occasion agreeable and even jolly. Both by training and temperament he was masterful, and at times autocratic and arbitrary.[14] But he was a just man, and on the whole managed to get along well with the miners and to command their respect and a measure of their affection.[15] He worked hard, and even hostile critics admitted that he possessed "considerable energy, with some ability and power of organization." Though these critics constantly harp on the idea that he was unfit for office because of having "lived beyond the pale of civilized life for more than thirty years", they concede that he was "not indifferent to mental culture," and that since becoming governor "he has read hard for information."[16]

One of the best ways by which to get a just view of the real

---

[13] *British Columbia Proclamations*, pp. 23-27.

[14] In the San Juan affair, for example, the conduct of Douglas was precipitate and arbitrary, most serious consequences were averted mainly through the moderation of the officers of the British fleet. Governor Douglas had given Captain Hornby authority to prevent the landing of the United States troops and the erection of military works See letter to Cap Hornby, *Correspondence Book*, MS., 2nd of Aug 1859. Again, writing to Mr. Chartres Brew concerning the payment of miners' licenses the Governor wrote, "The miners must be prepared with coin to pay their dues when demanded. The time of the officers cannot be taken up in weighing out small portions of gold dust."—*Miscel. Letters*, MS, Vol. I, p. 215.

[15] "The moral habit of the man was justice",—Letter of Mr. G. M. Sproat to Mr. E. O. L. Scholefield; "The boys all thought a good deal of him",—*Reminiscences* of Wm. Stout, MS.

[16] Macfie, *Van Id. and Br. Col.*, pp. 363-95, McDonald, *Br. Col and Van, Id.*, p. 272. A friendly observer wrote that "it seems astonishing how he gets through his work; but, as he sticks close, at it early and late, I suppose an active life suits him."—The London *Times*, Jan. 19, 1859.

character of Governor Douglas is by the perusal of the letters in his Correspondence Book, 1859–1864, which is in the provincial archives at Victoria. These letters were, for the most part, informal, many of them being written to friends. Humor is lacking in them, though there is an occasional touch of sarcasm. But there is in them no trace of lamentation, conceit, maliciousness, or unmanliness. They show constant courtesy, very considerable thoughtfulness and kindliness, rather wide perspective, and some capacity for enthusiasm, together with a measure of characteristic pompousness; and, in general, they are sincere, vigorous, wholesome. While for the composition of his letters he may have at times relied upon others, often he wrote them himself, and he had command of plain, direct English.[17] There was no doubt of the whole-hearted devotion of Governor Douglas to his work: "I cannot express," he wrote near the close of his official career, "the interest I feel in the welfare of these colonies, they have for years been the objects of my tenderest care. Every step in the process of construction has been anxiously studied".[18] The estimate of Governor Douglas's work by the Imperial Government was shown by his being created Companion of the Bath and later raised to be Knight Commander of the Bath.

Through most of the career of Sir James Douglas in the service of the Crown, however, he encountered much obloquy and opposition. This was, in part, due to the formation in Victoria of a factious opposition party, headed by James Cooper, Harbour master of Victoria, and Amor De Cosmos, editor of the British Colonist; in part, to a real grievance of the people of British Columbia.[19]

---

[17] For example in a letter, apparently of his own composition, he wrote to a magistrate: "I must enjoin upon you and all other magistrates in British Columbia to permit no relaxation in the laws of the land; let their provisions be rigidly enforced and all the powers of justice arrayed against offenders in order that rogues and vagabonds of every degree especially thieves and gamblers may be rooted out of the country".—Letter to Mr. Bevis, *Miscl. Letters*, MS., Vol. I, p 63. Mr. G. M. Sproat says that he had seen Douglas revise the drafts of some of his letters five or six times.—Note from Judge F. W. Howay.

[18] Letter to Mr. Good, *Correspondence Book*, Dec. 10, 1863.

[19] De Cosmos' own account of his warfare against Douglas carries rather a flippant tone. He was a native of Nova Scotia who had gone to California, and from there "sick and tired of the heat of the interior," had come to

The people of that colony (whose demands were voiced, in particular, by New Westminster), disliked to be ruled by a Governor who resided most of the time at Victoria and whose interests, they thought, would lead him to favor the merchants of Victoria at the expense of British Columbia.[20] Moreover, it was asserted that a free British people were under an autocratic rule and were refused representative institutions—how different, they said, was the condition in the American territories— and that Governor Douglas desired to perpetuate this state of affairs. The Governor believed that representative government was not feasible, until the British element in the colony would become stronger.[21] Moreover he was probably not averse to autocratic rule. "I, James Douglas" was prominent at the heads of his proclamations. His powers, indeed, were very extensive: he issued a proclamation enabling the Governor to convey Crown lands and followed that by an ordinance on the same subject; the full power of taxation was in his hands, and he raised large sums; he incurred an indebtedness of more than half a million dollars; and he promulgated a code of laws for the mining regions, and created an effective administration system for carrying it into effect.[22] While there was danger of abuse in such powers if exercised unworthily, and while Governor Douglas persisted, perhaps, somewhat too long in postponing representative institutions, yet some sound arguments may be adduced in defense of such a system for newly-formed mining communities, as he administered. A thoughtful observer wrote as follows concerning conditions in the mining com-

---

Victoria. He had been but few months in Victoria when he prepared a petition for the removal of Governor Douglas on the ground that he was obnoxious to the people and that in him the Hudson's Bay Company interests predominated, and he obtained for the petition one hundred seventeen names. "That agitation", says De Cosmos, "went on from year to year. It did not have any effect."—De Cosmos, *Governments of British Columbia*. MS.

[20] See supra, p. 113. Indeed it did seem strange for the Governor of British Columbia to issue a proclamation for legalizing acts of His Honor Chief Justice Begbie, while the latter was in Victoria. *British Columbia Proclamations*, p. 32.

[21] *British Columbian*, Feb. 28, 1861.

[22] *British Columbia Proclamations*, pp. 55, 67, 121, 129, 139, and 142. One extreme form of tax was that of $5 upon every load of a pack animal proceeding to the mines; such an outcry was raised against this tax both by the miners and by the merchants of Victoria, that it was never put into force, *Id.*, p. 73; San Francisco *Daily Bulletin*, Apr. 2, 1860.

munities south of the Line: "The people east of the Cascades are wanting in some of the most essential elements and conditions for a successful representative government. They are mostly scattered about in mining camps without families or any of the conservative influences of home, or on the road going to and fro in search of better luck. The majority of them are in no way attached to the soil, and may be in Cariboo or Australia a year hence. Yet of all people, they have most need of a government—not the complex and elegant machinery of a representative one, commencing with a primary meeting and ending in a legislative enactment a year afterwards, but a simple executive government with ample power for emergencies and a somewhat summary method."[23] The unprejudiced historian may, perhaps, wisely sum up the matter in the words of one, who, while naturally favoring Governor Douglas, yet presents reasonable considerations: "The necessity of a representative government has been urged upon arguments which, however legitimate in themselves, become fallacious under certain circumstances. Indeed, it is difficult to perceive how, with hastily accumulated population, chiefly consisting of foreigners of many nationalities, it would have been possible to organize a system of representation adequate to the end in view. It may further be questioned whether any purely representative government, hastily convened, could have accomplished so speedily, and it has proved judiciously, that which has been effected under a system, which, if less accordant with our constitutional ideas, has certainly in the present case, answered the desired end."[24]

One fact, at any rate, stands out prominently in any comparison between the executive government of British Columbia and those formed on the representative principle in the American territories: namely, that in British Columbia, crime was promptly and justly dealt with, and that there never was a lynching nor a vigilante committee, nor occasion for either; while in the American Territories there was scarcely one important camp which did not have some "statistics of blood" and where there

---
[23] Correspondent of San Francisco *Daily Bulletin*, June 30, 1863.
[24] Anderson, Alexander Caulfield, *History of the Northwest Coast*, MS.

was not some sort of lynching or some form of a vigilante committee.[25] Not that there were no murders in British Columbia, for there were such occasionally, and criminals sometimes escaped across the border; but generally on the committing of a crime a magistrate was soon on the spot, and instant measures were taken for bringing culprits to justice without delay and without interference of the people. It is safe to say, I think, that order was as well kept and law as well administered in British Columbia during the mining rushes, as in any older community having good law and order. It is fair, on the other hand, to remember that the United States was in the midst of a trying war, and that the best administrators of the northwest had been withdrawn for service in the war, but still the difference is so pronounced as to suggest that it arose mainly from the differences between the systems of government in the two regions. There was no essential difference in the characteristics of the mining populations; Cariboo in the United States would have been an ideal field for road-agents and vigilante committies, and Kootenay was near the border. But in British Columbia there was Law, and an Executive, and a Chief Justice, and a Magistracy that expected obedience, and the mining population rendered obedience willingly.

Of all the forces that in the mining camps of British Columbia made for law and order none was more potent than the work of His Honor, Matthew Baillie Begbie, Judge of the Supreme Court. Something of the character of the man we catch in a letter to Judge Begbie from Governor Douglas,—written near the close of the latter's term of office,—which does honor to both men: "I may truly say that my official intercourse with you has been profitable and of the most agreeable character, and when differences of opinion have arisen, they never gave rise to asperity of feeling or language, being I am persuaded in every case the result of honest conviction and of a sincere desire to promote the public good."[26] Active, indefatigable, decisive, yet rea-

---

[25] One Instance of a lynching in British Columbia is narrated by Johnson, *Very Far West Indeed;* but this author, as before mentioned (p. 52, note), needs corroboration, and in this instance the story is without any corroboration whatever.

[26] *Correspondence Book,* Oct. 28, 1863, MS.

sonable, quick to seize on the most telling mode of punishment, the judge traversed the great highways and the rough trails, holding his assizes in every important town, now sentencing a Chinaman to imprisonment for assaulting another, now cautioning an Indian "very seriously" and sentencing another to have his hair cut off, again fining heavily a white man for selling liquor to Indians or giving judgment in some mining dispute. Untrammeled by those niceties of legal verbiage which, in the United States, so often become the mumbo-jumboes of the lawyers, he dispensed a robust and honest justice which made him a terror to evildoers and, in the eyes of the law-abiding, a worthy representative of a great governing race.[27]

In respect to fostering development of the country, on the other hand, the American territorial system contrasted favorably with the English colonial system as applied in British Columbia. The Imperial Government was willing to furnish protection from outside powers, but insisted that the colony from the start should be self-supporting with respect to internal affairs. Lytton repeatedly wrote to Douglas that the colony must not look to the mother-country for financial help; such help would "interfere with the healthy action by which a new community provides, step by step, for its own requirements. It is on the character of the inhabitants that we must rest our hopes for the land we redeem from the wilderness."[28] An English author of the time commented on this policy as follows: "The contrast between the United States and England in caring for the growth of new territories is decidedly unfavorable to the latter, England in defining land to be erected into a colony and passing an act of parliament to that effect, leaves to the settlers, however few and impotent they may be, the task of establishing leading communications, executing surveys, and completing postal arrangements. If the population be unequal to these undertakings, they must be postponed till colonial finances become capable of sustaining them. The Federal Government, on

---

[27] Some of the items of this characterization are drawn from the old Police Record Book from Hope, which His Honour, Judge Frederick W. Howay, of New Westminster, permitted me to use.

[28] Quoted by Macfie, *Van. Id. and Br. Col.*, p. 509.

the other hand, assumes the responsibility of giving effect to all works of magnitude necessary to bring an infant settlement to maturity, and indemnifies itself for the outlay incurred, by mortgaging the lands and the revenues derivable from the customs and other territorial sources." "It invariably turns out that works urgent and useful, thus undertaken, are speedily made to defray the cost of construction. The Americans have learned that whatever contributes to augment national wealth by developing the resources of new territory is not inconsistent with public economy."[29] "The English," wrote General Harney on a visit to Victoria in 1859, "cannot colonize successfully so near our people; they are too exacting."[30] The sentiment in favor of annexation to the United States, which was at times quite apparent in British Columbia during the colonial period, was in part due, probably, to the conviction that the colony would be more prosperous as a territory. Such a colony as British Columbia, as a matter of fact, had very different relations with the mother country, as compared with those existing between an American territory and the Federal Government: the territory was directly dependent upon the central government, and differentiation between the activities and functions of that government and those local to the territory is difficult to trace clearly; but the government of the British Colony had powers and, correspondingly, responsibilities in internal affairs nearly those of a nation (as, for example, the collection of customs and the establishment of a postal system) and the operations of the central power and those of the colonial administration are easily distinguishable.

The instrument which the Imperial Government had ever at hand for the protection of the infant colony was the fleet, but the fleet, in reality, afforded something more than protection against outside powers. One of Her Majesty's vessels, as we have before mentioned, was stationed at the mouth of the Fraser to enforce the collection of licenses from the miners. The marines were available for the prompt aid in case of any serious outbreak,—how effective that aid might be was apparent in

---
[29] Macfie, *Van. Id. and Br. Col.*, pp. 511-12.
[30] Thirty-sixth Cong., 2 sess., Sen. Doc., 2 No. 2, p. 109.

the case of the so-called McGowan riot at Hill's Bar. Moreover, besides support to the civil authority, other advantages were derived from the presence of vessels of the fleet, though these applied most directly to Victoria. In the first place, there was the expenditure of money in the colony. Again, "the security given by the presence or proximity of a strong naval force inspires confidence in legislation, in Government, in all the varied interests of life, in short; while to the success of commerce this security is peculiarly essential." Then, too, "the good effects on social life of friendly intercourse with so many educated men, possessing the manners and habits of gentlemen, as compose the body of officers in a squadron, need only to be mentioned to be understood." [31]

In the process of shaping forms of government both north and south of the Line there was, in one respect, an interesting and important similarity. Just as Iowa copied her forms of law and administration in part from New York, and Idaho and Montana imitated California and Nevada, so British Columbia derived perhaps the most important portion of her law and administrative system—that having to do with mines— from Australia and New Zealand. Both the colony and the territories, moreover, showed some preference for the latest models; in the case of the territories, for that of Nevada, in that of British Columbia for New Zealand. The derivation of the British Columbia code is clearly revealed in a letter of Governor Douglas. August sixth, 1860, to Sir Henry Barkly, K. C., Governor of the Colony of Victoria, which reads as follows: "I have the honor to acknowledge the receipt of your Excellency's Despatch of the 4th of May, 1859, date Melbourne, Victoria, No. 9, together with ample stores of information which you have been kind enough to enclose.

"It was found imperatively necessary to proceed to legislation here, with as little delay as possible. Accordingly, therefore, before the arrival of the full and minute particulars which your Excellency has so kindly procured and arranged, a code of Laws was published on the 31st of August last, and

---

[31] The London *Times*, Aug. 14, 1863.

the 7th of September last, a few further rules and regulations being added on the 6th of January last. I have the honor to enclose copies.

"It will be apparent to your Excellency that these have been framed on the experience of the Australian Colonies, and principally on that of Victoria. *The precedent chiefly followed was the New Zealand Code, which in fact had, equally with this Colony, the benefit of the previous legislation in Victoria and New South Wales.*[32] And in addition to the New Zealand Code, of which a copy had been procured, portions of the Codes in Victoria and New South Wales were also consulted, although only portions and those not of the latest dates were procurable."[33]

Another portion of this illuminating letter reveals a pride in law and order on the part of the English administrators scarcely characteristic of American territorial governors. It is as follows: "I most sincerely congratulate your Excellency upon the condition of the Criminal Calendars in Victoria to which you refer. It is with heart-felt satisfaction that I can for my part refer to those in British Columbia, where the only two serious offences committed by white men since the proclamation of the Colony (19th Nov., 1858) have been one burglary in which the criminals were seized and delivered up to the regular authorities by the inhabitants; and one murder committed at Lytton about a month ago, in which there is reason to believe that the criminal immediately escaped beyond the frontier. The only other cases have been a few petty thefts.

"There are seven Justices of the Peace and about fifteen constables in the entire Colony, scattered over a difficult country, about five hundred miles in length.

"I venture to think that such a state of circumstances speaks volumes for the readiness with which a politically disaffected population acknowledges the general good tendency of the English Law; and I submit that the very heterogeneous and roving population of British Columbia may claim to be at least on a par with that of the Victoria Gold Fields."[34]

---
[32] Italics not in MS.
[33] *Correspondence Book*, MS., pp. 44–47.
[34] *Id.*

The most important administrative feature of the system derived as above was the constitution of gold commissioners for the mining regions. There were no officials such as these in the United States, although the need for them was recognized, particularly for the purpose of gathering reliable data.[35] The general outline of the system, as at first conceived, included the appointment of a gold commissioner who was to have entire supervision over all the gold fields, including the direction of assistant gold commissioners in the various districts; but this central office seems early to have lapsed.[36] The subordinates in the field reported directly to the governor or to the colonial secretary, and they were styled gold commissioners. These commissioners were appointed to office and assigned to their districts by the governor. The system, as finally worked out, included the division of the mining regions into a few large districts and the assignment to each district of a gold commissioner, who was closely dependent upon and responsible to the central authority.

The powers of a gold commissioner within his district were great. Save for right of appeal to the supreme court in certain cases, subordination to the governor, and in districts where mining boards were constituted some limitation of activities, his authority was absolute.[37] In cases and suits "the gold commissioner alone, without a jury, shall be the sole judge of law and fact;" and he had power to compel attendance of witnesses and production of documents.[38] In contrast to legal procedure in the American territories, "it shall not be necessary for the

---

[35] It was felt in the United States, however, that the system was not exactly "adapted to our mineral regions, or to the habits and customs of our people". Still, "A permanent system like this, established upon a somewhat different basis, is greatly needed in our country."—J. Ross Brown, *Mineral Resources of the United States*, 1867, p. 8. But no such system was put into operation in the United States.

[36] Mr. Chartres Brew was appointed first general Gold Commissioner of British Columbia. His powers were defined in a communication which is found in *Miscl. Letters*, 1, 72-74, MS. Mr. Brew was consulted in working out the beginnings of this mining law of British Columbia. *Letters of Douglas to Brew, Id.* 1, pp. 102-105, and 123.

[37] The fame of the absolute powers and summary methods of the Gold Commissioners of British Columbia was well spread in the mining camps south of the Line, and "hard cases" avoided going there. In the eyes of American miners the Gold Commissioners had the powers of a Czar. Remarks of Judge W. Y. Pemberton of Helena.

[38] *The Gold Fields Act of 1859*, clause 22 and 23.

gold commissioner in any proceedings before him to follow any set forms, provided that the substance of the things done and to be done be therein expressed; nor shall any proceedings before any gold commissioner be liable to be set aside for any want of form, so long as matters of substance have not been omitted."[39] On appeal to the supreme court, "no objection shall be allowed to the conviction on any matter of form or insufficiency of statement, provided it shall appear to the said supreme court that the defendant has been sufficiently informed of the charge to be made against him, and that the conviction was proper on the merits of the case."[40] On complaint of wrongful encroachment ("jumping a claim") the gold commissioner was to "proceed forthwith" to the place of alleged encroachment, "and thereafter, on view of the premises and on such evidence as to such gold commissioner shall seem sufficient," shall "hear and determine the dispute in a summary way," * * * and whether all parties in difference shall appear or not, and in a summary way cause such encroachment to be abated, and to restore to the person who shall be entitled thereto full possession of the claim, ditch or other matter encroached upon."[41] In the gold commissioner of British Columbia, in fact, were centered the powers of the American mining camp and of a British magistrate. He recorded all claims, assessed all damages, and marked out plots for gardening purposes; he constituted mining boards and might fill vacancies; he had jurisdiction over all disputes as to titles, boundaries and contracts, whether relating to mines, bed rock flumes, or mining drains; he had power to try persons for breach of the rules and regulations of the Governor's Proclamation; and he had all the authority and jurisdiction of a justice of the peace.[42]

The duties and responsibilities of the gold commissioner were even more multifarious than his powers would indicate. The "pressing calls of the public service," in the "early condition

---

[39] *Id*, 24
[40] *Id.*, 29.
[41] *Id.*, XXVI.
[42] A summary of the powers of the Gold Commissioner in British Columbia may be found in Park, Joseph, *A Practical View of the Mining Laws of British Columbia*, pp 46-50.

of the colony, before institutions are formed and Departments fully organized," "necessitated that each officer be a "General Government Agent" ready to "afford his assistance in every way possible."[43] The gold commissioner might be required to see to the mail, try a man for allowing a pig to trespass, take charge of a dead man's effects, see that a sick man was taken care of, recover a stolen horse, fine a drunken Chinaman, and contract for large expenditures on the roads. Very careful and detailed reports were to be made monthly. His Excellency wanted to know of Mr. O'Reilly when the latter was stationed at Ft. Hope the number of miners at work on each bar, their average earnings, the discovery of any new mining ground, the state of trade, the price of provisions, the arrival or exodus of miners, and general information.[44] All items of expenditure were reported down to the smallest details and, also, all receipts. Elaborate printed forms for reports were furnished to the gold commissioners, and they were expected to use official stationery even when stationed in remote Cariboo. The communications of the officials, other than tabulations, were expressed in clear, good English, with a noteworthy lack of slang, but with some lapses in punctuation. As before remarked, these reports of the gold commissioners constitute one of the most valuable sources for the mining history of British Columbia.

While the gold commissioners were central factors in the government of the mining communities of British Columbia, yet there were the beginnings of local popular government in the constitution of mining boards. Upon the petition of one hundred and one registered free miners in any district, and due authentication by the gold commissioner of the district, the governor might direct the commissioner to constitute a local board. The board consisted of six to twelve members (according to population), and the members were elected by the votes of the registered free miners of three months' standing. It is interesting

---

[43] Letters of Douglas to Hicks, Sanders, and O'Reilly, *Miscl. Letters*, MS. I, pp. 7, 160, 185. The concentration of offices in one person was carried much farther than in the States. Thus Mr. O'Reilly besides being Gold Commissioner was High Sheriff of British Columbia. Mr. Chartres Brew was Chief Inspector of Police.

[44] Letter to P. O'Reilly, Apr. 7, 1860, MS.

to notice that voting was not limited to nationals. The mining board had power to make by-laws and to alter and repeal existing by-laws "regulating size of claims and sluices, mode in which claims may be registered, worked, held and forfeited, and all other matters in the district. *Provided that none shall have force unless and until approved by the Governor.*"[45] Acts of the mining boards were to be valid, "notwithstanding any informality or irregularity in the mode of election, or of the meeting of such mining board, or in the passing of any such acts." It was a characteristic principle of the administrative system of British Columbia, that regulations were so shaped as to incite miners to obey the statutes and the laws. This attitude of expectancy, if I may so phrase it—an attitude lacking in the States—is illustrated in the requirement that, if any member of a mining board should cease to be a free registered miner in the district, "or shall be convicted of any misdemeanor or felony, or of any assault, being armed with a lethal weapon or of any willful and malicious contravention of this act, or of any bylaw in force in his district, he shall *ipso facto* vacate his seat in each case."[46]

Another feature of the administrative machinery of British Columbia, unknown in the American territories, was the gold escort. The escort was designed to facilitate the carriage of gold from the mining regions, and to secure safety, while at the same time it was thought the display of a disciplined and uniformed force would have a salutary effect. The escort was given a semi-military organization, and consisted of a superintendent, first and second officers, and a dozen or more men.[47] Its establishment seems to have been urged more by merchants of Victoria and of Hope and Yale than by the miners. It was or-

---

[45] Italics are mine. Moreover, the Gold Commissioner had a veto power upon the resolutions of a Mining Board, but this might be overcome by a vote of two thirds of the members.

[46] *Gold Fields Act of 1859*, clauses XXIX to XXXVIII. I have treated of the Mining Boards as outlined in this act, though there were some slight modifications by Governor Douglas in the *Gold Fields Act of 1864*. I have not sought to trace their later development.

[47] *General Rules and Regulations for the Guidance of the Officer in Command of the Gold Escort*, June 4 1863, MS; also *Journal of Daily Proceedings of the Gold Escort first trip*, 1863.

ganized several summers, but it was not very successful because the government did not guarantee safe delivery, merchants and -packers had their own facilities, and claim owners could hire guards.[48] The escort appears to have been inferior in efficiency to the private express companies which operated everywhere through the mining regions south of the Line.[49]

Passing, now, from the mechanism of administration as revealed in gold commissioners, mining boards and the gold escort to the content of mining law, we find one class of persons, and only one, which was legally recognized as having the right to mine under the British Columbia code. These were the free miners. A free miner was a "person named in and lawfully possessed of an existing valid free miners' certificate." A free miner's certificate was in the following form:

BRITISH COLUMBIA.

Free Miner's Certificate.

Date   No.

Not transferable.

Valid for one year.

This is to certify that A. B. of .... has paid me this day the sum of one pound sterling, and is entitled to all the rights and privileges of a free miner for one year from the date hereof.

(Countersigned A. B.)   (Signed) G. B.
Signature of free miner.

                         Chief Gold Commissioner, or assistant Gold Commissioner or Justice of the Peace, as the case may be.

Every free miner during the term of his certificate had the right to "enter on and mine the waste lands of the Crown, not lawfully occupied by any other person." He might then become a

---

[48] Report of P. O Reilly, July 1863, MS.
[49] To a less degree, also, in British Columbia.

registered free miner, "entitled in his own right to any claim, lease of auriferous earth, ditch or water privilege."[50] He now, moreover, acquired other rights; he might vote for members of the mining board or become a member of that board; and, in case of his death, his claim could not be occupied by another for non-representation, but it might be kept afoot by the gold commissioner or sold for the benefit of the heirs. But miners not possessing valid certificates had no rights, as miners, whatever. If the claim of such an one were "jumped" by one possessing a certificate, the gold commissioner would recognize the title of the intruder; in case of dispute the uncertificated miner had no standing in court; he could hope for no lease of mining ground, nor could he become a member of a mining co-partnership or of a bed-rock flume company; and he was not entitled to receive water from a ditch (and water was indispensable for mining operations). Lists of all free miners in a district were kept by the gold commissioners, and revised quarterly; also, the names of those legally entitled to work claims were to be conspicuously posted by the gold commissioner on each claim.[51] By this system of licenses very effective control over the miners was secured by the Government.

We shall not attempt a study in detail of the ordinances in accordance with which the free miners of British Columbia worked, but certain of these laws are of special interest in illustrating the regulated relations of the individual miner to the society of which he was a part.

It was lawful for any gold commissioner to mark out for the use of any free registered miner in his district land not exceeding five acres, for a garden plot or residence. Such plots (but not for more than one acre) might also be marked out for any

---

[50] "The amount of interest which a free miner has in a claim, save as against Her Majesty, shall be deemed a chattel interest equivalent to a lease for a year, renewable at the end of the first and every subsequent year, subject to the conditions as to forfeiture, working, representation, registration and otherwise for the time being in force with respect to such claim or interest under any law or rule regulating the same, Provided: that every forfeiture under any such law or rule shall be absolute, any rule of law or equity to the contrary notwithstanding." *Gold Fields' Act, 1864*, clause 45.

[51] The above paragraph is based on the *Gold Field's Acts* of 1859 and of 1864, and on the *Rules and Regulations for the Working of Gold Mines, Issued in Conformity with the Gold Fields' Act, 1859*.

one intending to carry on temporary trade. But rights to such plots were valid only for so long as the miner was a "registered free miner of the district", and for so long as the trader had all license dues paid up. The British Columbia government gave no countenance to "squatting"; land occupation of all sorts was to be under some legal sanction. Moreover, the interests of the community were to be guarded: in staking out plots of land for gardening and residential purposes the gold commissioner "is to keep in view the general interests of all the miners in that locality, the general principle being that every garden benefits indirectly that whole locality, and also that the earlier application is to be preferred; but where the eligible plots of land are few, or of scanty dimensions, and especially where they are themselves auriferous, it may be injudicious that the whole or the greater part should fall into the hands of one or two persons."[52]

The very important matter of ditch or water privileges was carefully regulated. Any person desiring exclusive privileges of this nature was required to make application to the gold commissioner, and to state full details, including the amount of water to be used and, if the water was to be sold, the price proposed. Rent was to be paid at the rate of one day's receipts per month. Effort was made to guard against waste and monopoly; "If any person shall refuse or neglect," said the statute, "to take within the time mentioned in the application, or within an extension of time at the discretion of the Gold Commissioner the whole of the water applied for, he shall be entitled only to the quantity actually taken by him." Moreover, "every owner of a ditch or water privilege shall be bound to take all reasonable means for utilizing the water granted to and taken by him, and if any owner shall wilfully take and waste any unreasonable quantity of water, he shall be charged with the full rent, as if he had sold the same at a full price. And it shall be lawful for the Gold Commissioner, if such offense be persisted in, to declare all rights to the water forfeited." Finally, "the owner of any ditch or water privilege shall be bound to supply

---

[52] *Gold Fields' Act*, 1859, clauses XXVII and XXVIII; *Rules and Regulations in Conformity with Gold Fields' Act* 1859, clause XVII.

water to all applicants, being free miners, in a fair proportion, and shall not demand more from one person than from another."[53]

There were provisions, likewise, against obstructions and dangerous works. In no case were "deads or leavings, forkings from sluices, waste dirt, large stones or tailings to be allowed to accumulate so as to obstruct the natural course" of a stream, and free miners were not to obstruct a bed-rock flume by rocks or boulders "or otherwise unnecessarily." Danger to the public was to be guarded against; upon complaint, gold commissioners were empowered "to order all mining works to be carried out in such manner as he shall think necessary for the safety of the public, or the protection of their rights, or of the interest of adjoining or affected claims, and to cause abandoned works to be filled or guarded." Any one who has traversed some of the gulches south of the Line which were worked by old-time miners, and has seen unguarded shafts yawning twenty or thirty feet deep within a few yards of a public highway, will realize the advisability of the latter requirement.

Public interests were guarded, also, in the granting of leases. Leases were to be granted for a term of not more than ten years and they were applicable to not more than ten acres of alluvial soil, one-half mile of unworked quartz, or one and one-half miles of unworked quartz, "that shall have been attempted and abandoned by individual claim owners." Individual free miners were to have the first chance; leases, in general were not to be granted of "any land, alluvium or quartz, which shall be considered to be immediately available for being worked by free miners or holders of individual claims," and in no case were individual free miners in actual occupation to be disturbed. Every such lease was to contain "all reasonable provisions for securing to the public rights of way and water, save insofar as shall be necessary for the miner-like working of the premises thereby devised, and also for preventing damage to persons or property of others than lessee." Conservation of the mineral resources was to be a principle of leases, and, "every such lease shall contain a covenant by the lessee to mine the said premises

---

[53] *Gold Fields' Act, 1859*, clauses XXVII and XXVIII; *Rules and Regulations in Conformity with Gold Fields' Act, 1859*, clause XVII.

in a miner-like way.'' In case of refusal or neglect to perform any and all covenants, the lease was to be voided.

In summing up the tendency of the above-stated provisions of the British Columbia code, it may be seen that, while the priority of the rights of the individual miners was recognized and guarded, yet there was a plain tendency to restrain individualism in the interests of the public good.

There remains one further inquiry in regard to this, on the whole, admirably conceived system of government in British Columbia—that is, as to its cost.

To American observers of the time, who had in mind salaries paid officials in the United States, the cost seemed excessive. The correspondent of the New York Tribune, Mr. Richardson, noted that while populous New York paid her governor $4,000, scantily populated British Columbia paid hers $15,000.[54] Another American wrote that notwithstanding the comparative scantiness and poverty of the population, "both at Victoria and New Westminster there was set up the cumbersome and expensive system of English colonial governments. The governors were almost more numerous than the governed, and the latter made bitter complaint of the severe taxes that were levied upon them for the benefit of the former. The year we were there (1869) nearly half a million dollars had been squeezed out of the people of little Victoria alone by a system of taxation much more burdensome than our civil war had thrown upon the American people and including a tax on all sales, special licenses for every kind of business, and an income tax at the end. The taxation in one province averaged $100 a year to each inhabitant, and in the other $70. Since 1865, the two provinces have been consolidated, and one set of Government machinery saved; but the governor of these ten or twelve thousand people still has a salary equal to that of the President of the United States, and his subordinates are paid in proportion."[55] These observations, however, were made in the years of decadence following the most prosperous era, and besides, in any comparisons between the British Colonies and American states or territories some discrim-

---
[54] Richardson, *Beyond the Mississippi*, p 417.
[55] Bowles, *Our New West*, pp. 466-68.

inations need to be made. In order to arrive at somewhat more precise ideas, let us make some comparison between the revenues and expenditures of British Columbia in the period prior to Union and some of the adjoining territorial divisions of the United States.

First, as to revenue. In 1859 the total revenue of British Columbia was £47,600 ($230,860), of which sum £17,000 ($82,450) was derived from the customs, £18,841 ($91,378.85) from land sales, and £11,759 ($57,151.15) from licenses and miscellaneous sources.[56] In 1863 the revenue exclusive of that derived from bonds and loans, amounted to £110,000 ($533,500) and in 1864 to £104,000 ($504,400).[57] That of the latter year was derived from customs £73,000 ($354,050), land sales £3,973 ($19,269.05), free miners certificates £3,540 ($17,169) general mining receipts £6,000 ($29,100), and the rest from miscellaneous sources.[58] The various sources of revenue in the mining districts themselves included miners' certificates, fees for recording mining claims, bills of sale, water rights and land claims, liquor and trading licenses, sale of lands, duty on wood, and Crown rents.[59] In comparison with the amount of revenue raised in British Columbia, that received in nearby American states and territories was small. The revenues of the State of Oregon in two years Sept. 1862 to Sept. 1864, produced $164,999.[60] In Washington Territory the total receipts in 1860 were $1,715, in 1861 $2,226, in 1862 $2,500, and in 1863, $4,777, and the total actual cash received into treasury from the organization of the Territory in 1853 to 1863 was $16,459.[61] The Territory of Idaho makes a somewhat better

---

[56] McDonald, *Br Col. and Van. Id.*, p. 37-8.

[57] *Government Gazette*, Jan. 23, 1864 and Aug. 26, 1865. For 1860 the revenue was £53,286 ($258,427.10)—Hazlitt, Cariboo, p. 110. I have not been able to secure statements for 1861 and 1862, but those cited seem sufficient for purposes of comparison with American conditions.

[58] The item of £3,540 for free miners' certificates would indicate that either there were no more than 708 miners in British Columbia in 1864, or that the law in regard to licenses was not fully enforced.

[59] *Abstract of the Hope Collectorate for 1860*, MS; *Report of John C. Hayne from Kootenay for the month of November, 1864*, MS.

[60] *Proceedings of the House of the Legislative Assembly, Report of the Treasurer*, Ap. p. 85.

[61] *House Journal, Treasurer's Reports, 1860, 1861, 1862, and 1863; Statement of Joint Committee on Ways and Means*, 1863, p. 260.

showing: the total receipts from the organization of the Territory in 1863 to Dec. 4, 1865 amounted to $20,999, and for 1866 (including delinquencies) to $33,511.[62] Delinquencies gave constant trouble and amounted at times to large proportions of the whole revenue; in Idaho there was backstanding in 1866 $10.145, and in Washington in 1863 $11,063. The chief cause of delinquency seems to have been in the fitfulness and, sometimes, the reluctance of the county treasurers in remitting. In fact, government in the territories as revealed in financial affairs appears to have been illjointed, in comparison with the well-knit system put into operation in British Columbia.[63] Certainly the amounts of revenue collected in the territories seem insignificant compared to the sums realized in British Columbia. But some large allowances must be made. The main sources of income in the territories were the property tax, poll tax, tax on "foreign" miners, percentages on franchises, and licenses for many sorts of business; and it will be observed that the most important items of revenue in British Columbia were lacking in the American territories—namely, the revenues from customs and from land sales.[64] Deducting these two items from the revenues of 1859 and 1864, respectively, we have left £11,761 ($57,040) and £28,027 ($135,930), On the other hand, large sums in the territories were contributed to the Federal government. To segregate the amounts paid for customs, indeed, by any single territory would be difficult, if not impossible; but as example of direct taxation by the Federal government (outside of excise on liquors) we find that Montana paid for the fiscal year ending June 30, 1866, $113,134, and for the next year the assessment was about the same. The territorial government for the same years, respectively, received $23,316 and $56,326. That a careful system brought satisfactory returns is shown both by the increasing effectiveness of territorial taxation as government became better ordered, and by the fact that 99¾ per cent. of the Fed-

---

[62] Hailey, *History of Idaho*, pp. 118 and 133.
[63] In British Columbia there were no counties at this period.
[64] The difficulty of effective taxation was increased in the American territories by the fact that comparatively little land was patented or deeded.

eral tax leviable was collected.[65] Moreover, it should be remembered that in British Columbia most of the local taxation was included in the colonial revenues, while in the territories county and, more, town taxation was very considerable; and, finally, that taxation in the forms of tolls levied by owners of franchises for ferries, bridges, and roads seems to have been decidedly less in the former. On the other hand, the Federal taxation in the territories was on a war basis. The only way in which we could arrive at exact comparisons would be to figure all items to a per capita conclusion, but this, because of the involved relations of the Federal and territorial governments, is impossible. On the whole, however, one gets the impression that, while taxation in British Columbia was proportionately in excess of that in the United States, the difference was by no means so pronounced as it seems at first glance.[66]

Comparison of expenditures in the two regions yields no more conclusive results than in the case of revenues. In British Columbia the colonial government, indeed, spent sums in comparison to which the expenditures of the territorial governments were insignificant; but here, again, there is no common plane for comparison. For the colonial government spent large sums on roads and means of transportation, provided mail facilities (though inadequate compared to those furnished by the Federal government), met the expenses of the land officials, paid most of the cost of military expeditions, and bore many expenditures provided for by local authorities in the United States. On the other hand, the Federal government in the territories spent a large amount for military protection, and on Indians, provided postal facilities and land surveys, built roads, paid the salaries (in large part) of the more important officials, built government buildings, and, in fact, furnished far the larger proportion of governmental expenditure

---

[65] Items in regard to receipts from taxation in Montana are derived from the message of Governor Green Clay Smith for 1866 and from the Treasurer's Report for 1867, *Con. His Soc. Mon.*, Vol. V, pp. 130–131 and 156–7.

[66] It was urged in British Columbia, in defense of rigid taxation of miners, that, while the miners received the good of such improvements as roads, etc., for which heavy indebtedness was incurred, many of them were likely to go away, leaving to the more stable inhabitants the payment of the debts.

within the territories.[67] In the matter of salaries, however, interesting comparisons are possible. The Governor of British Columbia in 1863 received £3,000 ($14,550), the Judge of the Supreme Court £1,200 ($5,820), and the Colonial Secretary £811 ($3,880).[68] Governor Seymour, however, the successor of Governor Douglas received a total sum of £5,450 ($26,432.50), the items of which were for transport £1,000, furnishing of residence £1,000, and salary £3,450.[69] Such a salary for a colony having less than fifteen thousand population certainly did not accord with American ideals. The Governor of Idaho received from the Federal government a salary of $2,500, the Chief Justice and two associate justices each $2,500 and the Secretary $2,000. But these salaries represented much less in reality, because of being paid in depreciated greenbacks, while those of British Columbia were paid at par.[70] Extra compensation, however, was voted by the territorial legislature, the governor receiving $2,111, the supreme judges $9,229 and the secretary $2,754.[71] Except for the great discrepancy in the governor's salaries the salaries of the other officials, with the extra compensation, were not greatly different; and the Governor of British Columbia was expected to meet expenses such as did not ordinarily fall to the governors of territories.[72] Moreover, the expenses of the territoral legislatures were not inconsiderable; in addition to $4 per day and transportation at the rate of $4 for every twenty miles travelled for each member, the first two sessions of the Idaho legislature cost in extra compensations more than eighteen thousand dollars.[73]

---

[67] There was some mention in 1861 of making Washington Territory a state, but the *Overland Press* argued that the territorial condition was to be preferred, because the United States government bore nineteen-twentieths of the expense. *Overland Press*, Nov. 21, 1861.
[68] *Schedule of Salaries*, 1863, MS.
[69] Ordinance to grant to Her Majesty £135,639 for 1864. *Government Gazette*, Feb. 20, 1864.
[70] *Organic Act of Idaho*.
[71] Hailey, *His. of Idaho*, p. 119.
[72] Of course the extra compensation could not always be depended upon, and it was ordered discontinued by Congress in 1870.
[73] Hailey, *His. of Idaho*, p. 119. No blame attaches to members of the Legislature, for expenses of all sorts were very high. In fact salary schedules applicable to agricultural territories were very inadequate for mining regions.

CHAPTER XII.

THE EVOLUTION OF ORDER AND LAW IN THE AMERICAN TERRITORIES

In the establishment of forms of order for the society which the mining advance deposited among the mountains south of the Line,, two forces worked. The one was extraneous and of national origin, the other indigenous to the mountain regions and derived from California; the one was the United States territorial form of government, the other the forms of organization characteristic of mining camps. Let us consider first the former.

1. The territorial form of Government.

The mining advance brought about the organization of two new territories. The rush to the Nez Percés mines in 1861 and to Salmon River in 1862 resulted in the passage by Congress, March 3, 1863, of the act creating the Territory of Idaho, and the rush to Grasshopper Creek and to Alder Gulch in 1862, and 1863, brought about, May 26, 1864, the creation of the territory of Montana.

Prior to the formation of Idaho Territory, the mining regions later embraced in it (and also that part of Montana lying west of the Rocky Mountains) were in the Territory of Washington; and the first steps toward governmental control of these regions. therefore, fell to that Territory. The Washington Legislature, previous to the division of the Territory, created the counties of Shoshone, Nez Perce, Idaho, Boise, and Missoula, all of which were more or less effectively organized, and from most of these members were sent to the legislature. In the governor's message for 1861 attention was called to the necessity for a code of mining laws for "the great. the controlling interest of our Territory," and it was suggested that the laws should be liberal and just, "such as have been found to work well in California and other mining districts." Many franchises for roads, ferries, and bridges were granted at different sessions. One important deficiency in the working of territorial government was indicated in the message of Governor Pickering, in 1862, in which he mentioned the lack of sets of the territorial laws, particularly in the new counties. The Federal government was urged by the territorial legislature to secure to miners the right to work in the Nez Percés country which, it was asserted, was covered by "improvident and unjust treaties," and to extinguish the Indian title to the Boise country. But while the legislature was thus zealous on behalf of the mining regions, political control by the Puget Sound country was endangered by the rapid growth of population in the eastern section of the territory, and division of the territory was agitated. In the interior the project was favored by Lewiston which hoped to be the capital of the new territory, but opposed by Walla Walla which hoped to become the capital of the old territory; while on the Sound the people perceived the danger that the capital might be removed, and that they might be included in inconvenient taxation.[1] Division was favored, also, by W. H. Wallace, territorial delegate to Congress (who became the first governor of Idaho Territory), and it met finally with general acquiescence. Thus came into being the new Territory of Idaho.

The creation of the Territory of Montana appears to have been a simple process springing directly from the exigencies of the mining advance. Hon. Sidney Edgerton, who had been appointed the first Chief Justice of Idaho Territory, arrived at East Bannack in the fall of 1863. The great rush to Alder Gulch was at that time in full tide, and thousands of persons were living on a spot that a few months before was but a wilderness. In the stern conflict which took place in the next few months following Judge Egerton's arrival between the elemental forces of order and disorder the authority of the chief justice does not seem to have been asserted. Judge Edgerton was a man

---

[1] *Overland Press*, Mch. 3, 1862; San Francisco *Daily Bulletin*, Jan. 7, 1863.

not lacking in ability and decision, but the office of territorial justice did not carry with it as much weight and fitness for dealing with crises as did that of judge in British Columbia. The citizens of Bannack and of Virginia, remote from the capital of the territory and involved in a critical struggle between the forces of order and disorder, felt that there was need for a new territory and requested Judge Edgerton to lay their case before the authorities at the national capital. A winter journey back to Washington resulted in the Organic Act for Montana Territory, and in Judge Edgerton being appointed the first Governor.[2]

In delimiting the new territories little or no attention was given to natural physiographic boundaries. The worst disregard of physiographic considerations occurred in the case of Idaho, where regions decisively separated physiographically and affiliated naturally with adjacent regions in other territories, were joined together. There early began in this territory a movement for the formation of a new territory more conformed to physiography, which has persisted in varying ways to the present day. A proposition was made in 1865 to create such a division by running a line from the southwest corner of Montana along the Salmon River Range, to the line of the Columbia and the Okanogan. "This would embrace," declared *The Lewiston Radiator* which was the champion of redivision, "that section of country which by physical formation and identity of interest among its population, naturally belongs to one political community, to a great degree separated from Boise on the south, Washington on the west, Montana on the east, and barred from political affinity with the people of the north by the British line." The population of the new territory would be 8,000 or 9,000 at the start, and territorial organization would soon be followed by statehood. The region would thus become better known, and immigration would in-

---

[2] *Contr. His. Soc. Mont.*, Vol. III, pp. 336-338. Congress was not averse to forming new territories at this period, since the administrative offices could be filled by Union men, and the Republican party organization thereby strengthened.

The origin of the names Montana and Idaho has been a matter of considerable dispute; they seem first to have gained currency in Colorado.

crease. "Nature herself," the article continued, "has marked out the boundaries of the Territory proposed as shown, and it matters not how much man may attempt to improve upon her work, he cannot neglect to follow her and succeed in such manner as obedience to her teachings will warrant."[3] Opposing arguments were put forth by *The Idaho World*, which intimated that the project arose from the disappointed ambitions of aspiring gentlemen, because of the removal of the capital from Lewiston to Boise. The territory was large, it was admitted, but the material interests (mainly mining) were more nearly identical than those of any territory or state on the Coast. "Western and eastern Oregon are not homogeneous; California has its mineral districts and its 'Cow Country'; Washington Territory its Sound interests and those of a distant interior. Still, they all manage to exist and prosper—and so has Idaho. If strict identity of interest is to prevail in the location of boundaries, every mining camp and school district would be entitled to a separate Territorial existence."[4]

Perhaps it was the desire to overcome the effects of physiographic separation which induced the Republicans of Idaho to hold their second territorial Convention at a remote spot on the trail from Lewiston to Idaho City, and about one hundred miles from the latter place.[5] The blare of bands, the gatherings in hotels, and the stir and noise of great crowds were absent at this convention. The only buildings anywhere around was Packer John's cabin, a small log hut roofed with shakes. The delegates ate in this cabin and slept under the trees adjoining, while their horses grazed peacefully around. The great work of the convention was the selection of a nominee for delegate to Congress, this office then being very highly prized.[6] In the first election in Idaho Territory, when the majority of the people were in the northern part, the Republicans had been

---
[3] Lewiston *Radiator*, Feb. 4, 1865, in San Francisco *Daily Bulletin*, Mch. 7, 1865.
[4] The Idaho *World*, Feb. 4, 1865.
[5] A description of this Convention is found in Goulder's *Reminiscences*, pp. 280-287.
[6] Governor Stevens of Washington Territory and Governor Wallace of Idaho Territory resigned the office of Governor in order to be elected as congressional delegate.

successful; but the discovery of the Boise mines drew thither many people from Missouri, and their arrival, with some contributing causes, made the Territory Democratic for several decades. Montana also was Democratic during the early mining period. In both territories conventions were regularly held almost from the start, and regular party machinery was organized. This party method of arriving at the will of the people and of carrying on government was in decided contrast to the simple and swift procedure that obtained in British Columbia.

In connection with the organization of parties in the new territories the question arises as to the prevalence of secession sentiment in these territories. As was natural, people who came from the border states, or from farther south, were earnestly sympathetic with the Confederacy; and it was natural, also, that this sympathy should find expression, and that there should be more or less friction with ardent Unionists (of whom there were many), and with the Federal administration. Sentiment among the American miners in British Columbia was clearly for the Union, and citizens of Victoria made contributions to the care of Union soldiers and to Lancashire sufferers—to the latter $12,000.[7] In northern Idaho sentiment was more divided and passions seemed to deepen, as the war went on, and people came in from the East. "Among the people at the mines and along the line of March," wrote a newspaper correspondent in 1861, "I heard but little of Union or Disunion. Those from the Seceding States had not much to say beyond sad regrets that the country should deliberately go to war with itself.[8] There were, however, at the mines occasional "rough scenes and personal collisions," sometimes attended by fatal consequences.[9] Yet the fiercest secessionists and the most uncompromising abolitionists were often the closest of friends. In southern Idaho, however, passion ran much more high. "The left wing of Price's army," as the Union men styled the rougher element from the border states, contained undoubtedly many reckless men accustomed to vio-

---

[7] San Francisco *Daily Bulletin*, Mch 23, 1863.
[8] *Id.*, July 28, 1861.
[9] Goulder. *Reminiscenses*, p. 207.

lence, who tried to terrorize Union men.[10] Affrays and duels were not uncommon. The most noteworthy of these (and one which brought the community to the verge of deplorable conflict) was that between Pinkham, a Union man originally from Maine, and Ferd Patterson, a secessionist born in Tennessee, which resulted in the death of the former.[11] In both Idaho and Montana determined objection was made to the iron-clad oath by some of the members of the legislatures.[12] The attitude of some of the members of the legislature in Idaho may be learned from the majority report of the Committee on Military and Indian Affairs, concerning a bill providing bounties for territorial volunteers who might have been wanted for garrison duty in the territory. Governor Lyon in urging the matter said, in his characteristic fashion, "I feel it will be a rare privilege for the great hearted, whole-souled mountaineers, ranchmen, and miners, to contribute in this way their support to a government beneath whose starry flag their cradles were rocked and that still flings its protecting shadow over their fathers' graves." The report of the committee, however, asserted that from the third of March, 1863, to December seventh, 1863, "more than 30,000 persons, thrown promiscuously together, into a crude and most irregular form of society, were obliged to remain in the same chaotic condition, without judicial tribunals, without officers, without law;" and the first evidence given that the General Government intended to exercise any care over them, was the advent of a class of political hackneys, sent among them by the Administration at Washington, "a set of officials more intent on securing personal advantage than on promoting the welfare of the individual community."

"Has the Mother Government grown so weak and become so impoverished during the 'sixty days' rebellion" the report continued, "that it can exercise no care over the people of the provinces, except to send tax gatherers and officials to rule over them and eat out their substance?" The bill failed to pass. In

---

[10] Butler, J. S., *Life and Times in Idaho*, MS.
[11] An account of this celebrated case may be found in Langford, *Vigilante Days and Ways*, Vol I, pp. 182–211.
[12] *Journals of the Council and House of Representatives of Idaho Territory*, 4th session, pp 208–9.

Montana, while there was some friction, on the whole, a happier state of affairs prevailed, particularly in the relations of the citizens to each other. Possibly the acute conflict there waged with the criminal element helped to allay controversy.[13] A careful characterization of Montana conditions has been left by Col. W. F. Sanders, who described them as follows. "There was considerable bad blood extant concerning the war, about which the communities radically differed. I think upon the whole as much philosophy and good nature was manifested as under the circumstances we had any right to expect. There were, of course, some hot headed men who would have been glad to have created trouble, but the good sense of the more moderate people prevailed and matters did not culminate in any difficulty."[14]

In the appointment of territorial officials by the United States government a prime qualification was staunch Unionism. Not that the appointees lacked ability; although part of them were mediocre, others were men of energy and of some distinction, who grasped quickly the conditions surrounding them and strove honestly to fill worthily their offices.[15] But there was constant going and coming, there was not time for eastern men to become familar with western conditions, and there was no such identification with and devotion to the community, as characterized the work of Governor Douglas and of Judge Begbie in British Columbia.[16] One misses, especially, in officials in the territories, the firm assertion of authority and the insistence upon obedience to law which was characteristic of the government of British Columbia. Leniency to criminals, acquiescence in punishment directly inflicted by the people, lack of decision in treating grave crimes, and over attention to minor obliquities (such as prize-

---

[13] *Contr. His. Soc. Mon.*, Vol. 4, p. 127.

[14] *Sketches of Early Settlers in Montana*, Col. W. F. Sanders, MS. The above extract, written by a pronounced Republican, was read by me to Judge W. Y. Pemberton, of opposite political affiliations, who gave it unqualified endorsement.

[15] There was one noteworthy defalcation in the case of Horace C. Gilson, Secretary of Idaho Territory, who absconded with twenty-five thousand dollars That such crimes were not lacking in British Columbia, also, would appear from a report of the British Columbian that within a few weeks the Post Master General, Harbour Master, and Colonial Treasurer became defaulters. *British Columbian*, Jan. 2, 1862.

[16] For a resumé of the officials of Idaho and a characterization of a number of them consult Hailey, *History of Idaho*, Chap. XXXV.

fighting, gambling, and Sabbath breaking) were apparent in administration, south of the Line. The comparative levity of American officials towards the most grave transgressions of order is illustrated in an incident narrated in the biography of Governor James M. Ashley. It would be a mistake to think of Mr. Ashley as a weakling or a coward; for he was a noted fighter for abolition and the rights of negroes, long a member of Congress, chairman of the Committee on Territories, and always an uncompromising radical. The quotation is as follows: "One of his most interesting experiences was connected with an old fashioned western lynching. A miner near Helena had 'struck it rich', and brought his gold into town to exchange it for greenbacks. This done he went to the nearest saloon and proudly exhibited his roll, with the natural result that he was followed from the saloon to a quiet spot outside of the city and there assaulted and robbed. He lived long enough to give a description of his murderers. These were soon apprehended by a vigilance committee and brought to trial in the most public way—in a large hall in Helena. Governor Ashley knew of this, but recognizing the absolute necessity of protection being afforded the miners, who for the most part lived in lonely cabins, and knowing the lack of a secure jail to hold criminals for a long time which the regular process of courts allow the criminal on trial, and also, aware of his inability to cope with the vigilantes even if he so desired, he did not try to interfere. At this juncture a New England lawyer appeared on the scene, whose name, according to the writer's best recollection, was Judge Gillette. The judge was horror struck at the idea of any man being tried except by the regular course, like most other New Englanders who have gone a long way from the recollection of the Boston Tea Party, and other similar informal events that took place in good old Massachusetts, and it was hard for him to imagine that any state of affairs admitted of any departure from the strict rules of the law. He, therefore, called upon Governor Ashley and made a typical academic law and order speech. The Governor suppressing his strong tendency to laugh, made a rejoinder with all earnestness.

"Now, Judge," said he, "you must see how helpless I am. I

have no force capable of dealing with these vigilantes, and if I should go down to the hall and make any attempt to stop the proceedings, it would simply result in a disgraceful showing of contempt for my authority; but I know these people are liberal, and that they would be willing to hear what anybody has to say on the subject. Now, suppose you go down to the hall and ask to be heard, and make them the same kind of a speech you have made me. I think they will listen to you, and we will see what the result is.'' Gillette thought the suggestion a good one, obtained a hearing and made a speech. After he concluded his stirring appeal for law and order there was a moment's silence and some man in the rear yelled out: ''Judge, that's a damn fine speech. *Go on with the trial!*''

''The next morning the Governor became aware that something exciting was going on across the gulch which lay in the rear of his house, and emerging from the kitchen door and shading his eyes, he looked across and saw hanging from ''Hangman's Tree'' the bodies of two men, while a large concourse in the vicinity were indulging in foot races and other amusements. After uttering a slight exclamation the Governor turned around, went in the house, and the affair was a closed incident so far as he was concerned.''[17] Looking at this occurrence from the point of view usual in the American territories, Governor Ashley's conduct was reasonable and defensible; from the point of view of government in British Columbia it is incomprehensible. Magistrate O'Reilly or Judge Begbie, it may safely be affirmed, would have been instant and strenuous in asserting the dignity and supremacy of the law, and Governor Douglas would have exhausted every resource in supporting these officials. But in truth the American officials lacked authority and prestige.

The most vital and the widest authority south of the Line was that of the Legislature, but this authority was not administrative and was shared, formally, by the Governor. The Organic Act of Idaho declared that the legislative power should extend to ''all rightful subjects of legislation consistent with the Con-

---

[17] *Governor James M. Ashley's Biography and Messages, Contr. His. Soc. Mon.* Vol. VI, p. 192–3. Cf., also, Charge to the Grand Jury, 1864 and 1866, by Chief Justice H. L. Hosmer; *Pioneer Reminiscences* by Lyman E. Munson, *Id.* Vol. V, pp. 235–252 and p. 209.

stitution of the United States and the provisions of this Act"; but no law was to be passed "interfering with the primary disposal of the soil", and it was provided further, "That, whereas slavery is prohibited in said territory by the act of Congress of June nineteenth, 1862, nothing herein contained shall be construed to authorize or permit its existence therein."

In exercising their authority, the legislatures both of Idaho and Montana adopted the Common Law of England, "so far as the same is applicable, and of a general nature, and not in conflict with the special enactments of this territory." They also provided practice acts. Some classes of laws passed by these legislatures are of special interest.

One of these groups was with regard to occupation of the public lands. The object was to secure to the occupants peaceable possession and as much of title as could be given prior to patent from the United States; in other words, the object sought was a legalization of squatters' rights. The law of Montana, conceding to the United States paramount right, gave rights to the occupant against all others. It sanctioned a claim of one hundred and sixty acres on declaration and record; such a claim was declared a "chattel real, possessing the character of real estate," could be sold by deed, and was subject to execution. Mining locations were excepted from agricultural occupancy.[18]

In Idaho there was an "Act for Maintaining and Defending Possessory Actions on the Public Land in this Territory." Claims were to be of not more than 160 acres, in compact form and clearly bounded; within 90 days after recording, improvements to the value of $200 were to be made. Any citizen, or one who had declared his intention to become a citizen, might maintain action for interference with or injury to the possession of land. Miners, however, might go upon such lands, if they contained mines of any precious metals, and work such mines "as fully as if no such claim for agriculture or grazing purpose had been made thereon;" provided, however, compensation were made for crops planted prior to location.[19]

An Act of the Territory of Montana had reference to an

---
[18] The Montana *Post*, Jan. 21, 1865.
[19] *Laws of Idaho, Second session*, p 421-2

interesting custom, not without significance in the evolution of law. This act forbade ranchmen and stable keepers from using stock left with them, without the consent of the owner. Since the prices of feed in the mining camps prohibited keeping animals in towns for any length of time, persons found it profitable to establish ranches a few miles from the towns, where horses and pack animals might be corraled and herded. A ranch generally had an agent in the town to whom the stock was intrusted, and who was notified when the owner was in need of it. Not infrequently both ranch keeper and agent were in league with road agents, and in consequence, it was often a matter of great difficulty for a man who desired to carry treasure without the gang knowing it. Moreover, if a man had a good horse, it was not unlikely to be used by the ranchman or his friends or to become permanently "sick" or "lost". On the other hand, when vigilantes arose, it was difficult for roughs in town to leave unobserved, and an honest ranchman might furnish mounts for vigilantes who needed them.[20]

One of the most striking and important features of territorial legislation in connection with the mining advance was the granting of numerous franchises for roads, ferries, and bridges. These franchises, of course, conferred monopolistic privileges, and they were the subject of much execration. Conditions in respect to franchises, from the point of view of opponents, were discussed by Governor Ashley, of Montana, as follows: "A large majority of these private acts conferred extraordinary privileges on a few individuals, and, of necessity, excluded from the enjoyment the great body of our citizens. And I speak with moderation when I say that many of these so-called laws authorized persons to do acts which were little better than legalized highway robbery. The whole territory was shingled with special franchises so that travelers and packers, and freighters, found in every canyon, on almost every water-course, and on many broad and level plains, a toll collector, who demanded, as a condition to the passing of each, from *one* to *three* dollars. The smallest amount demanded at any toll gate, as a rule *is one dollar*.

---

[20] McConnell, W. J., *Idaho Inferno*, MS. p 4; *Contr. His. Soc. Mon.*, Vol VI, p. 279-80.

At rickety bridges, which are often unsafe for man or beast, from one to three dollars." A majority of all the acts, memorials, and joint resolutions passed by the early Montana Legislatures, the Governor claimed, were of a private character. Congress finally amended the Organic Act so as to prohibit special charters.[21] Washington Territory, (during the period when it included the mining regions) and Idaho Territory were just as lavish.[22]

Valid grounds for defense of the conduct of the legislatures, however, are not lacking. There was very urgent need for roads, ferries, and bridges in the mining regions. If one can imagine how the country was when civilized society entered it, how formidable were the obstacles to communication, and how difficult and even dangerous traveling was, he can more readily understand how natural and insistent were the demands of the mining population upon the legislatures. How were these demands to be met? Recourse could be had to the Federal government for these purposes only rarely on the plea of military or postal necessity, and the aid given was far too slow for the needs of a mining people; the legislatures on their part had, as we have seen, extremely scanty revenues, and the expense of getting work done was great on account of the high prices in the mining districts. Shrewd men, of course, were willing under special privileges to undertake the work, because of the prospect of good gains, and many of the honored names of the territories were to be found among the owners of franchises. It should be noted also that limitations were generally placed upon franchises by the legislatures, especially upon such as were of special importance. The rates of toll to be charged were often specified, and generally these rules were to be subject after a year or two to the control of the county commissioners. There was always a time limitation of ten, fifteen, or twenty years, and sometimes it was provided that the county commissioners could take over roads, bridges, or ferries on payment of cost. Failure to make

---

[21] Ibid.

[22] Another practice of the territorial legislatures, which was reprobated by executives was the granting of divorces. The Legislature of Montana at its first session granted 9 divorces, and the practice was persisted in by the Legislature of Washington in spite of earnest opposition by governors.

improvements within the specified time might result in voidance of the franchise and certainly in the lapse of legal right to collect tolls. Generally there was some special taxation, though not very heavy. There was a tendency, moreover, to place all such special acts under general law, and also to relegate such matters largely to the county commissioners.[23]

Notwithstanding its imperfections, the machinery of American territorial government in the mining regions worked gradually toward ordered processes of law. As a matter of fact, whatever might have been, it *was* the means through which these territories settled down to the conditions usually obtaining in American communities. But the great defect lay in the slowness of administration in comparison to the sudden needs of mining camps. While Congress was legislating for one set of conditions and officials journeying slowly over the plains, conventions and elections being held, legislatures gathering and county organizations being effected, the mining population might jump hundreds of miles in a week, fill a gulch with unorganized society, and create conditions imperatively demanding instant readjustment in the application of the forces of government. The fundamental trouble was that a system of government which had been evolved for the needs of an agricultural population, in regions generally not rugged, failed to meet the demands of communities of miners in mountainous regions. In the one case, population came in leisurely, with the intention of permanency, and did not concentrate densely; in the other it came in with utmost haste, having little idea of abiding, and gathered in more compact communities.

II. Forms of organization characteristic of mining camps.

The looseness and ineffectiveness of the American territorial machinery which, when revealed in the lack of control of crime, made imperative the robust procedure of the mining camps, may be illustrated by a report from the county auditor of Madison County, then in Idaho Territory, to the territorial auditor:

---

[23] *Laws of Washington Territory*, 1858–1861, Vol. II, pp. 86, 116, and 130; *Laws of Idaho Territory*, First Session, pp. 645 and 647.

Virginia City, Idaho Territory,
Aug. 3rd, 1864.

B. F. Lambkin,
    Territorial Auditor,
        Lewiston, Idaho.

Dear Sir:—

Enclosed find simply a report of the amount of money received by the County Treasurer of Madison County. We have a rebellion here and can do nothing with the revenue law of the Territory. Our merchants have held indignation meetings and all refuse to pay the license, and about nine tenths refuse to pay the poll tax. The laws are very odious and unpopular with the whole people, and what makes it worse is the fact we are separated from you and are soon to be organized as Montana Territory. The Governor is already here and another drawback is, we have no published copy of the law, and we cannot show authority for collecting taxes. We have nothing but an old bill introduced into the House or Council but is not a certified copy of the law........ ....

Yours truly,
R. M. Hagaman.

Mr. Hagaman wrote again three weeks later that the Governor was about to commission the officers of the new territory, and added—, "this will dissolve I suppose our connection with Idaho."[24]

Still more significant of the weakness of the territorial system, when applied to criminal conditions, was a defect brought out in a decision of the supreme court of Idaho Territory. The decision dealt with the validity of criminal law in the territory between the passage by Congress of the Act creating the territory, March, 1863, and the enactment of a criminal code by the first legislature in the session which began in December. It will be recalled that this was just the period when thousands of adventurers rushed into Boise Basin, and when the need of law was very great. During this period two men had been tried for murder and adjudged guilty, the one re-

---

[24] *Report of the Territorial Auditor of Idaho Territory*, December 1, 1864, p. 8.

ceiving a sentence for imprisonment for ten years, the other for twenty. These men were brought before the Court in 1866 by writ of habeas corpus and were ordered released on the ground that, at the time the crimes were committed, no statute against this crime existed in the territory. The opinion of the court was based on the following considerations: By the Organic Act, Idaho was formed out of portions of Washington, Dakota, Nebraska, and Utah Territories. The Organic Acts of these territories in so far as they applied to the new Territory were at its formation repealed and became nullities. Hence, statutes based on them, so far as affecting this territory, were invalid, since the fountain of authority was stopped. "The uniform practice . . . conclusively establishes, we think, the principle that the laws of the old organization have no force in the new political community, unless by special provision." In the act organizing this territory there were no provisions recognizing former laws—an impossibility, indeed, since the territory was formed from four territories. Nor was there any similarity to conquered or ceded territory, in which case laws pass with the people and the soil, because this case was that of dismemberment of old territory. No statute, therefore, existed, and the court ordered these proven criminals set at liberty. No such incident occurred in British Columbia, nor would it seem a possibility there. While this decision may not directly have done serious damage in Idaho, yet this attitude on the part of those charged with administering law in preferring theoretical and technical considerations to plain, common-sense justice was particularly unfortunate in these mining communities in their formative period; and it made necessary forms of organization which should attain swiftly and more surely indispensable ends.[25]

The form of organization to which miners always turned naturally was that of the mining camp. A mining camp in the mineral regions of the United States, as is well understood, was not merely a collection of claims or of cabins but generally, also, an organized form of local government. Each

---

[25] The full text of this opinion is given in the Idaho *World*, Aug. 25, 1866.

camp—or, to use the more technical term, district—had its customs and rules, and to enforce them a judge, recorder, and some sort of executive officer. The position of Miner's Judge in a prosperous camp was very important, and he was generally kept busy continually hearing cases. All sorts of cases were tried before him and argued by attorneys, who were to be found in every large camp—cases of assault and battery, suits, and all the manifold disputes concerning rights to claims and to water which arose in the camp. Disputants might have a trial by jury, if they would agree to pay the jury enough to make up for loss of time on their claims. In case of dissatisfaction, appeal might be taken to a miner's meeting, which was the final source of authority. The miner's meeting was quite like a New England town meeting—except that it was frequently held on Sunday. In this meeting the district voted its rules and regulations, elected its officers, decided when claims should be laid over, heard appeals, organized for military purposes, and sometimes tried cases—especially the more serious ones, such as robbery or murder. Cases might be tried by the meeting itself, or left to a jury appointed by the meeting. This mining camp organization originated in California and spread thence everywhere with the mining advance in American territory; and even in British Columbia it began to be used by the miners before they learned that there it would not be needed. The mining camp was, as an institution, a remarkable example of the American instinct for order when formal law was dilatory and weak, and it contributed greatly to the evolution of law and order in the American territories.[26]

There is an interesting example of the informal working of the mining camp in an action of Brown's District, Bivens Gulch, Montana Territory, in 1864. The meeting was held in the saloon of J. H. Hughes in Bagdad City, for the purpose of settling a dispute between W. P. Allen and Company and Caleb Perry. Wila Huffaker was called to the Chair, and E. T. Headley was appointed Secretary. On motion, the Chair appointed six citizens as a committee to try the case and render

---

[26] A careful and interesting account of mining camps is that by Charles Howard Shinn, *Mining Camps. A study in American Frontier Government.*

a decision according to the evidence and testimony advanced before them. The committee reported that Allen and Company were entitled to receive $100 from Perry. Perry, however, declared that he would pay nothing. The following resolution was then adopted: "Whereas, It is a notorious fact that Caleb Perry will pay no debt unless by force; and

Whereas, after having agreed to abide by the decision of a jury of six men appointed to make such decision, and then disputing the right of such jury to try the case, and refusing to make any settlement,

Resolved, That the miners of this district put Mr. Allen in possession of the claims of Caleb Perry and assist and protect him in working the same, until he shall have taken out $100 clear of expenses." Perry was then notified that unless he complied with the decision within twenty minutes Mr. Allen should be put in possession the following day. Perry refused to comply, and a committee was appointed to carry out the will of the meeting. Perry, however, promised next day to pay Allen from the first dust taken out, but on leniency being shown, paid other debts first. Another meeting was held, and it was resolved to put Allen and Company at once in possession. Perry was called in, and the resolution was read to him, "to his great disgust." The resolution was carried out.[27]

But local government by the miners had its defects.

In the first place, charges of monopolization of mining ground were repeatedly made in all sections of the mining regions south of the Line. In Owyhee on Jordan Creek the first twenty-nine discoverers appropriated all of the available ground by making mining laws which allowed to each a discovery claim of three hundred feet, a location claim of the same size, and in addition three hundred feet for a friend.[28] In Boise Basin there was much outcry against monopoly.[28a] An expedition of forty-two miners which prospected in 1863 far up the South Snake, thinking that prospects were favorable for good dig-

---

[27] The Montana *Post*, Nov 3, and 26, 1864.
[28] Maize, *Early Events in Idaho*, MS, San Francisco *Daily Bulletin*, June 6, 1864.
[28a] "Such land monopoly [as at Boise] and such mining laws were never heard of," San Francisco *Daily Bulletin*, Oct. 20, 1863.

gings, organized into a miners' meeting and adopted the following regulations:

1. That every person present should be regarded as a discoverer, in each and every gulch found by any party or member of a party.

2. That each member, as discoverer, should be entitled to five claims of 200 feet each along the gulch—*viz.*, "a discovery claim and a pre-emption claim in the main gulch, a bar claim, a hill claim, and a patch claim." "These liberal and disinterested regulations," one of the party wrote, "were voted in the affirmative with gratifying unanimity and the chairman was just about to put the question to the meeting whether there was any more business before it, when a big burly Scotchman named Brown, who had apparently been turning the subject over in his mind, jumped up and inquired with great earnestness, "But Mr. Chairman, what shall we do with the rest of it?" The question, it was reported, was received with roars of laughter.[29] A mining convention in Summit District, Montana, asserted that legislation was needed to regulate the district laws and the power to make them; "Fifty men may make the laws of a gulch which may contain ten times that number before the end of the month."[30] In the region around Helena, a correspondent wrote to Judge Hosmer, "A perfect monopoly exists among the early claimants. Some 20 or 25 persons first preempted Last Chance Gulch and when they had exhausted the names, they went above or below and formed new districts, and thus they continued, carrying their exclusiveness into other gulches in the vicinity, as they were discovered; and to enable them to hold this number of claims they passed laws to suit themselves, postponing representation to suit their convenience."[31] At a "miner's mass meeting" at Helena, at which there were said to have been 800 people present, the principle was expressed that no man should "hold more claims than he can represent by actual labor," and the determination was announced to break down these "gambling-speculative paper

---

[29] *Contr. His. Soc. Mont.*, Vol I, pp. 113-143.
[30] *The Montana Post*, Dec. 10, 1864.
[31] *The Montana Post*, Feb. 25, 1865.

titles and put picks and shovels in their place.'' The evidence from so many localities would indicate that, in the American system of free competition in the exploitation of the public domain, as manifested in the mining camps, there was a perceptible tendency to petty monopolization—a tendency under general governmental regulation from the start in British Columbia.

Something is to be said, however, on the other side. It was true that, so far as the rules went in some of the mining districts, a man could hold claims in more than one district, and that the requirements of representation were not strict; but, as a matter of fact, very few men did hold claims in more than one district. Why were not alert men, moreover, who prospected far at much expense, or who got up in the middle of the night to take part in a stampede, entitled to special privileges? Here were fellows, on the other hand, who loafed around for a week to see whether new ground would turn out to be good, and then wanted a share of the rewards of the energetic, and would try to get a majority in miners' meeting in order to reduce the size of claims. It was well to remember what the crowd got that tried to jump the claims of some discoverers across the Prickly Pear—three or four of them were killed, and the rest stampeded. There were always people who were discontented with other people because they had something, and there were always natural agitators glib of tongue, and sometimes intelligent men and skilled miners, who liked to get up mass meetings and try to overthrow established ways. In reality, there was no such thing as monopoly in the mines.[32]

Another, and a real, defect of the system of local mining law was that the miner's meetings were, like all popular bodies, liable to gusts of feeling, and sometimes made sudden reversals of judgment. For example, when, at Virginia City, two desperadoes had been condemned to death for a flagrant murder and were on the point of being executed, because of the clamors of some women and the intercession and sharp practices of

---

[32] I have tried in this paragraph to express the views of practical miners. For some of the considerations I am indebted to Judge Pemberton of Helena.

friends, they were let off.[33] It is not denied, of course, that there were executions firmly and justly conducted by miner's courts. But there might come times when the roughs were so numerous and so well-organized as fairly to dominate for a while the mining community—and then society fell back upon that summary instrument for protecting itself, the vigilante organization.

At the outset of our discussion of this interesting phase of the evolution of law and order in the American mining camps, it is well to make clear the difference in the procedure of the vigilantes and that of the ordinary miners' courts or meetings. When a man was arrested by authority of the latter organizations, he was brought to trial, and the determination of the case, finally, was in the body of the people; when a man was arrested by the vigilante organization, his trial had already been held and the punishment determined in secret by a few citizens. The mysteriousness, swiftness, and certainty with which the vigilantes worked awed the most formidable desperadoes. It is not the purpose of this work, however, to give a circumstantial account of the thrilling and picturesque achievements of the various vigilante organizations which came into being in the mining regions of our study, but to try to set forth some of the conditions which produced them and determined their efficiency and, especially, to describe so far as our material will permit their methods of organization.[34] Since the conditions in Montana were such as to produce a remarkably thorough and effective vigilante organization, let us turn our attention to the organization in that territory first.

Nowhere was the inadequacy of the territorial system in the mining regions attended by more grave consequences than in western Montana. When, in 1862, the mining movement thither began to assume noticeable proportions, that part west of the Rocky Mountains was in Washington Territory and dependent for authority to form legal local government upon the legisla-

---

[33] Langford, *Vigilante Days and Ways*, Vol. I, p. 359-70.
[34] For narratives and descriptions of the deeds of the desperadoes and of the circumstances of their punishment the reader is referred to the following works: Dimsdale, *The Vigilantes of Montana;* Langford, *Vigilante Days and Ways;* Bancroft, *Popular Tribunals.*

ture which met on Puget Sound; the part east of the mountains, on the other hand, belonged to Dakota Territory, whose legislature convened at Yankton a thousand miles or more down the Missouri. The mining community which was forming on Grasshopper Creek was, therefore, within the jurisdiction of the latter. There was a constant tendency in the criminal element of mining camps, it may be observed at this point, to migrate from older camps where order had begun to evolve to these new camps, where, for a while at least, unrestrained by authority, they might commit crime. On the other hand, it was very difficult for the honest miners and citizens in these exposed camps, having come from many and diverse sections, and therefore being unacquainted with each other—each intent, moreover, on his own work and purposing to make as much money as he could and get away as soon as possible—it was difficult for these to organize in opposition to violent and desperate men. Such organization became doubly difficult and dangerous when the roughs themselves were leagued together. Such was the case in East Bannock in 1862-3. A gang of ruffians gathered there, coming immediately from Florence, Lewiston, or Walla Walla, but with a schooling in crime that extended back to Nevada and California. Some of them had learned disrespect for law by experience of its leniency as administered by regularly constituted authorities. Qualities of manhood were not wanting among some of their number; courage, skill in the use of arms, education, ability to use good language, fidelity to friends, personal attractiveness, and social charm—qualities which gave to them so wide a circle of friends as to make harder the task of punishing them for their villanies. But robbery and murder became with them a business. They bound themselves together by oath, adopted special marks of identification, and arranged means of communication.[35] Their chief was Henry Plummer. Plummer was a man of good manners, somewhat fastidious as to dress, usually quiet in demeanor and self-controlled, a good student of human nature, and keen to direct and take advantage of public opinion; but

---

[35] The names of the gang and a description of their organization may be found in Langford, *Vigilante Days and Ways*, Vol. II, p 93.

he was also venomous in animosity and so unscrupulous and determined as to let nothing stand in his way, and he was noted for his skill with the revolver. This remarkable man so ingratiated himself with the community as to be elected miner's sheriff, and he chose as some of his deputies members of his own gang.[36] The inclusion of East Bannock and neighboring camps in the new territory of Idaho in the spring of 1863, did not weaken the power of the band; for Lewiston, the first capital, was on the other side of almost impassable mountains, and the legislature did not meet until the next winter. The discovery of Alder Gulch that same spring, on the other hand, the inrush of thousands of people (many of them unused to Western ways), and the production, circulation, and transportation of many thousands of dollars worth of gold dust gave to the desperadoes opportunity for more bold and extensive operations. Villianies multiplied. No traveler was safe from attack; merchants were compelled to extend credit with no hope of repayment; men who knew the authors of the outrages were killed, driven away, or silenced by threats; citizens who made any open stand for law were marked for death. The miners' meetings and juries were swayed by the desperadoes and their friends, or terrorized. Robberies, assassinations, and murders became increasingly common and wanton; the criminals more defiant and insolent. The total number of men killed mounted to over one hundred.

The crisis came, December, 1863, in the murder in an atrocious manner of a young German. George Ives, a prepossessing member of the gang, conspicuous for the number and boldness of his crimes, was brought to trial for this crime before a great miners' meeting at Nevada City. An advisory commission was chosen, and lawyers appeared for the prosecution and defense. Delay of more than a day by bickering and altercations was ended by the announcement of the miners that the case must close at a certain hour. The commission, with the exception of one man, voted guilty. Then came a period

---

[36] Plummer was not a county sheriff under regular legal authorization He even schemed to become deputy United States Marshall, and nearly all the members of the Union League at Bannack favored his appointment; id. Vol. I, p. 382.

of hesitation such as had before unnerved the friends of justice. The crowd swayed to and fro, the friends of the prisoner swore that he should not die, everywhere were confusion, doubt, and anxiety. The occasion demanded a leader of more than ordinary courage and decision. It was at this juncture that Col. W. F. Sanders moved "That George Ives be forthwith hanged by the neck until he is dead." The motion was carried, and Ives was hanged within an hour.

Some account, at this point, of the character and career of the man whose leadership at this critical time was so decisive for the cause of order, may not be amiss. Wilbur F. Sanders was born May 2, 1834, at Leon, New York, of New England ancestry, and he was educated at Phelps Academy. He removed at the age of twenty to Akron, Ohio, where he taught school and studied law, being admitted to the bar in 1856. At the outbreak of the Civil War he recruited a company of infantry and enlisted in the 64th O. V. I. He was in active service until ill health compelled him to resign, and he then went in company with his uncle, Judge (afterward Governor) Edgerton to Montana. In the formative era of Montana—from the mining camp stage, through the territorial period, to established statehood—no man more devotedly labored for the best interests of the community nor better served the cause of law and order than did Colonel Sanders. A candidate for Congress several times, though unsuccessful, at the entrance of Montana to statehood he became United States Senator. He died July 7, 1905.[37]

Senator Sanders was a man of great vigor, activity, and power of initiative. His two leading characteristics were intrepidity and honesty. He was a "superb warrior" and delighted in fighting in a minority, if he believed that he was in the right. His was not a nature given to compromise, and he spoke out fearlessly against corruption. The very intensity of his courage and integrity, however, made him sometimes not absolutely just, and the poignancy of his speech produced enemies. His power as an orator was very great. Men who heard him at the time of the Ives trial say that his eloquence

---

[37] Mr. Sanders was also President of the State Historical Society and Past Grand Master of the Masonic order.

was terrible. He had a marvelously modulated voice and an exceptionally easy and precise command of English. His addresses on historical and social themes reveal power to discern conditions clearly, breadth and vividness of characterization, profound comprehension of contemporary tendencies, and much social earnestness. The style of these addresses, even in the reading, compels one's attention by its rapidity and breadth.[38] The main tendency of the life of this pioneer leader may be learned from some words written by him about the time Montana became a state. The man "who does nothing to make the community wiser and better," he wrote, "will never know the real luxury that pertains to identification with the founders of these communities." The labor of the first pioneers he explains, has been accomplished, but there now remains the founding of the State. "It will be a very unsatisfying consciousness when we recur to the present time if we shall only have it to say that we made a fortune for ourselves, that we were a mere observer of events, when we are also conscious that we did nothing to strengthen the intellectual and moral force that out of the chaos of incoherent life is to evolve law and order."[39]

A stern and, under the circumstances, a necessary first step in the evolution of law and order in Montana was the formation of a vigilante organization. A few of the citizens of Nevada and Virginia started the movement the day after the execution of Ives, and the organization spread secretly and swiftly, until it came to embrace a majority of the citizens in the different camps who were resolute to bring about a better state of affairs. Paris S. Pfouts, a merchant of Virginia City, it is now known, was president of the vigilantes, and Col. Sanders was legal adviser and, as one pioneer recently expressed it, "the life of the thing." Among the executive officers were John X. Beidler, Neil Howie, and John Featherston—a trio unsurpassed for coolness and daring, to whom Montana owes

---
[38] For example consult *Con. His Soc. Mon.* Vol. IV, pp. 38–48 and 122–148.
[39] *Sketches of Early Settlers in Montana*, by Col. W. F. Sanders, MS My chief sources for the above characterization are conversations with Judge W. Y. Pemberton and James U. Sanders, son of Col. Sanders; also the Maryville *Mountaineer*, July 13, 1905, and the Butte *Miner*, July 8, 1905.

much for brave enforcement of order against desperate odds.[40] Other leaders or "captains" were James Williams and Richard Kenyon. Among these leaders were both ardent secessionists and unionists. The main headquarters were at Pfouts's store in Virginia City, and a notice of a meeting was given by posting the symbol, 3—7—77. Miners formed the rank and file of the organization.

The vigilantes went promptly to work, with the purpose not simply of driving the murderous crew to other communities (as was the effect of some vigilante movements), but to end the careers of the criminals. "If a man a'int fit to live here," remarked one vigilante, "he a'int fit to live nowhere." One of the desperadoes earliest captured revealed the names and the method of organization of the gang.[41] Within a month more than a score of criminals were summarily executed, including Plummer. The work was done for the most part quietly and by small groups of men.[42] One must admire not only the valor of these American citizens in risking their lives to effect the capture and execution of these desperadoes, but also their determination in making long journeys in the depth of a severe winter. The effect of this heroic work was healthful. Criminals were cowed, and reckless young men who were drifting toward crime were appalled. Violent crimes for awhile ceased, and citizens worked and traded and traveled in comparative security. "There was an omnipresent spirit of protection, akin to that omnipresent spirit of law which pervaded older civilized communities."[43] Summary methods of American citizens in the mining regions attained by a more difficult and dangerous process ends not unlike those attained by summary government in British Columbia.

Two documents have survived which reveal something of methods of organization of the vigilantes in Alder Gulch.

---

[40] Photographs of these men are reproduced in *Contr. His. Soc. Mon.* Vol. V, op p. 210.

[41] Dimsdale, *Vigilantes of Mont.* (ed. 1882) p. 120-21.

[42] On occasion, as at the capture and execution of five of the band at Virginia City, the miners assembled in large numbers and acted in military formation

[43] Langford, *Vigilante Days and Ways*, Vol. II, p 232

The first is a copy of their regulations and by-laws, and is as follows:

"This committee shall consist of a President or Chief, an Executive officer, Secretary, Treasurer, Executive committee Captains and Lieutenants of Companies, and such gentlemen of known worth and integrity, as the Captains, Lieutenants and other officers enumerated above may deem worthy of being made members.

"The President shall be the supreme ruler of the committee, shall reside in Virginia City, and shall have power to appoint Captains to raise Companies wherever and whenever he deems the interests of the committee require the same to call together the Executive Committee whenever the same should be convened to order the arrest of any suspicious or guilty person, to preside at all meetings whenever present, and to have such other powers as would naturally devolve upon one occupying his position.

"A majority of votes of the Executive Committee shall constitute an election for President and he shall hold the office until his successor is appointed and accepts the position.

"The Executive officer shall have the government and control of all Captains, Lieutenants, and companies, shall see that all orders of Chief and Executive committee are duly executed, shall have the selections of all persons sent out upon any expeditions of the Executive committee and choose a leader for the same and in case of the death or absence of the chief shall assume the duties of the office of President, until a new President is chosen. The Secretary shall keep a correct record of all things proper to be written, the names of the Chief, Executive officer, Secretary, Treasurer Executive committee and the names of the Captain and Lieutenants of Companies.

"The Treasurer shall receive all monies belonging to the committee, keep a true account of the same and pay them out again upon orders of the Executive committee attested by the Secretary.

"The Executive shall consist of seventeen members to wit: The President, Executive officer, Treasurer, Secretary of the Committee, four persons to be selected from Virginia City, three from Nevada, one from Junction, one from Highland, one from Pine Grove, two from Summit, and one from Bivins Gulch, any eight of whom shall constitute a quorum. It shall be the duty of the Executive committee to legislate for the good of the whole committee, to try all criminals that may be arrested, to pass upon all accounts that may be presented, and if just to order the same paid by the Treasurer and to take a general supervision of all criminal acts that may be committed within this Territory or come under their notice.

"The Captain of Companies may be appointed by the President, or the Executive officer, who shall hold their offices until elected by the Companies themselves, every Captain shall have power to appoint one or more Lieutenants. The Captains and Lieutenants shall have power to recruit their companies from men of integrity living in their midst, and when any one company outside of Virginia City numbers over fifty effective men a division should be made, and two companies formed from the same and officers elected from each.

"It shall be the duty of the members to attach themselves to some company and whenever any criminal act shall come to their knowledge to inform his Captain or Lieutenant of the same, when the officers so informed shall call together the members of his company, (unless the Company has chosen a committee for such purpose) when they shall proceed to investigate the case, and elicit the facts and should the said company conclude that the person charged with any offense, should be punished by the committee, the Captain or Lieutenant will first take steps to arrest the criminal and then report the same with proof to the Chief who will thereupon call a meeting of the Executive and the judgment of said executive committee shall be final.

"The only punishment that shall be inflicted by this committee is DEATH."[44] The property of any person executed by this committee shall be immediately seized upon and disposed of by the Executive Committee for the purpose of paying the expense of the Committee, and should the person executed have

---

[44] As a matter of fact, there were exceptions. Two lawyers, Smith and Thurmond, who sympathized with and defended the criminals, were banished, and one man was whipped. Imprisonment was impossible, because there were no jails.

creditors living in the Territory, it shall be the duty of the committee to first pay the expenses of the committee and Executive and funeral expenses afterwards, pay the residue over to some one for the benefit of said creditor."

The second document is the Vigilante oath, as subscribed to by one of the "companies," and was as follows:

"We the undersigned uniting ourselves in a party for the Laudible purpos of arresting thievs and & murderers & recovering stollen propperty do pledge ourselvs upon our sacred honor each to all others & solemnly swear that. we will reveal no secrets, violate no laws of right & not desert each other or our standerd of justice so help us God as witness our hand & seal this 23 of December 1863."[46]

Justifiable as the organization of the Vigilantes of Montana undoubtedly was under the circumstances, nevertheless there was felt to be danger of misdirection or of misuse of a weapon so terrible; and this was the more true after the most critical time had passed, and careful citizens were again intent on their own business. In some cases,—more conspicuous elsewhere than in Montana,—men of criminal character would join the organization as a shield for their own misdeeds, and these, with other despicable or chance characters, might work excess. One man was executed at Nevada, the victim of whose shooting afterwards recovered; and another was hanged at Helena after trial by the civil authorities, sentence for three years, and pardon by the Executive. Because of past cases of doubtful or wrongful justice in the infliction of the death penalty, some of the old Californians in Montana were opposed to the organization of a vigilante committee; and the well meaning citizens who took part in the movement were zealous to uphold the regular civil authority and willing to quit their organization, when that authority proved itself thoroughly competent to maintain order.

But the civil authorities had first to establish their competence. In the meantime, the people, realizing the beneficence of

---

[46] Original copies of the Constitution and Oath given above are in the Montana Historical and Miscellaneous Library The oath itself and the signatures of the signers (of whom there were twenty-four) are in the cramped writing of hands more used to the pick than to the pen.

the work done by the vigilantes, were inclined to uphold them. The judges, themselves, recognized the temporary necessity for the work of the vigilantes. Judge Munson, insisting in a conference with other judges that the courts should take cognizance of some of the executions, was told by one of the judges: "I am content to let the vigilantes go on for the present; they can attend to this branch of jurisprudence cheaper, quicker and better than it can be done by the courts—besides we have no secure jails in which to confine criminals." [46] A grand jury in one of the districts is reported to have presented to the court in lieu of an indictment,—"That it is better to leave the punishment of criminal offenders to the Vigilantes, who always act impartially, and who would not permit the escape of proved criminals on technical and absurd grounds." [47] The Montana Post claimed that there was "No jury as immovably fair, impartial and unassailable, as the cold, stern, lynx-eyed, iron-willed and even-handed Executive Committee." [48]

In other localities covered by the mining advance besides Montana there was recourse, as occasion demanded, to vigilante organization. At Lewiston there was a Protective Association composed of two hundred and fifty good citizens, which had a president, secretary, and executive committee, and was modeled on the plan of the San Francisco Vigilante Committee. It was said to have hanged three murderers and to have exiled about two hundred thieves and gamblers.[49] Renegades from the mines were active in Walla Walla, and stockmen were especially troubled by their running off stock from the neighboring hills and selling it in Walla Walla. Summary executions brought order.[50] At La Grande, Oregon, a vigilante "lodge" was formed having as some of its leading members the Meachem Brothers, Doctor E. A. Stockton, and Lawyer Bacon.[51]

In Southern Idaho, unity such as prevailed among the supporters of law and order in Montana, was, unfortunately, lack-

---
[46] *Contr. His. Soc. Mon.*, Vol. V., p 209.
[47] *Id.*
[48] Quoted in the Idaho *World*, May 26, 1866.
[49] San Francisco *Daily Bulletin*, May 5, 1863.
[50] Ritz, *Settlement of the Great Northern Interior*, MS., p. 19.
[51] McConnell, *Idaho Inferno*, MS, p. 54.

ing. The situation here was complicated, and it is only with difficulty that one can arrive with some clearness at certain phases of the situation, which need careful elucidation as part of our study.[52]

It seems certain that in Southern Idaho, crime was prevalent to a degree such as in other communities had been held to warrant the formation of a vigilante committee. There was frequent mention in the papers of murders and robberies. The district attorney stated in the district court in 1865 that, since the organization of Boise County, there had been sixty deaths from violence, and yet not a single conviction.[53] *The Idaho World*, the leading Democratic paper and an opponent of the vigilante organizations, while attributing the lack of legal executions to the delay in organizing the territory and the courts, admitted that no one had been hanged for murder by due process, and that the 'vigilantes had hanged none but roughs.[54] These latter were undoubtedly numerous, some of them congregating at road houses along the thoroughfares and others in the towns. The livery stable of David Updyke at Boise City, in particular, had the reputation of being a rendezvous for a bad crowd.[55]

The first movement toward vigilante methods of suppression occurred among the ranchers of the Payette Valley, who had lost considerable stock at the hands of insolent ruffians and could get little satisfaction from lawful authorities. As an example of the inutility of legal procedure at the time, the case of one gentleman may be mentioned who, when a horse worth fifty dollars was stolen and taken to Boise City, sued out an attachment and recovered the animal, but at an expense of seventy dollars. A small organization of the ranchers was effected, thieves were pursued long distances, several of them were executed, and thievery in the valley was summarily checked.[56] The

---

[52] The main trouble is that politics entered into the situation, and that the sources are influenced by political affiliations.
[53] The Idaho *Statesman*, Sept. 3, 1865.
[54] The Idaho *World*, Oct. 2, 1865; April 28, 1866.
[55] As to the career of Updyke, see Langford, *Vigilante Days and Ways*, Vol. II, Chap XXII.
[56] The leading spirit of this organization was Mr. W. J. McConnell, who gives an interesting account under the caption of *Idaho Inferno*, MS. Mr. McConnell later became Governor of Idaho and United States Senator.

vigilante movement was manifested again in August, 1865, in the attempt to take Patterson from jail; and an atrocious murder in Boise City at Updyke's barn (April, 1866,) was followed by prompt hanging at the hands of a vigilante committee. A little later Updyke himself was hanged with a companion on the Rocky Bar Road; some authorities claim that this was done by the Boise vigilantes, others by an organization of Overland employes.[57]

Updyke had been the Sheriff of Ada County, regularly elected as such, but being charged with embezzlement he had resigned. He was a man of genial character, who made many friends, and he was a leading Democratic politician. *The Idaho World* claimed that his execution was really a murder, having for its object getting possession of the money that was on his person, "gratification of personal hate, and to get a powerful political foe out of the way." The organization of a vigilance committee, the *World* claimed was mainly for the purpose of carrying the summer elections against the Democratic party.[58] This charge that the vigilante organizations of Southern Idaho were political in purpose and inimical to the Democratic party, was again and again reiterated. The *World* admitted, however, that at the time of the Patterson affair, "There were undoubtedly many who went into the organization with the laudable desire of freeing the community of much which is deservedly the object of reprobation with every good citizen, having no ulterior objects in view other than that of the good society." But there was a legally constituted government in Idaho, so the Democrats argued, and the majority of the people were in favor of civil government, not of mob rule.[59] On the other hand, the Republicans charged that the Democratic political organization, having the power, did not enforce the laws; "make the people believe that you are in good faith trying to enforce it (the law)," said *The Statesman*, "and we shall hear no more of vigilance committees and lynch law."[60] The situation appears to have

---
[57] The latter view, for example, by McConnell, p. 55; the former by Langford, Vol. II, p. 352.
[58] The Idaho *World*, April 14, 1866
[59] *Id*, Oct. 2, 1865.
[60] The Idaho *Weekly Statesman*, Sept. 3, 1865.

been that there were politicians in both parties who were willing to place party advantage above the good of the community, but that the majority of the number of both parties were sincerely desirous of more orderly government; that those of the people who tried to act through vigilante organization were confronted by the fact that they put themselves in an attitude of antagonism to the regular authorities, while the people who upheld the authorities, and particularly the political organization of the dominant party, were hampered by the fact that they were in political affiliation with, and dependent upon, men for votes, whose character they could not defend. At any rate, the situation was such that neither the extra legal organization nor the legal authorities could deal decisively with the criminal element, and so the evolution of law and order in Idaho was slower and more confused than in Montana.[61]

Reviewing in conclusion, the prominent features of the different governmental forms applied under the British and under the American auspices in the mining advance, we see, on the one hand, government concentrated largely in the hands of an efficient executive, who made laws and organized administration on summary methods; on the other, representative government, under hampering conditions, working tardily and painfully towards order, and meeting local or occasional reinforcement. Under the former society was from the first under control, and there was a tendency to restrain individuals for the benefit of society—a restraint at times verging to over repression; under the latter individualism was feebly controlled from above, but

---

[61] A curious fact in the party politics of Idaho at this time is the connection between Fenianism and the Democratic party. The leaders of that party in Boise County (which was far the most populous county in the Territory at that time and with political power proportionate to population) were on close terms with or members of the Fenian Organization. On the Invitation and Reception Committees of a Grand Fenian Ball given by the Emmett Life Guards were E. D. Holbrook, Democratic candidate for Delegate to Congress, James Crutcher, Democratic Sheriff, Street, the Editor of the World, Mix, nominee for representative, and a number of other prominent Democrats. John M. Murphy, the Secretary of the Democratic Territorial Central Committee, was the State Centre of the Fenian Brotherhood. For substantiation of these statements compare lists of Democratic nominees in the *Idaho World*, May 12 and June 26, 1866, with the leaders at the Fenian Ball, published June 30, 1866. It was charged by Republicans that Fenianism was being used by Democrat politicians. *Idaho Weekly Statesman*, April 22, 1866.

had to generate within itself forces of order, and it tended to undue license hurtful to society. The American system developed a country the more swiftly, the British the more safely. Under both systems strong men labored courageously and well to adjust forms of order to unorganized society.

A SELECTED BIBLIOGRAPHY

I. Manuscript Sources

The most important manuscripts for this study are located in three libraries specified below. Only manuscripts of chief weight for this work are mentioned.

1. The Montana Historical Library at Helena.

Bradley, Lieut. James H.
- (a) *Affairs at Ft. Benton 1831—1864.*
- (b) *Effects at Ft. Benton of the Gold Excitement in Montana.*
- (c) *A General View of the Settlement of Montana.*

Benedict, Gilbert.
Diary of an Immigrant of 1864.

Haskell, Wm. S.
Pilgrimage to the Gold Regions, 1864.

Howie, Neil, *Letters.*

Hough, Rev. A. M.
The Establishment of our Mission in Montana—Notes from my Diary.

Morley, J. H.—*Diary.* (Of special value for Bannack and Alder Gulch.)

Sanders, Senator W. F.
Sketches of Early Settlers in Montana.

Williams, Capt. James.
Interview and Autobiographical Sketch.

Williams, A. M. and Wheeler, Wm. F.
History of Mining in Montana.

Vigilante Constitution and Oath.

2. The Library of the Academy of Pacific Coast History (The Bancroft Collection).

> Ainsworth, Capt. J. C. *Statement.* (Refers particularly to O. S. N. Co.)
> Anderson, Alexander Caulfield. *History of the Northwest Coast.*
> Ballou, William T.—*Adventures.*
> Braunstetter, J. H. *The First Discovery of Boise Basin.*
> Bristol, Sherlock. *Idaho Nomenclature.*
> Butler, J. S. *Life and Times in Idaho.*
> Coghanour, David. *Boise Basin.*
> Deady, M. P. *History of the Progress of Oregon after 1845.*
> De Cosmos, Amor. *The Governments of Vancouver Island and British Columbia.*
> Douglas, Sir James. *Diary of Gold Discovery on Fraser River. Private Papers.*
> Evans, Elwood. *The Fraser River Excitement.*
> Farnham, Edwin. *Statement.* (Concerning Salmon River and Warren's)
> Finlayson, Roderick. *The History of Vancouver Island and the Northwest Coast.*
> Hofen, Leo. *History of Idaho County.*
> Hutton, James H. *Early Events in Northern Idaho.*
> Joset, Father. *The War of 1855—58.*
> Knapp, Henry H. *Statement of Events in Idaho.*
> Maize, H. B. *Early Events in Idaho.* (Deals particularly with Owyhee)
> McConnell, W. J. *The Idaho Inferno.*
> Ritz, Philip. *Settlement of the Great Northern Interior.*
> Roder, Capt. Henry. *Narrative Concerning Bellingham Bay.*
> Schultze, Mrs. Theodore. *Anecdotes of the Early Settlement of Northern Idaho.*

3. Provincial Library and Archives of British Columbia, Victoria.

There are two classes of material here which deserve special consideration. The first pertains closely to Sir James Douglas and includes his Letters and Proclamations. The letters are found mainly in his *Miscellaneous Letters* and in his *Correspondence Book*.

Douglas's letters to the gold commissioners and magistrates in the various mining districts in British Columbia very urgently required these subordinates to furnish full and detailed reports. After a persistent search, which was made possible by the help of the officials of the Parliament buildings (and in particular by the courtesy of Mr. Arthur Campbell Reddie, Assistant Provincal Secretary), these reports and letters from the gold commissioners were found among a mass of material in the archives of the secretary's office. They constitute a most satisfactory and reliable source for the history of the early period of British Columbia mining. The commissioners were men of considerable education, who were placed in positions of responsibility wherein it was more to their interest to give a true account of what was occurring than to exaggerate, and their letters were not intended for publication. If these letters could be sorted out, edited, and published, they would furnish valuable material not only for British Columbia history but for the general history of the precious metal industry.

II. Newspapers

One of the significant features of the mining advance was the swift establishment of newspapers in all important centers. The mining population wanted the news and was willing to pay for it; in particular there was demand for news of the Civil War. The following newspapers were selected as representative:

The Washington Statesman. (Walla Walla)
The Idaho World. (Idaho City)
The Boise *Statesman.* (Boise)
The Owyhee Avalanche. (Silver City)
The Montana Post. (Virginia City)
The British Columbian. (New Westminster)
The Cariboo Sentinel. (Barkerville)

Other papers of the mining regions were the *Golden Age*, (Lewiston), *The Rocky Mountain Gazette*, (Helena), and The Dalles *Mountaineer*.

Papers more remote from the mining region were in direct touch with them and contain much valuable information. Of this character were the Victoria *Gazette and Colonist.* In the Sound country, among others, were the Puget Sound *Herald* (Steilacoom), and *The Pioneer* and *Democrat* (Olympia). At Portland was *The Oregonian*, with correspondents in many camps. The San Francisco *Daily Bulletin*, whose columns ranged the whole vast mining field, is the best single newspaper source. The wide sweep of its news items and of its editorial surveys emphasizes the fact that San Francisco was the metropolis of the American mining movement. The London *Times* contained reports from correspondents in British Columbia and valuable comments on conditions. Mention should also be made of *The Mining and Scientific Press*, a magazine published at San Francisco.[1]

III. Contemporary Documents and Books

1. *Government Reports.*

Up to the outbreak of the Civil War comprehensive information was furnished by the army administrators. Their reports are to be found in *The Reports of the Secretary of War.* The sudden dearth that falls on the opening of the war is significant as revealing the withdrawal of these trained administrators. About the same time came the officials of the Indian department, whose reports are to be found in *The Reports of the Commissioner of Indian Affairs.* In 1866, with the appointment of Mr. J. Ross Browne as United States Commissioner of Mining Statistics, came new and indispensable sources. The reports of Mr. Browne and of his successor Mr. R. W. Raymond, entitled *Mineral Resources of the United States* appeared from 1867 to 1876, and these must be studied by any one wishing to know the mining history of the period. Other important sources are the Journals, Records, Session Laws and Reports of the legislative bodies and officials of Oregon, Washington, Idaho, and Montana.

For British Columbia we have *Papers regarding British Co-*

---
[1] Hon. C. B. Bagley, of Seattle, possesses one of the most valuable collections of newspapers on the Pacific Coast. I am greatly indebted to him for cordially allowing me to use it.

lumbia presented to Parliament by Command of her Majesty. The official *Gazette,* published at New Westminster, is also important. Of a semi-official character and valuable are the *Occasional Papers* of the Columbian Mission. On the Indian question invaluable are the *Papers relating to the Indian Land Question.*

2. Private publications.

A noticeable feature of the bibliographical material for British Columbia is the large number of books concerning that colony, which were published in Great Britain during the early years of the colony,—a fact indicating the great interest of the public and the government. Some of them are as follows:

Barret-Lennard, Capt. C. E. *Travels in British Columbia.* (London, 1862)

Cornwallis, Kinahan, *The New Eldorado.* (London, 1858)

Emmerson, John, *British Columbia and Vancouver Island.* (Durham, 1865)

Hazlitt, W. C. *British Columbia and Vancouver Island.* (London, 1858)

Hazlitt, W. C. *The Great Gold Fields of Cariboo.* (London, 1862)

Johnson, R. Byron. *Very Far West Indeed.* (London, 1872)

MacDonald, D. G. F. *British Columbia and Vancouver Island.* (London, 1862)

Macfie, M. *Vancouver Island and British Columbia.* (London, 1865)

Mayne. R. C. *Four years in British Columbia and Vancouver Island.* (London, 1862)

Milton and Cheadle. *The Northwest Passage by Land.* (London, 1865)

Rattray, A. *Vancouver Island and British Columbia.* (London, 1862)

Wyld's *New Map of the Gold Fields on the Fraser's River.* Printed at London 1858 and 1859 by James Wyld, Geographer to the Queen.

A number of pamphlets concerning British Columbia were issued from Ottawa, New Westminster and Victoria. References to some of these are found in the text.

In the American territories works by contemporary observers were rare. Mention may be made of the following pamphlets.

Angelo, C. *Idaho.*

Campbell, J. S. *Six Months in the New Gold Diggings.*

Dimsdale, T. J. *The Vigilantes of Montana.*

Leighton, Mrs. Caroline C. *Life at Puget Sound, with Sketches of Travel.*

Langley, *Pacific Coast Directory.*

Mullan, John. *Miner's and Traveller's Guide.*

There are valuable passages also in *Our New West*, by Samuel Bowles and in *Our New States and Territories* and *Beyond the Mississippi* by Albert D. Richardson.

Some comparatively recent publications give satisfying material for the earlier time. Of these the *Contributions to the Historical Society of Montana* are very serviceable. Valuable articles have been published also in the Oregon Historical Quarterly. Hailey's *History of Idaho* and Goulder's *Reminiscences* furnish suggestive and important material.

3. General and Secondary Works.

Bancroft, H. H. *British Columbia.* 1792—1887

Bancroft, H. H. *Washington, Idaho and Montana.*

Bancroft, H. H. *Popular Tribunals.*

Begg, A. *History of British Columbia from the Earliest Discovery to the Present Time.*

Lyman, W. D. *The Columbia River; its History, its Myths, its Scenery, its Commerce.*

Meany, E. S. *History of the State of Washington.*

Schafer, Joseph. *History of the Pacific Northwest.*

On mining law the following may be consulted:

Davis, John F. *Historical Sketch of the Mining Law in California.*

Lindley, Curtis Holbrook. *A Treatise on the American Law Relating to Mines and Mineral Lands within the public land States and Territories and governing the acquisition and enjoyment of Mining Rights in the Public Domain.* (Contains a succinct and scholarly historical review, Vol I pp. 5–115.)

Yale, Gregory. *Legal titles to Mining Claims and Water Rights in California under the Mining Law of Congress of July, 1866.*